COST-EFFECTIVENESS AND EDUCATIONAL POLICY

2002 YEARBOOK OF THE AMERICAN EDUCATION FINANCE ASSOCIATION

Henry M. Levin
Teachers College, Columbia University

Patrick J. McEwan
University of Illinois at Urbana-Champaign

Editors

D1319423

EYE ON EDUCATION

EYE ON EDUCATION
6 DEPOT WAY WEST
LARCHMONT, NY 10538
(914) 833-0551
(914) 833-0761 fax
www.eyeoneducation.com

For information about permission to reproduce selections from this book, write:
Eye On Education, Permissions Dept., Suite 106, 6 Depot Way West, Larchmont, NY 10538

Library of Congress Cataloging-in-Publication Data

ISSN pending

10 9 8 7 6 5 4 3 2

Editorial and production services provided by
City Desktop Productions, LLC
10127 Northwestern Avenue, Franksville, WI 53126
(262-884-8822)

CONTRIBUTORS

COEDITORS

Henry M. Levin is the William Heard Kilpatrick Professor of Economics and Education at Teachers College, Columbia University and the Director of the National Center for the Study of Privatization in Education. He is also the David Jacks Professor Emeritus of Higher Education and Economics at Stanford University.

Patrick J. McEwan is an Assistant Professor of Educational Policy Studies and Economics at the University of Illinois at Urbana-Champaign.

CONTRIBUTORS

W. Steven Barnett is a Professor in the Graduate School of Education and the Director of the Center for Early Education Research, Rutgers University.

Clive Belfield is the Assistant Director for Research at the National Center for the Study of Privatization in Education, Teachers College, Columbia University.

Celia Brown is a Research Fellow in the Economics of Education at the School of Education, University of Birmingham.

William H. Clune is the William Voss-Bascom Professor Emeritus of Law at the University of Wisconsin-Madison and the Co-Director of the Study for Systemic Reform in the Milwaukee Public Schools.

David Grissmer is a Senior Management Scientist at RAND.

Doug Harris is an Education Economist at the Economic Policy Institute.

Leonard N. Masse is a public school teacher and a Research Associate at the Center for Early Education Research, Rutgers University.

Jennifer King Rice is an Assistant Professor in the Department of Education Policy and Leadership at the University of Maryland.

Mun C. Tsang is a Professor of Education and Economics at Teachers College, Columbia University and the Director of the Center on Chinese Education.

TABLE OF CONTENTS

1

COST-EFFECTIVENESS AND EDUCATIONAL POLICY

Henry M. Levin and Patrick J. McEwan

Two women of a certain age are at a Catskills mountain resort, and one of them says: "Boy, the food at this place is really terrible." The other one says, "Yeah, and the portions are so small."

Annie Hall, 1977

INTRODUCTION

Woody Allen was not referring to cost-effectiveness analysis, but his lament is appropriate to that topic. Existing cost-effectiveness studies are often lacking in quality and there are relatively few of them. This is surprising given the enormous demands that education makes on society's resources, and the constant quest to obtain educational improvements from the same or even fewer resources. Estimates of the total costs of the educational sector including elementary and secondary education, higher education, and other forms of education and training are thought to be on the order of $750 billion a year or more. Even an improvement of just 2 percent in efficiency would yield a dividend of $15 billion. Many observers believe that possibilities for improving resource allocation far exceed this amount. By viewing educational decisions in terms of both their costs and outcomes, decision-makers can select those educational approaches that are most promising in their use of resources—that is, the most cost-effective ones.

To assist in making cost-effective decisions, researchers in both education and health have devised and honed the tools of cost-effectiveness analysis (CEA).[1] These tools provide the means of estimating the costs of two or more educational alternatives, as well as the effectiveness of each alternative in producing a common outcome, such as reading or mathematics achievement. With this information in hand, one can determine which alternative yields the highest educational effectiveness for a given cost or the lowest cost for any given level of educational

---

1 For methodological discussions in education, see Levin (1975, 1983) and Levin and McEwan (2001). In health, see Drummond, O'Brien, Stoddart, and Torrance (1997); Gold, Siegel, Russell, and Weinstein (1996); and Sloan (1995).

performance. CEA is closely related to cost-benefit analysis (CBA), in which both costs and outcomes are expressed in monetary terms. But, only in special circumstances can educational results be expressed in monetary terms. The enduring appeal of CEA lies in the fact that educational outcomes can be evaluated in forms such as achievement tests and dropout rates.

The terminology of cost-effectiveness is so common in contemporary debates about education that one might expect it to occupy an important place in the tool-kits of researchers. Yet, it is relatively rare in educational evaluation and research. The first author began devising methods for carrying out educational CEA about 30 years ago (Levin, 1975), culminating with the publication of a methodological primer (Levin, 1983). What has happened since then? A recent overview of the field suggests that the term has strongly entered into the public vocabulary, and that the amount of applied work has slowly increased (Levin and McEwan, 2001). However, the body of cost-effectiveness analysis studies in education still appears to be unimpressive in both quantity and quality.

Of course, it is easy to engage in rueful commentary like Woody Allen. It is more difficult to construct a useful research program. Towards doing so, the collected papers of this volume have three main purposes. Chapters 2–4 attempt to provide an assessment of the state-of-the-art of cost-effectiveness analysis in education, reviewing the quantity and quality of existing studies.[2] Chapters 5–7 push this assessment even further, identifying key issues that need to be considered in the conduct of good cost-effectiveness analyses. These issues are illustrated with critical reviews of the cost-effectiveness literature on commonly proposed solutions to low educational quality, such as whole-school reform, class size reduction, and private schooling. Finally, Chapters 8–10 present original empirical studies in cost-effectiveness and cost-benefit analysis that model some of the best practices referred to in previous chapters.

Since each chapter in this yearbook uses a common set of concepts and methods related to cost-effectiveness analysis, the next sections will provide some additional background on these tools.[3] Section 2 provides a basic overview of cost-effectiveness and cost-benefit analysis and the key analytical questions that they are suited to answering. Section 3 describes the economic approach to cost estimation, including the important concept of opportunity cost, while Section 4 reviews some basic concepts in the estimation of effectiveness and benefits. Section 5 discusses approaches to jointly interpreting measures of costs and outcomes. The final three sections will describe the particular contributions of each chapter to the three goals just described.

TWO MODES OF COST ANALYSIS

COST-EFFECTIVENESS ANALYSIS

Cost-effectiveness analysis compares two or more educational programs according to their effectiveness and costs in accomplishing a particular objective (e.g.,

---

2 Similar reviews are already available in health (Gerard, 1992; Salkeld, Davey, and Arnolda, 1995; Udvarhelyi, Colditz, Rai, and Epstein, 1992).

3 Naturally, this discussion will be limited by space and it can hardly purport to give a thorough grounding in the concepts and methods of cost-effectiveness analysis. For that, the reader is advised to consult other sources (see especially Drummond et al., 1997; Levin and McEwan, 2001).

raising student mathematics achievement). By combining information on effectiveness and costs, the evaluator can determine which program provides a given level of effectiveness at the lowest cost or, conversely, which program provides the highest level of effectiveness for a given cost. Cost-effectiveness analysis is a fundamentally comparative endeavor. That is, it allows us to choose which of two or more alternatives is relatively more cost-effective, but it does not tell us whether an alternative is worthwhile in some absolute sense.

The approach's key strength is that it can be easily reconciled with standard evaluation designs in education. Furthermore, it is useful for evaluating alternatives that have a limited number of objectives (and measures of effectiveness). When there are multiple measures, however, a cost-effectiveness analysis becomes unwieldy. It may conclude, for example, that one alternative is more cost-effective in raising mathematics achievement, but that another is the most cost-effective means of raising reading achievement. Without further analytical tools, we have no decision rule for choosing between alternatives.[4]

COST-BENEFIT ANALYSIS

In a cost-benefit analysis, the outcomes of an educational alternative are directly expressed in monetary terms. Presuming that monetary benefits can be fully measured, they can be directly compared to monetary costs. In the educational context, this is most often the case with alternatives that are designed to affect outcomes in the labor market. A clear benefit is the increased earnings that may accrue to participants from education and training, although researchers have used creative techniques to place monetary values on a wide range of outcomes (Chapter 9 will provide an excellent example of this).

When CBA is feasible, it has a clear advantage over other techniques of cost analysis. It can be used to assess directly whether benefits outweigh costs, allowing a clear statement of whether the program is desirable in an absolute sense. The results of a cost-benefit analysis can also be compared to other cost-benefit results for a wide range of alternative programs, in education and other fields such as health. With these advantages come important limitations. In many fields, particularly education, it is rarely feasible to express outcomes in monetary terms. Thus, a cost-benefit analysis often focuses on a narrow range of outcomes—such as job earnings—and risks understating the existence and magnitudes of other benefits.

ESTIMATING COSTS

Every intervention uses resources that have valuable alternative uses. For example, a program for raising student achievement requires personnel, facilities, and

---

4 One set of tools for doing so is referred to as cost-utility analysis. This technique involves assigning "importance weights" to various measures of effectiveness, which are then used to obtain an overall measure of utility, or satisfaction with the alternative. To implement the technique, many analytical decisions need to be made. For example, whose preferences should be used to gauge the "importance" of various objectives? How should their preferences be measured? Although researchers in decision analysis and health-care use the techniques frequently, the use of cost-utility analysis in education is still rare. For an overview, see Levin and McEwan (2001, Chap. 8).

materials that can be applied to other educational and non-educational endeavors. By devoting these resources to a particular activity we are sacrificing the gains that could be obtained from using them for some other purpose. Thus, the "cost" of pursuing the intervention is the value of what we must sacrifice by not using these resources in some other way. Economists define the cost of an intervention as the value of all of the resources that it utilizes had they been assigned to their most valuable alternative uses. Defined in this sense, all costs represent the sacrifice of an opportunity that has been forgone. It is this notion of opportunity cost that lies at the base of cost analysis in evaluation.

Although this may appear to be a peculiar way to view costs, it is probably more familiar to each of us than appears at first glance. It is usually true that when we refer to costs, we refer to the expenditure that we must make to purchase a particular good or service as reflected in the statement, "the cost of the meal was $15." In cases in which the only cost is the expenditure of funds that could have been used for other goods and services, the sacrifice or cost can be stated in terms of expenditure. However, in daily usage we also make statements like, "it cost me a full day to prepare for my vacation," or "it cost me two lucrative sales," in the case of a salesperson who missed two sales appointments because he or she was tied up in a traffic jam. In some cases we may even find that the pursuit of an activity "cost us a friendship."

In each of these cases a loss is incurred, which is viewed as the value of opportunities that were sacrificed. Thus the cost of a particular activity was viewed as its "opportunity cost." Of course, this does not mean that we can always easily place a dollar value on that cost. In the case of losing a day of work, one can probably say that the sacrifice or opportunity cost was equal to what could have been earned. In the case of the missed appointments, one can probably make some estimate of what the sales and commissions would have been had the appointments been kept. However, in the case of the lost friendship, it is clearly much more difficult to make a monetary assessment of costs. In cost analysis a similar approach is taken, in that we wish to ascertain the cost of an intervention in terms of the value of the resources that were used or lost by applying them in one way rather than in another. To do this we use a straightforward approach called the "ingredients" method.

THE INGREDIENTS METHOD

The ingredients method relies upon the notion that every intervention uses ingredients that have a value or cost.[5] If specific ingredients can be identified and their costs can be ascertained, we can estimate the total costs of the intervention as well as the cost-per-unit of effectiveness, utility, or benefit. We can also ascertain how the cost burden is distributed among the sponsoring agency, funding agencies, donors, and clients.

---

5 For detailed descriptions of the ingredients method, see Levin (1975, 1988) and Levin and McEwan (2001, Chap. 3–5). The reader should be aware that this approach to cost analysis goes by other names in the literature. For example, it is often referred to as the resource cost model (see Chambers and Parrish, 1994a, b). At their core, the ingredients and resource cost approaches are very similar.

The first step in applying the method is to identify the ingredients that are used. This entails the determination of what ingredients are required to create or replicate the interventions that are being evaluated, casting as wide a net as possible. It is obvious that even contributed or donated resources such as volunteers must be included as ingredients according to such an approach, for such resources will contribute to the outcome of the intervention, even if they are not included in budgetary expenditures.

In order to identify the ingredients that are necessary for cost estimation, it is important to be clear about the scope of the intervention. One type of confusion that sometimes arises is the difficulty of separating the ingredients of a specific intervention from the ingredients required for the more general program that contains the intervention. This might be illustrated by the following situation. Two programs for reducing school dropouts are being considered by a school district. The first program provides additional counselors for dropout-prone youngsters. The second program provides peer tutoring by fellow potential dropouts as well as special enrichment courses to stimulate interest in further education. The question that arises is whether one should include all school resources in the analysis as well as those required for the interventions, or just the ingredients that comprise the interventions. We are concerned with the additional or incremental services that will be used in order to provide the alternative dropout-reduction programs. Thus, in this case one should consider only the incremental ingredients that are required for the interventions that are being evaluated.

SPECIFICATION OF INGREDIENTS

The identification and specification of ingredients is often facilitated by dividing ingredients into four or five main categories that have common properties. A typical breakdown would include (1) personnel, (2) facilities, (3) equipment and materials, (4) other program inputs, and (5) client inputs.

PERSONNEL

Personnel ingredients include all of the human resources required for each of the alternatives that will be evaluated. This category includes not only full-time personnel, but part-time employees, consultants, and volunteers. All personnel should be listed according to their roles, qualifications, and time commitments. Roles refer to their responsibilities, such as administration, coordination, teaching, teacher training, curriculum design, secretarial services, and so on. Qualifications refer to the training, experience, and specialized skills required for the positions. Time commitments refer to the amount of time that each person devotes to the intervention in terms of percentage of a full-time position. In the latter case there may be certain employees, consultants, and volunteers who allocate only a portion of a full workweek or workyear to the intervention.

FACILITIES

Facilities refer to the physical space required for the intervention. This category includes any classroom space, offices, storage areas, play or recreational facilities, and other building requirements, whether paid for by the project or not. Even donated facilities must be specified. All such requirements must be listed according to their dimensions and characteristics, along with other information that is important for identifying their value. For example, facilities that are air-conditioned have a different value than those that are not. Any facilities that are jointly used with other programs should be identified according to the portion of use that is allocated to the intervention.

EQUIPMENT AND MATERIALS

These refer to furnishings, instructional equipment, and materials that are used for the intervention, whether covered by project expenditures or donated by other entities. Specifically, they would include classroom and office furniture as well as such instructional equipment as computers, audiovisual equipment, scientific apparatus, books and other printed materials, office machines, paper, commercial tests, and other supplies. Both the specific equipment and materials solely allocated to the intervention and those that are shared with other activities should be noted.

OTHER INPUTS

This category refers to all other ingredients that do not fit readily into the categories set out above. For example, it might include any extra liability or theft insurance that is required; or it might include the cost of training sessions at a local college or university. Other possible ingredients might include telephone service, electricity, heating, internet access fees, and so forth. Any ingredients that are included in this category should be specified clearly with a statement of their purpose.

REQUIRED CLIENT INPUTS

This category of ingredients includes any contributions that are required of the clients or their families. For example, if an educational alternative requires the family to provide transportation, books, uniforms, equipment, food, or other student services, these should be included under this classification. The purpose of including such inputs is that the success of an intervention may depend crucially on such resources whether provided by families or schools. To provide an accurate picture of the resources that are required to replicate any intervention that requires client inputs, it is important to include them in the analysis.

CONSIDERATIONS IN SPECIFYING INGREDIENTS

There are three overriding considerations that should be recognized in identifying and specifying ingredients. First, the ingredients should be specified in sufficient detail that their value can be ascertained in the next stage of the analysis. Thus it is important that the qualifications of staff, characteristics of physical facilities, types of equipment, and other inputs be specified with enough precision that it is possible to place reasonably accurate cost values on them.

Second, the categories into which ingredients are placed should be consistent; but there is no single approach to categorization that will be suitable in all cases. The one that was set out above is a general classification scheme that is rather typical. It is possible, however, that there need be no "other inputs" category if all ingredients can be assigned to other classifications. For example, insurance coverage can be included with facilities and equipment to the degree that it is associated with the costs of those categories. Likewise, if parents are required to provide volunteer time, that ingredient can be placed under client inputs rather than under personnel. The categories are designed to be functionally useful rather than orthodox distinctions that should never be violated.

Third, the degree of specificity and accuracy in listing ingredients should depend upon their overall contribution to the total cost of the intervention. Personnel inputs represent three-quarters or more of the costs of educational and social service interventions. Accordingly, they should be given the most attention. Facilities and equipment may also be important. However, supplies can often be estimated with much less attention to detail, since they do not weigh heavily in overall costs.

COSTING OUT THE INGREDIENTS

At this second stage a cost-value is placed on each ingredient or resource. Since the emphasis is typically on annual costs for educational interventions rather than costs of a longer time horizon or the life of the project, the analysis is often limited to yearly costs. However, projects of longer duration can be analyzed as well as long as the time pattern of costs is accounted for by a discounting procedure.[6] It is important to note that what is called cost is really a cost-value rather than the more familiar notion of cost in terms of "what was paid for it." The reason for this is that many resources are not found in standard expenditure or budget documents, and even when they are included, their costs are sometimes stated inaccurately from a value perspective. For example, donated inputs such as volunteers or in-kind contributions are not found in any official reporting of expenditures or costs. Investments in capital renovations which typically last many years, such as major facility improvements, are often paid for and shown as a cost in a single year, even though they may have a life of 20 to 30 years over which costs must be amortized.

Personnel costs are relatively easy to estimate by combining salaries and benefits, if personnel are hired from reasonably competitive labor markets. Unfortunately, a portion of personnel benefits is often found in other parts of the budget than salaries. For example, the traditional system used by educational agencies for expenditure accounting has a category called "fixed charges" that includes insurance expenses including those that comprise staff insurance benefits. In some states, retirement benefits are paid fully or partly by the state to a state retirement fund, so they do not appear on the expenditure statements of local school districts. Thus, personnel costs should include the full market value of what it takes to obtain persons with the qualities and training that are desired.

Facilities costs are usually more of a challenge because many educational entities already "own" their facilities, so it is not obvious what the cost-value amounts to of the use of any particular portion of the facilities. Standard techniques for estimating their annualized value include determination of what it would cost to lease them as well as methods of determining annual costs by estimating replacement value. The annualized value of a facility comprises the cost of depreciation (that is, how much is "used up" in a given year of a facility with a fixed life) and the interest forgone on the undepreciated portion. In principle, a facility with a 30-year life

---

6 This chapter does not describe the procedures of discounting in any detail. For details, see Levin and McEwan (2001, pp. 90–94).

will lose one-thirtieth of its value each year in depreciation cost. Furthermore, since the undepreciated investment cannot be invested elsewhere, it implies an additional cost of forgone interest income. The same is true of equipment such as furniture and computers or materials such as textbooks that have a usable life of more than one year. Consumable inputs such as energy and telephone costs or supplies can be readily obtained from expenditures.

In short, there are standard methods for estimating the costs of each of the ingredients. The total costs of an intervention—usually the "incremental" costs of adding an intervention to existing operations—are divided by the total number of students who benefit from the intervention to get an additional cost per student. To carry out these analyses, a standard worksheet format can be applied (for examples, see Levin and McEwan, 2001). The worksheet can be easily replicated with a spreadsheet package such as Microsoft Excel.

By itself, a cost analysis can provide valuable information. It can tell us whether a program is feasible, in that it can be carried out within a budget constraint. With further analysis, it can also tell us how costs are distributed across various stakeholders that participate in a program, and hence whether they are likely to evince support for it. However, a cost analysis alone cannot tell us whether a particular alternative is relatively more desirable than another, or whether it is worthwhile in an absolute sense. For that, we must begin to incorporate information on the effectiveness or benefits of educational alternatives.

ESTIMATING EFFECTIVENESS AND BENEFITS

EFFECTIVENESS

In most evaluation studies, effectiveness is an overarching theme. It is no less important in the conduct of a cost-effectiveness analysis. The fundamental challenge lies in identifying the causal relationship between an educational alternative and a measure of effectiveness. "Alternatives" may be construed narrowly (e.g., the use of new textbooks) or broadly (e.g., a whole-school reform that transforms many facets of school operations). This is determined by the particular context of the cost-effectiveness evaluation. Similarly, measures of effectiveness are determined by the objectives of the alternative. They have often included student outcomes on standardized tests, but a wide range of other measures could be employed.

To assess whether individuals reap better educational outcomes from participating in an educational intervention, we require some estimate of how they would have fared in the absence of the program. Identifying such a "counterfactual" lies at the heart of the evaluative endeavor. One of the best approaches for doing so is the randomized experiment.[7] Individuals, classrooms, schools, or some other unit are randomly assigned to either participate in the alternative (the "treatment" group), or to not participate (the "control" group). If both groups are sufficiently large, randomization ensures that the two groups are essentially the same before an alternative is implemented. Thus, the control group serves as a good estimate of the

---

7 For an overview of experimental methods, see Boruch (1997); Orr (1999); and Shadish, Cook, and Campbell (2002).

counterfactual, and any subsequent differences between the groups can be attributed with great confidence to the impact of the alternative.

If randomization is not possible, there are other approaches. In quasi-experimental evaluations, evaluators have some purposive involvement in assigning individuals to participate or not participate in an alternative (that, nonetheless, does not extend to randomized assignment). Among the many quasi-experimental approaches, a common one relies on matching each student that participates in an alternative with another, non-participating student, according to observed characteristics like socioeconomic status.[8] The weakness of the approach almost always lies in the fact that matching may still produce treatment and comparison groups different in unobservable ways. These unobserved characteristics may also affect group outcomes, and hence confound attempts to isolate the causal impact of an educational alternative.

In non-experimental approaches, evaluators have no control over how alternatives are allocated to schools, classrooms, or students. Instead, they rely on statistical techniques like multiple regression analysis to control for individual characteristics that affect outcomes, but may also determine the likelihood that individuals participate in an alternative. Again, this is almost always problematic, because we have few guarantees that controls are adequate. If they are not, then program effects may be confused with other factors. Even so, economists and statisticians have devoted considerable effort to devising techniques that will still allow non-experimental data to yield useful causal findings (for an overview, see Angrist and Krueger, 1999). At their core, many of these techniques—such as instrumental variables—require researchers to identify "natural" experiments, in which some element of randomness, usually unintended, was involved in determining which individuals received a treatment.

For further discussion of these issues in the context of cost-effectiveness analysis, see Levin and McEwan (2001, Chap. 6). For general discussions, readers should consult almost any volume on evaluation and research design (e.g., Boruch, 1997; Cook and Campbell, 1979; Light, Singer, and Willett, 1990; Orr, 1999; Rossi and Freeman, 1993; Shadish et al., 2002).

BENEFITS

In some cases, educational outcomes can be expressed in monetary terms, and benefits can be estimated with the evaluation approaches described in the previous section. For example, there are several well-known evaluations of job training programs that are expressly aimed at improving labor market earnings. An experimental evaluation of the Job Training Partnership Act (JTPA) randomly assigned individuals to receive training or serve in a control group (Orr et al., 1996). The earnings of each group were traced during the ensuing months, and the difference provided a useful measure of program benefits.

Even when outcomes are not measured in monetary terms, they can often be readily converted. In an evaluation of a dropout prevention program, outcomes were initially measured in the number of dropouts prevented in a quasi-experimental framework (Stern, Dayton, Paik, and Weisberg, 1989). Given the well-known

---

8 For overviews of quasi-experimental techniques, see Cook and Campbell (1979) and Shadish et al. (2002).

relationship between earnings and high school graduation, the evaluators then derived a monetary estimate of program benefits. In his cost-benefit analysis of the Perry Preschool Program, Barnett (1996b) concluded that participants reaped a variety of positive outcomes. Among others, student performance improved in K-12 education and participants were less likely to commit crimes later in life. In both cases, Barnett obtained estimates of monetary benefits (or averted costs), because individuals were less likely to use costly special education services or inflict costly crimes upon others. A very similar approach is used in Masse and Barnett's evaluation of the Abecedarian early childhood program in Chapter 9.

There are other methods for estimating the monetary benefits of education, but they are rarely applied. In contingent valuation, researchers obtain direct estimates of educational benefits from individuals, using a variety of survey techniques. Although variants of this approach are commonly applied in environmental economics (e.g., Mitchell and Carson, 1989), it has almost never been applied in education (see Escobar, Barnett, and Keith, 1988 for one of the few examples).

Another approach attempts to infer benefits from individuals' observed behavior in the marketplace. For example, individuals consider a variety of factors when purchasing a home. Most are tied directly to features of the home itself, such as size and quality of construction. But some are related to surrounding amenities, such as the quality of the local public school district. It is unlikely that a family will be indifferent between two identical homes, if one has access to better-quality schools. The difference in purchase price between the homes can be interpreted as families' implicit willingness to pay for school quality. It also represents an estimate of monetary benefits. Economists have used extensive data on home prices and school quality, in concert with statistical methods, to infer estimates of schooling benefits (e.g., Black, 1999). While almost never done, these estimates could be incorporated into an educational cost-benefit analysis.

JOINT INTERPRETATION OF COSTS AND OUTCOMES

Once estimates of costs and outcomes are in hand, they must be jointly interpreted in order to rank alternatives from most desirable to least desirable. This is determined by calculating a ratio of costs to outcomes. In a cost-effectiveness analysis, the cost-effectiveness ratio of each alternative is obtained by dividing the cost of each alternative by its effectiveness. It is interpreted as the cost of obtaining an additional unit of effectiveness. When ratios are calculated for each alternative, they should be rank-ordered from smallest to largest. Those alternatives with smaller ratios are relatively more cost-effective; that is, they provide a given effectiveness at a lower cost than others and are the best candidates for new investments.[9]

In cost-benefit analysis, the researcher has a wider array of options. The ratio of costs to benefits provides a simple gauge of program desirability. They are interpreted

---

9 It is also common for cost-effectiveness studies to calculate effectiveness-cost ratios (E/C) for each alternative. This ratio indicates the units of effectiveness that are obtained for each unit of cost that is incurred (generally a dollar or a multiple of a dollar). While the interpretation of these ratios is different, they will lead to the same conclusions about the relative cost-effectiveness of alternatives. For purposes of consistency, it is generally preferable to present cost-effectiveness ratios (C/E).

in a similar fashion to the cost-effectiveness ratio. The goal is to choose the alternatives that exhibit the lowest cost per unit of benefits. Because a cost-benefit analysis expresses outcomes in monetary terms, however, the cost-benefit ratio has an additional interpretation. We should not implement any alternative for which the costs outweigh the benefits (i.e., C/B>1). Thus, we can assess the overall worth of an alternative, in addition to its desirability relative to other alternatives.[10]

Because a cost-benefit analysis expresses outcomes in pecuniary terms, there are several alternative measures of project worth that can be employed, including the net present value and the internal rate of return. Each has its own decision rules, and is subject to strengths and weaknesses. For a summary, see Levin and McEwan (2001, Chap. 7) and Boardman, Greenberg, Vining, and Weimer (1996).

It is a rare (or perhaps nonexistent) cost analysis that is not subject to some measure of uncertainty. This can stem from any component of the analysis, including the estimates of effectiveness or benefits; the cost ingredients that comprise each alternative; or the discount rate. In some cases, uncertainty is a natural component of the analysis, as with estimates of program impact that are derived from statistical samples of individuals. In other cases, uncertainty is a direct reflection of our ignorance regarding a component of the analysis, such as the price of a cost ingredient.

There are multiple techniques for assessing whether uncertainty may invalidate the conclusions of a cost analysis.[11] The simplest is known as one-way sensitivity analysis, and it is an indispensable part of the evaluator's toolkit. One identifies a parameter for which there is uncertainty and specifies a range of plausible values. Generally the "middle" estimate is the original estimate, while "low" and "high" estimates are derived from more and less conservative assumptions. Using this range of parameter values, the evaluator calculates a series of cost-effectiveness ratios for a particular alternative. Ideally, the ratio's magnitude will not be extremely sensitive, and the overall cost-effectiveness rankings will be unchanged. When cost-effectiveness rankings do change, it may prod the evaluator to seek better data on some aspect of the analysis. Minimally, it warrants a larger dose of caution when interpreting the results and making policy recommendations.

THE QUANTITY AND QUALITY OF RESEARCH

In a very general way, the previous sections described some of the best practices in conducting a cost-effectiveness or cost-benefit analysis. The first objective of this volume is to inquire whether these techniques are commonly applied, and whether

---

10 The scale of the intervention must be considered, too. Educational projects with large fixed costs and low variable costs such as educational television will have lower costs per student at higher enrollments. In contrast, those interventions that have high variable costs (e.g. reduced class size) will not experience declining costs.

11 Besides sensitivity analysis, another useful but rarely applied tool is a Monte Carlo analysis, in which statistical distributions are specified for each uncertain parameter in the analysis (see Boardman et al., 1996). After taking random draws from each distribution, one calculates a cost-effectiveness ratio. The process is repeated many times, yielding multiple cost-effectiveness ratios. If the ratios are clustered tightly around a single value, then uncertainty does not greatly alter the conclusions. If they range widely, then conclusions are less robust.

they are applied correctly. The conclusions of the authors in Chapters 2–4 do not leave us with much optimism that the quantity or quality of studies is sufficient to provide high-quality advice to policymakers about the most efficient allocation of educational resources.

In Chapter 2, Jennifer King Rice assesses whether, in fact, cost analysis is conducted less frequently in education than in other fields of public policy. This has been frequently conjectured, but there is little systematic evidence to that effect. Thus, Rice reviews the recent publications of four scholarly journals in educational policy, educational economics, health economics, and the more general field of public policy analysis. On average, she finds that articles in education policy are the most likely to avoid any discussion of costs. Between 1996 and 2000, for example, 55 percent of the evaluations in *Educational Evaluation and Policy Analysis* ignored costs completely, and another 34 percent provided a simple treatment with little or no analysis. These trends appear to have remained fairly steady during the last decade.

Among the small number of papers that do provide some extended treatment of costs, the good news is that there does not seem to be an appreciable difference between the quality of cost analyses in education and other fields, and quality appears to have increased slightly during the last decade (although these judgments are limited to five basic criteria). The bad news is that none of the fields seem to provide many exemplars for methodological rigor. For example, no more than a third of cost studies in any field make a comprehensive attempt to include difficult-to-value resources such as volunteers.

Chapter 3, by Patrick McEwan, focuses more intently on the issue of quality, using a sample of 54 studies that attempt to compare the costs and outcomes of one or more educational alternatives. Using a detailed set of methodological criteria, he finds that cost analyses often fall short of minimal standards. For example, 54 percent of studies do not provide a complete description of the educational alternatives, making it difficult to understand what exactly is being evaluated. Only 31 percent undertook a comprehensive description and valuation of costs using some approximation of the ingredients method. Twenty-eight percent applied some other method, often excluding or misvaluing key categories of ingredients such as volunteers and facilities, and 11 percent provided no details on the costing method at all. Fully half of the analyses do not account for uncertainty in their analyses by assessing whether their conclusions are sensitive to key assumptions about costs or outcomes.

McEwan concludes that these shortcomings should not be taken lightly when making policy decisions. In the prominent case of private-school vouchers, for example, he argues that the existing base of evidence is not appropriate to judge whether private schooling is more or less cost-effective than public schooling, because of flaws in existing research—a point reiterated by Mun Tsang later in the volume.

In Chapter 4, William Clune uses yet another sample of studies, drawn from the ERIC database of educational research, to review the quantity and quality of research. Between 1991 and 1996, he found 541 studies that purported to conduct a cost-effectiveness study in K-12 education. Based on a review of abstracts, however, 83 percent used the term as a rhetorical device or made a very minimal attempt to compare costs and outcomes. Just 2 percent of abstracts were classified as "plausible" or "partially plausible" attempts. Upon examining a subsample of complete studies, the quality ratings declined even further. Even so, Clune draws considerably more optimistic conclusions than McEwan about the usefulness of this highly imperfect research base, arguing that it might still yield useful policy conclusions. He reviews a small number of studies from his sample in greater detail suggesting that they can provide some guide to resource allocation even if parts of each study are viewed with a grain of salt.

Notwithstanding Clune's optimism, the cost-effectiveness literature provides little cause for celebration. Despite different samples and measures of quality, Chapters 2–4 all point to a similar conclusion. As a term, "cost-effectiveness" is used frequently, but it is rarely accompanied by a systematic empirical study. When a study is carried out, it often fails to meet a fairly minimal set of quality standards.

KEY ISSUES IN CONDUCTING RESEARCH

The previous chapters assess the quality of research in very general terms, and they paint a depressing portrait. Though helpful in assessing the overall health of the field, the findings still provide little concrete guidance to researchers who are interested in improving the quality of research. Thus, Chapters 5–7 pursue more specific, and perhaps more constructive, lines of inquiry. Each chapter identifies key issues in the conduct of good cost-effectiveness analyses, motivating the discussion by focusing on a particular area of policy. The chapters establish whether the issues have been treated adequately (or inadequately) in a particular body of cost-effectiveness research, and how this may alter policy conclusions about resource allocation.

In Chapter 5, Henry Levin analyzes the contentious issue of which of the popular whole-school reform initiatives (e.g., Coalition of Essential Schools, Core Knowledge, America's Choice, Success for All, Comer schools, the Accelerated Schools Project) provides the most cost-effective means of improving student outcomes. He concludes that existing evidence is mostly insufficient to provide reasonable guidance. Some of the reasons are fairly straightforward, and would apply to cost-effectiveness analyses in almost any area. For example, there is a growing literature that evaluates whether these reforms are effective in raising a variety of student outcomes. Yet, there are only a few high-quality experimental studies, and many other studies provide few details on how treatment and comparison schools were chosen, even when there are strong *a priori* reasons to suspect that treatment schools are "special" in some unobserved way.[12] Even when evaluation designs are strong, comparisons of effectiveness are still challenging because whole-school reforms sometimes pursue multiple objectives that are not shared across all reforms.

Cost analysis turns out to be just as problematic. Although there are two pioneering studies of the costs of whole-school reforms (Barnett, 1996a; King, 1994), neither relied heavily on direct observations of cost ingredients in schools or was able to combine cost information with effectiveness. Levin further notes that the implementation of some whole-school reforms relies upon reallocations of resources from other activities within the school (e.g., from Title I expenditures). It is common to treat these reallocations as "costless," an unlikely assumption. A comprehensive

---

12 For example, most of the reforms require substantial support (or "buy-in") within the school before the reform can be applied. This is suggestive that only the most motivated or able schools end up participating.

evaluation should search for evidence that such reallocations do not impinge upon other important school goals, but this has been little explored.

David Grissmer reviews a broad range of cost-effectiveness and cost-benefit evidence in Chapter 6. In doing so, he makes a simple, but often neglected point: the effectiveness of educational interventions can differ dramatically among different populations of students. By failing to assess the differential effectiveness of interventions, we risk drawing erroneous conclusions about the cost-effectiveness of some alternatives.[13] In other research with the National Assessment of Educational Progress (NAEP), Grissmer and colleagues found that investing in additional teacher resources—but not class size reduction—was the most cost-effective means of raising achievement (Grissmer, Flanagan, Kawata, and Williamson, 2000).

However, these conclusions are reversed when the analysis allows class size effects to vary across subsamples of students. In fact, class size reduction turns out to be one of the most cost-effective interventions in states with a high proportion of disadvantaged students and already large classes. Besides the obvious implications for conducting research, Grissmer notes that constructing efficient policies will depend on finding good mechanisms for identifying and targeting special populations of students. He suggests that effective targeting is most likely to occur at the local level.

In Chapter 7, Mun Tsang examines the pitfalls to comparing the costs of private and public schools in developing countries. As he notes, the relative merits of private and public schools are hotly debated throughout the world, and much of the debate turns on the relative cost-effectiveness of private schools. Unfortunately, the cost side of the analysis has often been treated with less care than the effectiveness side. Tsang describes how a careful ingredients-based approach might approach a comparison of public and private costs.

On a number of fronts, he argues that this approach is usually not applied well. For example, Tsang reviews a large body of evidence showing that the private sector costs account for a substantial portion of overall school costs in both private and public schools (even when public schools are nominally "free"). These costs include the direct and indirect costs to parents, as well as other private contributions that subsidize school operations. For many reasons—but often because of poor data—these costs are estimated with error, if at all. Unfortunately, their exclusion or understatement is not innocuous. Because costs to the private sector are relatively higher in the private schools, incomplete cost comparisons will usually favor private schools. This could yield substantially misleading advice about whether privatization of schooling will lead to increased efficiency.

NEW EMPIRICAL EVIDENCE

Lest the complaints of Chapters 2–4 appear unhelpful, Chapters 8–10 attempt to provide new evidence from cost-effectiveness and cost-benefit analyses, modeling some of the best practices described in previous chapters. At the beginning of Chapter 8, Brown and Belfield note the frequent laments about the lack of cost-effectiveness research, and observe that an efficient response is to take advantage of extant research on effectiveness, in concert with new information on costs. They

---

13 Also see Levin and McEwan (2001, pp. 132–135).

gather the existing body of research on the effectiveness of several modes of imparting information—relative to the "traditional" mode of lectures—including personalized instruction, discussion modes, and independent study. Much of the evidence is drawn from randomized experiments. Referring to the original studies, they devise a procedure to estimate the costs of each intervention relative to lectures using a cost template based on the ingredients method. Perhaps contrary to conventional wisdom, no particular mode emerges as clearly more cost-effective than lectures, and there is considerable variance in cost-effectiveness even within categories. A sensitivity analysis sought to assess whether these conclusions were robust to alternative assumptions about costs, but the fundamental results were similar.

Barnett's (1996b) cost-benefit analysis of the Perry Preschool Program is often cited as a best practice in the cost-benefit analysis of early childhood programs. In Chapter 9, Leonard Masse and W. Steven Barnett pursue a similarly thorough research strategy in their evaluation of the Abecedarian early childhood intervention. The Abecedarian program provided full-day, year-round preschool services to children at risk of educational failure. Beginning in 1972, a randomized experiment was undertaken which established that treated children experienced gains in IQ and academic achievement. Masse and Barnett used findings from the experiment and other, supplemental data to compare program costs and benefits.

To estimate the costs of the program, they applied the ingredients method. The analysis is notable for its careful attempt to monetize costs that are frequently ignored (such as the parental time) and for its attempt to provide policy-relevant costs. Besides estimating costs in the original treatment environment, the authors estimate costs of replicating the program in public school and child care environments. Costs are compared with several categories of program benefits, including additional earnings that are projected to accrue to participants over their lifetimes; the earnings of future generations; the cost-savings incurred because participants were less likely to be placed in special education; health benefits due to lower smoking rates among participants; and increased maternal earnings. Over a wide range of discount rates, they find that the net present value of benefits outweighs costs.

Despite the positive results, Masse and Barnett conclude by noting that their cost-benefit analysis is hard-pressed to identify the optimal amount of an educational intervention that should be provided. Indeed, this is a problem common to all cost-effectiveness and cost-benefit analyses. By their nature, these analyses usually only consider discrete applications of particular interventions, but not what the "right" amount is. That is, they enable a comparison of alternatives and a ranking in terms of their effectiveness or benefits relative to their costs, but do not reveal the optimal level of use.

This is on of the primary motivations of Chapter 10 by Doug Harris. Based on his larger study of efficient resource allocation, the chapter reminds us that cost-effectiveness and cost-benefit analyses are based on economic principles, even if this is rarely stated explicitly. The presumption is that a decision maker at some level will choose the "optimal" resource allocation that maximized benefits, subject to resource constraints. Harris proposes that such an optimization model can be explicitly implemented, drawing upon accumulated evidence from education production functions and some assumptions.

His analysis attempts to identify the "optimal" levels of two common educational inputs: class size and teacher salaries. He finds that current class sizes already lie within a range of optimal values established by the model, but that teacher salaries are below the optimal range. His conclusion is that policymakers have gone too far in reducing class size, and that additional resources could be more efficiently allocated to interventions such as raising teacher salaries. With higher teacher salaries it is possible to draw a larger and higher quality pool of prospective teachers, and to maintain a more stable teaching force.

FUTURE DIRECTIONS

This volume raises serious questions about the amount and quality of existing cost-effectiveness studies. In response, it suggests a range of methodological considerations for expanding and improving the body of work in this field. Finally, it provides new examples of rigorous cost-effectiveness and cost-benefit studies in education. It is our hope that the various chapters provide useful information and examples that might inspire others to add to the literature so that the repast of cost-effectiveness endeavors available to policymakers will be more sumptuous and nutritious for educational policymakers than it has been in the past.

REFERENCES

Angrist, J. D., and Krueger, A. B. (1999). Empirical strategies in labor economics. In O. Ashenfelter and D. Card (Eds.), *Handbook of labor economics* (Vol. 3A, pp. 1277–1366). Amsterdam: Elsevier.

Barnett, W. S. (1996a). Economics of school reform: Three promising models. In H. F. Ladd (Ed.), *Holding schools accountable* (pp. 299–326). Washington, DC: The Brookings Institution.

Barnett, W. S. (1996b). *Lives in the balance: Age-27 benefit-cost analysis of the High/Scope Perry Preschool Program.* Ypsilanti, MI: High/Scope Press.

Black, S. E. (1999). Do better schools matter? Parental valuation of elementary education. *Quarterly Journal of Economics, 114*(2), 577–599.

Boardman, A. E., Greenberg, D. H., Vining, A. R., and Weimer, D. L. (1996). *Cost-benefit analysis: Concepts and practice.* Upper Saddle River, NJ: Prentice Hall.

Boruch, R. F. (1997). *Randomized experiments for planning and evaluation: A practical guide.* Thousand Oaks, CA: Sage.

Chambers, J., and Parrish, T. (1994a). Developing a resource cost database. In W. S. Barnett (Ed.), *Cost analysis for education decisions: Methods and examples* (Vol. 4, pp. 23–44). Greenwich, CT: JAI.

Chambers, J., and Parrish, T. (1994b). Modeling resource costs. In W. S. Barnett (Ed.), *Cost analysis for education decisions: Methods and examples* (Vol. 4, pp. 7–21). Greenwich, CT: JAI.

Cook, T. D., and Campbell, D. T. (1979). *Quasi-experimentation: Design and analysis for field studies.* Chicago: Rand McNally.

Drummond, M. F., O'Brien, B., Stoddart, G. L., and Torrance, G. W. (1997). *Methods for the economic evaluation of health care programmes* (2nd ed.). Oxford: Oxford University Press.

Escobar, C. M., Barnett, W. S., and Keith, J. E. (1988). A contingent valuation approach to measuring the benefits of preschool education. *Educational Evaluation and Policy Analysis, 10*(1), 13–22.

Gerard, K. (1992). Cost-utility in practice: A policy maker's guide to the state-of-the-art. *Health Policy, 21,* 249–279.

Gold, M. R., Siegel, J. E., Russell, L. B., and Weinstein, M. C. (Eds.). (1996). *Cost-effectiveness in health and medicine.* New York: Oxford University Press.

Grissmer, D. W., Flanagan, A., Kawata, J., and Williamson, S. (2000). *Improving student achievement: What NAEP state test scores tell us.* Santa Monica, CA: RAND.

King, J. (1994). Meeting the needs of at-risk students: A cost analysis of three models. *Educational Evaluation and Policy Analysis, 16*(1), 1–19.

Levin, H. M. (1975). Cost-effectiveness in evaluation research. In M. Guttentag and E. Struening (Eds.), *Handbook of evaluation research* (Vol. 2). Beverly Hills, CA: Sage.

Levin, H. M. (1983). *Cost-effectiveness: A primer.* Newbury Park, CA: Sage.

Levin, H. M. (1988). Cost-effectiveness and educational policy. *Educational Evaluation and Policy Analysis, 10*(1), 51–69.

Levin, H. M., and McEwan, P. J. (2001). *Cost-effectiveness analysis: Methods and applications* (2nd ed.). Thousand Oaks, CA: Sage.

Light, R. J., Singer, J. D., and Willett, J. B. (1990). *By design: Planning research on higher education.* Cambridge, MA: Harvard University Press.

Mitchell, R. C., and Carson, R. T. (1989). *Using surveys to value public goods: The contingent valuation method.* Washington, DC: Resources for the Future.

Orr, L. L. (1999). *Social experiments.* Thousand Oaks, CA: Sage.

Orr, L. L., Bloom, H. S., Bell, S. H., Doolittle, F., Lin, W., and Cave, G. (1996). *Does job training for the disadvantaged work? Evidence from the National JTPA Study.* Washington, DC: Urban Institute.

Rossi, P. H., and Freeman, H. E. (1993). *Evaluation: A systematic approach* (5th ed.). Newbury Park, CA: Sage.

Salkeld, G., Davey, P., and Arnolda, G. (1995). A critical review of health-related economic evaluations in Australia: Implications for health policy. *Health Policy, 31*(2), 111–125.

Shadish, W. R., Cook, T. D., and Campbell, D. T. (2002). *Experimental and quasi-experimental designs for generalized causal inference.* Boston: Houghton Mifflin.

Sloan, F. A. (Ed.). (1995). *Valuing health care: Costs, benefits, and effectiveness of pharmaceuticals and other medical technologies.* Cambridge: Cambridge University Press.

Stern, D., Dayton, C., Paik, I.-W., and Weisberg, A. (1989). Benefits and costs of dropout prevention in a high school program combining academic and vocational education: Third-year results from replications of the California Peninsula Academies. *Educational Evaluation and Policy Analysis, 11*(4), 405–416.

Udvarhelyi, I. S., Colditz, G. A., Rai, A., and Epstein, A. M. (1992). Cost-effectiveness and cost-benefit analyses in the medical literature: Are the methods being used correctly? *Annals of Internal Medicine, 116,* 238–244.

THE QUANTITY AND QUALITY OF RESEARCH

2

COST ANALYSIS IN EDUCATION POLICY RESEARCH: A COMPARATIVE ANALYSIS ACROSS FIELDS OF PUBLIC POLICY

Jennifer King Rice[*]

INTRODUCTION

Public education in the United States has been widely criticized for its apparent inefficient use of resources. At the national level, Hanushek (1994) shows evidence that per-pupil expenditures for education have increased dramatically over the past three decades, while student test scores have remained steady at best.[1] Further documenting the perception of widespread inefficiency in the administration of public education is the array of reforms aimed at improving the use of education resources to realize greater productivity. Reform initiatives like high stakes accountability systems, incentive programs for teachers and schools, and school choice plans all embody the assumption that restructuring the use of rewards and sanctions in education can induce higher levels of performance, even with little or no increase in spending. In fact, Hanushek (1996, p. 30) argues that additional funding to support education reform initiatives should be limited since "the problem is not a lack of resources but poor application of available resources." The nature of many of these reforms is to force policymakers and school leaders to be more disciplined in making difficult

---

[*] The author acknowledges Ed Pachetti for his valuable contributions as a graduate assistant on this project.

[1] Much debate surrounds the questions of how efficient or inefficient public education actually is (National Research Council, 1999). For instance, the claims of Hanushek (1994) have been criticized both for overestimating the increases in expenditures for public education (see, for example, Rothstein and Miles, 1995; Rothstein and Mishel, 1997) and for understating the achievement outcomes he reports (see, for examples, Berliner and Biddle, 1995; Bracey, 1995; Grissmer, 1998; and Grissmer, Flanagan, and Williamson, 1998). The point here is not to resolve this debate, but rather, to recognize efficiency as an issue that needs to be better addressed.

decisions among attractive but competing policy alternatives with the goal of finding more productive ways to use resources within their budgetary constraints.

One logical response to this call for greater efficiency would be for education researchers, policymakers, and leaders to base policy decisions on sound empirical evidence. Cost analysis—particularly approaches that compare the cost and effectiveness of multiple alternative courses of action—could be very powerful and persuasive given the current policy climate of increasing pressure on public education to accomplish an expanding array of goals often in the face of few additional resources. However, education research has traditionally been criticized for its under-utilization of this potentially powerful tool (Catterall, 1988; Haller, 1974; Hanushek, 1994; Levin, 1991).

While the need for cost analysis to inform decisions about how to most efficiently allocate limited resources is apparent, questions remain about how much attention is currently being devoted to cost analysis, how sophisticated the studies are, and what sorts of education policy issues are most likely to be evaluated using this analytic tool. This chapter uses three approaches to gauge the amount and the nature of cost analysis that is occurring in the field of education policy. First, it compares the use of cost analysis in education policy research to that in other fields of public policy, in order to document the extent to which the field of education stands alone in its apparent neglect of this potentially powerful analytic tool. Second, it examines how the use of cost analysis has changed over time, in order to assess whether education researchers are making more and/or better use of cost analysis than in the past. Finally, it explores the kinds of education policy issues that are most likely to be addressed using cost analysis to get a sense of the context in which this tool is most commonly used by education policy researchers. The overall purpose of the chapter is to profile the attentiveness to cost analysis in education policy research with an eye toward improving on its current use.

The next section of this chapter reviews what is known about the use of cost analysis in education policy research. The sections that follow describe the methodological approach used in this comparative study, and present the findings of the analysis. The chapter concludes with a discussion of the implications for the ongoing work of education policy analysts.

WHAT IS KNOWN ABOUT THE USE OF COST ANALYSIS IN EDUCATION POLICY RESEARCH?

While one would expect cost analysis to be a commonly used tool in education policy research, evidence suggests this kind of analysis is not characteristic of education evaluation studies. Levin (1991) found that between 1985 and 1988 fewer than 1 percent of the evaluations presented at the annual meetings of the American Educational Research Association included cost-effectiveness considerations. Monk and King (1993) examined evaluation studies in two scholarly journals to examine how the use of cost analysis in education compared to public policy in general. They found that 75 percent of the evaluations in the education journal ignored cost compared to 20 in the broader public policy journal. Despite these differences, the nature of the studies that were published in the two journals was comparable along a number of dimensions. Finally, Levin and McEwan (2001) contrast the limited use of cost analysis in education with the growing reliance on this analytic tool in health policy research. This apparent dearth of cost analysis in education policy research in the face of increasingly strained resources presents a paradox (Rice, 1997). As Levin and

McEwan (2001, p. xix) argue, "cost-effectiveness analysis should be more important than ever, particularly in education. At every level of government, administrators are being asked to accomplish more with the same or even fewer resources."

A number of explanations have been set forth to account for the limited attention to cost-effectiveness issues in education policy research. These include inappropriate training among education researchers and policymakers (Levin, 1983, 1991), inadequate understanding of the technical properties of the education production process (Barnett, 1993), as well as a number of difficulties that complicate the application of cost analysis to education policy (e.g., the identification and measurement of costs and effects, the distribution of costs and effects across individuals and organizations, and the limited generalizability of findings across sites) (Rice, 1997).

In sum, there is little question that cost analysis should be a consideration in education policy research, some evidence suggesting that it is uncommon, and a number of reasonable explanations for why this is the case.

METHOD

This study builds on earlier work by Monk and King (1993) that reviewed evaluation studies in two academic journals to draw conclusions about the frequency and sophistication of cost analysis in education compared to public policy in general. Like the Monk and King analysis, this study uses scholarly journals as the basis for the comparison and applies the two coding strategies used in that study. This chapter takes the analysis forward in several ways by: (1) refining the framework used in that study by adding additional components, (2) updating the analysis to the past five years, (3) expanding the comparison to additional journals, (4) adding a longitudinal component to examine trends over time, and (5) including a content analysis of the education evaluations to determine the types of issues most commonly considered using cost analysis. Below I describe the journals used in the analysis and the ways the evaluations published in those journals were coded for the study.

JOURNALS

The comparisons in this chapter are based on evaluation studies published in four reputable, peer-reviewed academic journals. Two journals are focused on education: *Educational Evaluation and Policy Analysis* (EEPA) and *Economics of Education Review* (EER). Both are well-respected education policy research journals. One emphasizes evaluation in general and the other is focused on economic issues related to education. Taken together, they represent primary outlets through which education policy researchers might publish cost evaluations. The other two journals provide the basis for comparing the use of cost analysis in education policy evaluations to that in other fields of public policy. The *Journal of Policy Analysis and Management* (JPAM) is a public policy journal that includes articles on a wide variety of issues permitting a comparison between education and public policy in general.[2] The *Journal of Health Economics* (JHE) provides an opportunity to compare education and health policy specifically. Levin and McEwan (2001) recognize the increasing reliance on cost analysis in health policy, a sharp contrast to their observations of education policy

---

2   While *JPAM* includes some articles on education, it tends to focus more on broader issues of public policy.

evaluation. *JHE* provides the basis for an empirical investigation of the frequency and sophistication of cost analysis in these two fields of public policy. The inclusion of *EER* and *JHE* also provide an opportunity to observe the extent to which analyses published in journals with an emphasis on economics differ from those published in more general policy analysis journals like *EEPA* and *JPAM*.

Several important reasons ground the decision to base the comparisons made in this chapter on work published in scholarly journals. First, defining the basis for this kind of comparison is a major challenge given that program evaluation is routinely conducted in many arenas including both public forums (like journals) and site-specific contexts which are generally not shared though public channels. Relying on a set of journals that are well-regarded outlets for evaluation research in education and other fields of public policy allows for an even-handed comparison of evaluations that have been released to the public domain. Second, all four of these journals engage in formal peer review processes that ensure some level of quality control over the studies they publish, offering a degree of validity to the comparisons made here. Finally, on a practical note, Monk and Rice's (1993) comparison used two of the journals included in this study—*EEPA* and *JPAM*—as the basis for their analysis. Since this chapter builds on that work, and draws on data from that analysis for longitudinal comparisons, consistency in the use of those two journals was essential.

While a variety of articles are routinely published in these four journals, I focused primarily on evaluation studies to assess the role that cost analysis plays. For the purposes of this analysis, evaluations were identified using three criteria: (1) the studies had an identifiable treatment or intervention (i.e., a policy, program, or practice) that was the subject of interest; (2) the studies identified some sort of measurable outcome hypothesized to be related to the intervention being studied (e.g., test scores, dropout rates, wages, medical procedure rates, welfare participation rates, crime rates); and (3) the studies were data-driven and employed a methodology that permitted the researcher to examine the relationship between the treatment and the outcomes. Each evaluation was coded using the three strategies described below. In addition to evaluations, I recorded the number of articles addressing methodological issues associated with cost analysis included in each of the journals over the period studied. While these articles were not the focus of the analysis, they do serve as an indicator of the degree to which cost analysis is receiving attention and being disseminated as an important tool in policy evaluation in the fields being compared.

The cross-field comparisons reviewed all volumes of each of the four journals over the five-year period between 1996 and 2000.[3] The longitudinal comparison combined the data from *EEPA* and *JPAM* generated for this study between 1993 and 2000 with previous data (1991–1992) from Monk and King (1993) to draw conclusions about how the use of cost analysis in education and public policy has evolved over the past decade (1991–2000).[4] The content analysis of education issues addressed using cost analysis also relied on studies published during the past decade.

---

3 This included *EEPA* volumes 18(1)–22(4), *EER* volumes 15(1)–19(4), *JPAM* volumes 15(1)–19(4), and *JHE* volumes 15(1)–19(6).

4 The 10-year comparison included *EEPA* volumes 13(1)–22(4), with 13(1)–14(3) coming from the Monk and Rice analysis. The *JPAM* volumes used in the longitudinal comparison included 10(1)–19(4), with 10(1)–11(4) drawn from the Monk and Rice comparison.

ANALYTIC FRAMEWORK

I use three typologies to assess (1) the attentiveness of policy evaluations to cost issues, (2) the dimensions of quality included in the studies, and (3) the type of cost analysis conducted. The first two of these coding rubrics were also used by Monk and King (1993) in their comparative analysis. Each of these typologies captures a different dimension of the use of cost analysis, and each is described below. In many cases, assigning codes to a particular evaluation was not straightforward. In general, we were liberal with inclusion criteria for assigning the various codes. As a result, this study presents a best-case scenario in terms of the use and sophistication of cost analysis in these journals.

ATTENTION TO COST

The first step of the analysis involved coding each evaluation according to the degree to which cost considerations were included in the study. Each study was assigned one of the following values: 0 = no mention of cost; 1 = a simple or cursory mention or cost but with little or no analysis); and 2 = some extended treatment of one or more aspects of cost. This categorization provided a basis for understanding how attentive education evaluation research is to cost issues relative to other fields of public policy and over time.

DIMENSIONS OF QUALITY

A second issue relates to the nature of the studies that are conducted. This part of the analysis included only those studies that were assigned a code of "2" in terms of attentiveness to cost. In other words, the focus is on studies that included some extended treatment of cost with the goal of understanding the nature of that treatment. The idea here was to assess the degree to which the cost studies included certain features generally recognized as quality standards (Gerard, 1992; Levin and McEwan, 2001; Salkeld, Davey, and Arnolda, 1995; Udvarhelyi, Colditz, Rai, and Epstein, 1992). The goal was not to evaluate the articles in terms of how well they delivered on these dimensions of quality, but rather to determine whether the studies made an effort to include such features.[5] Adhering to the coding strategy of Monk and King (1993), I used five types of treatment:

A = Includes difficult-to-value resources. Public policy interventions involve a variety of resources that can be hard to value (e.g., the donated time of parents, teachers and community members; the opportunity costs associated with students' and patients' time). An "A" was assigned to those studies that make efforts to include resources that are not easily valued in dollar terms.

B = Recognizes multiple perspectives. Public policy, including education and health policy, generally involves multiple stakeholder groups with the costs and benefits distributed across a variety of individuals and organizations. In the field of health, this might include patients, hospitals, and society (Udvarhelyi et al., 1992). Similarly, in education, costs and benefits are distributed across students, schools, communities, and the public treasury (Rice, 1997). A "B" was assigned to those studies that recognize this distribution of cost across a variety of parties.

---

5   We found a great deal of variability in the quality and sophistication of the analyses with respect to these features. In an effort to be as generous as possible, we included even limited attempts to recognize a particular dimension of quality.

C = Considers costs over time. The costs of an intervention are likely to change over time. For instance, start-up costs (e.g., development and implementation) are often high relative to the costs associated with the continuous operation of a fully implemented program. A "C" was assigned to those evaluation studies that include a longitudinal dimension for examining costs over time.

D = Compares costs with measures of effectiveness. Considered alone, information on the costs of an intervention can reveal important information on the feasibility of an intervention in terms of its resource requirements. However, studies that link costs with outcome measures can provide valuable information on how much it costs to accomplish specific goals, or what can be accomplished through a particular intervention at a set level of investment. A "D" was assigned to studies that explicitly link costs with measures of effectiveness.

E = Compares costs with effectiveness across multiple interventions. Studies that consider the cost-effectiveness trade-offs associated with multiple courses of action hold the most promise for improving the efficiency of an industry. These studies are intended to identify the policy alternative associated with the lowest cost per unit of effectiveness (or, alternatively, that yields that highest level of outcome per unit of cost). An "E" was assigned to evaluations that compared the cost-effectiveness (or cost-benefit) of multiple policy alternatives. Note that every study coded "E" must also be coded "D."

According to this coding rubric, a single study could be assigned multiple letter categories. In fact, it could be argued that the most sophisticated cost analyses are characterized by all five of these features. Since some studies were assigned multiple letter ratings, the sum of the letter columns exceeds the number of evaluations coded as "2" in terms of the attentiveness to cost.

TYPE OF ANALYSIS

In addition to the two coding rubrics that were used by Monk and King (1993), this chapter also accounted for the type of cost analyses that are conducted in education versus other fields of public policy. Four approaches to cost analysis frame this part of the study.

CE = Cost-effectiveness. This type of cost analysis addresses the question "Should we support this or that?" Cost-effectiveness studies integrate information on the costs and effects of various alternatives to identify the option that most efficiently utilizes resources to produce a particular outcome. Strictly defined, the interventions should be alternative ways to accomplish a single shared goal.

CU = Cost-utility. This type of cost analysis also addresses the "this versus that" question, but is used when the alternatives are intended to realize multiple outcomes. The various outcomes are weighted and are combined into a single measure of utility against which the costs are compared.

CB = Cost-benefit. These studies answer the question "Is this initiative worth the investment?" For the purpose of this type of analysis, costs and benefits are both measured in monetary units. To the degree that the benefits outweigh the costs, the initiative is desirable on economic grounds. Cost-benefit analyses can be applied to a single initiative or to inform decisions about competing investment alternatives with different goals (e.g., education versus health care).

CF = Cost-feasibility. These studies answer the question "How much does this intervention cost?" By providing information on the total cost of the intervention, cost-feasibility studies can provide decision makers with a sense of the array of resources required to accomplish the goals of the initiative.

These codes were assigned based on what the evaluation actually did, rather than what the authors claimed it would do.[6] This coding rubric was applied only to those evaluations that were assigned a "2" in terms of the attention to cost.

Findings

The findings of the analysis are presented in three sections. First, I discuss how education compares with other areas of public policy in terms of its use of cost analysis in evaluation research over the past five years. Next, I describe how the use of cost analysis has changed during the past decade. Finally, I describe the kinds of education policy issues identified as most likely to be the subject of cost analysis.

Education Versus Other Areas of Public Policy

Table 2.1 presents the findings that compare the use of cost analysis across the four journals during the five-year period ranging from 1996 to 2000. The first three columns provide the number and percentage of evaluation articles in terms of their attentiveness to cost considerations. The next five columns code those evaluations that do attend to cost (rated "2") according to the five dimensions of quality. The final four columns categorize the studies in terms of the type of cost analysis they represent.

Attentiveness to Cost

The first three columns of Table 2.1 reveal that both journals of education are less likely than the others to publish articles that devote extensive treatment to cost (as indicated by a code of "2"). Only 10 percent of the evaluations published in *EEPA* and 16 percent of those in *EER* paid serious attention to cost. In comparison, 21 percent of the evaluations published in *JPAM* and 30 percent of those in *JHE* included extended treatment of cost. Also of interest are comparisons of similar types of journals: general policy analysis journals (*EEPA* vs. *JPAM*) and economics-based journals (*EER* vs. *JHE*). Within each pair, the non-education journals were about twice as likely to include serious attention to cost issues than the education journals.

Likewise, education journals were more likely than similar types of non-education policy journals to neglect cost considerations completely (as indicated by a code of "0"). Overall, articles published in the general policy analysis journals (*EEPA* and *JPAM*) were more likely to include no mention of cost than those in the economics-based journals (*EER* and *JHE*). Within each journal type, the education journals were more likely to neglect cost. More than half (55 percent) of the evaluations published in *EEPA* included no mention of cost, compared to one-third of those included in *JPAM*. Thirty-two percent of the studies in *EER* ignored cost issues, compared to just 21 percent in *JHE*. With the exception of *EEPA*, the greatest tendency across the journals was to include some cursory mention of cost with limited if any evaluation (code of "1"). About half of the evaluations published in *EER*, *JPAM*, and *JHE* during the five-year period fell into this category.

---

6 A number of studies labeled cost-benefit analyses in their titles were actually cost-effectiveness or cost-utility analyses.

Table 2.1 Comparison of the Use of Cost Analysis in Education Policy Research Versus Other Fields of Public Policy, 1996–2000

	Attentiveness to Cost Issues[a]			Dimensions of Quality Represented in Cost Studies[b]					Type of Cost Analysis[c]			
	0	1	2	A	B	C	D	E	CE	CU	CB	CF
EEPA[d]												
Number of evaluations (n=58)	32	20	6	2	3	4	5	2	1	1	0	4
% of evaluations	55%	34%	10%									
% of evaluations rated 2 (n=6)				33%	50%	66%	83%	33%	17%	17%	0%	66%
EER[e]												
Number of evaluations (n=71)	23	37	11	2	5	2	10	7	7	0	1	3
% of evaluations	32%	52%	16%									
% of evaluations rated 2 (n=11)				18%	45%	18%	91%	63%	63%	0%	9%	27%
JPAM[f]												
Number of evaluations (n=57)	19	26	12	4	8	9	11	6	3	1	7	1
% of evaluations	33%	46%	21%									
% of evaluations rated 2 (n=12)				33%	66%	75%	92%	50%	25%	8%	58%	8%
JHE[g]												
Number of evaluations (n=57)	12	28	17	4	6	6	13	8	3	3	6	5
% of evaluations	21%	49%	30%									
% of evaluations rated 2 (n=10)				24%	35%	35%	76%	47%	18%	18%	36%	28%

a. 0=no attention to cost, 1=simple treatment of cost with little or no analysis, 2=some extended treatment of cost.

b. A=attends to difficult-to-value resources, B=recognized multiple perspectives, C=considers costs over time, D=compares costs with measures of effectiveness, E=compares cost with effectiveness across multiple alternatives.

c. CE=cost-effectiveness, CB=cost-benefit, CU=cost-utility, CF=cost-feasibility.

d. *Educational Evaluation and Policy Analysis*, 18(1)-22(4).

e. *Economics of Education Review*, 15(1)-19(4).

f. *Journal of Policy Analysis and Management*, 15(1)-19(4).

g. *Journal of Health Economics*, 15(1)-19(6).

DIMENSIONS OF QUALITY
OBSERVED IN THE STUDIES

The next step of the analysis was to examine the degree to which the cost studies that were identified in these journals included a variety of features typically associated with quality. The results are presented in the next five columns of Table 2.1. Recall, this component of the analysis focuses only on those studies that were assigned a code of "2" with respect to their attentiveness to cost issues. Interestingly, the differences observed in the percentage of studies reflecting these dimensions of quality tend to fall more along the lines of the type of journal (policy analysis vs. economics-based) than the policy field of the journal (education vs. health or general public policy).

The first dimension of quality is whether difficult-to-value resources are included in the study (coded "A"). Across all four journals, this quality dimension was among the least likely to be addressed in cost evaluations.[7] No difference was found in the percent of studies including difficult-to-value resources between the two general policy analysis journals; one-third of the cost analyses published in both *EEPA* and *JPAM* included attention to this dimension of quality. Economics-based journals were less likely to include attention to difficult-to-value resources. In the economics-based journals, attention to difficult-to-value resources was less apparent in the education journal (*EER*) than in the health journal (*JHE*).

The second dimension of quality is the recognition of multiple perspectives (coded "B"). The degree to which evaluations in the different journals attended to multiple perspectives did not reveal clear differences between education and other areas of public policy. Rather, the general policy analysis journals surfaced as more attentive to this issue than were the economics-based journals. More than half of the cost studies published in *EEPA* and *JPAM* included this feature, compared to 45 percent and 35 percent for *EER* and *JHE*, respectively. The economics-based journals tended to be more focused on the costs from a single perspective, often the firm (e.g., the school system, hospital, or HMO). The more general policy analysis journals, on the other hand, were more likely to recognize the multiple stakeholders in the context of the analysis.

The next feature related to the quality of a cost analysis is the extent to which the study considers cost over time (coded "C"). Once again, the observable differences seemed to be between the general policy analysis journals and the economics-based journals rather than between education and other fields of public policy. The two general policy analysis journals were quite attentive to costs over time; 66 percent of the *EEPA* studies and 75 percent of the *JPAM* studies included this feature. On the other hand, the analyses published in the economics-based journals were less likely to include a time dimension: only 18 percent of the *EER* studies and 35 percent of the *JHE* studies attended to this quality indicator. Note that within each type of journal, the studies published in the education journals were less likely than those in the non-education journals to include this feature.

Perhaps most impressive was the high proportion of evaluations that compared costs to measures of effectiveness (coded "D"). Over 75 percent of the cost analyses

---

7   The percentage of studies assigned a rating of "A" was tied with one other quality dimension in EEPA and EER.

published in all four journals attended to this dimension of quality. One explanation for this high rate is the selection process used for the study. Since the comparative analysis is limited to evaluation studies that were published in the journals, it stands to reason that most of the articles included attention to measures of effectiveness. Those that do not are typically some sort of cost feasibility study.

While the proportion of studies linking costs with effectiveness was impressive in all the journals examined here, it was less common for studies to go the next step to compare the cost-effectiveness (or cost-benefits) of multiple competing interventions (coded "E"). No clear pattern was evident with respect to this quality indicator. One-third of the cost studies published in *EEPA* and almost two-thirds of those included in *EER* compared costs and effectiveness across multiple interventions. About half of the cost analyses in the non-education policy journals (*JPAM* and *JHE*) included this feature.

TYPE OF COST ANALYSIS

The cost studies published in the various journals also differed in terms of their type. Two-thirds of the cost analyses published in *EEPA* during the five-year period were cost-feasibility studies (arguably the least sophisticated approach with limited potential for enhancing efficiency). The remaining third were cost-effectiveness and cost-utility studies. None of the *EEPA* cost analyses was a cost-benefit study. *EER* revealed a slightly different pattern. The majority of the cost analyses published in this journal (almost two-thirds) were cost-effectiveness studies that weighed the economic trade-offs of different alternatives. *EER* also included several cost-feasibility studies, and a single cost-benefit analysis.

In contrast, the majority (58 percent) of the cost studies published in *JPAM* were cost-benefit analyses with the remaining one-third split among the other types of analysis. Cost-benefit analysis was also a common approach in *JHE*, representing 36 percent of the cost studies. Another 36 percent of the *JHE* analyses were a combination of cost-effectiveness and cost-utility studies, and the remaining 28 percent were cost-feasibility studies. The relative prevalence of cost-benefit studies in *JPAM* and *JHE* compared with the education journals may indicate the difficulty of translating educational outcomes to the dollar metric. While labor market outcomes are a primary goal of education, the time and effort needed to connect education interventions with those long-term outcomes is often prohibitive. It may be that other fields of public policy (e.g., transportation, health, and welfare) may be better suited for cost-benefit analysis.

THE EVOLVING USE OF COST ANALYSIS

The next step in the study examined how the use of cost analysis in education versus public policy has changed over the past decade. Since the number of cost evaluations published in these journals during any single year was limited, I focused on five-year increments, comparing the use of cost analysis during the first half of the 1990s with that during the second half. This longitudinal component of the analysis focused only on *EEPA* and *JPAM* since I was able to draw on data from the Monk and King (1993) analysis that compared the use of cost analysis in these journals during the early years of the decade (1991–1992).[8]

---

8 The same coding conventions were used in these two studies, and much of the review of articles was conducted by the same individual, decreasing concerns about rater reliability.

Figure 2.1 presents the findings related to changes in the attentiveness of evaluations to cost issues over the past decade. The first column in each pair indicates the percent of evaluations assigned to a particular attentiveness category during the 1991–1995 period. The second is the comparable figure for 1996–2000. The first three pairs of columns presents the trends for *EEPA* and the last three pairs show the corresponding breakdowns for *JPAM*.

The findings here are disappointing from the perspective of those advocating more extensive use of cost analysis in public policy research. Neither journal evidenced an increase in the percentage of evaluations that devote significant attention to cost (assigned a rating of "2"); rather, both show a very slight decline. *EEPA*, however, also slightly decreased in the percentage of evaluations that give no attention to cost (rating of "0"), and showed a small increase in the percentage of articles giving cursory attention to cost (rating of "1"). While these changes are quite small, they may reflect a response to the growing public demand for accountability in that education policy studies are more likely than in the past to at least recognize (if not evaluate) the cost of the policy alternative being studied. A very small change was also observed in the use of cost analysis in evaluations published in *JPAM* during the first and second halves of the 1990s. The data show modest evidence of a decrease in the number of studies giving cursory attention to cost and a small increase in those giving no attention to cost. While studies published in *JPAM* continue to be more likely than those in *EEPA* to devote extensive treatment to cost considerations, the observed trends have narrowed this gap between the two journals over the past decade with respect to the percentage of studies that pay cursory attention to cost issues.

FIGURE 2.1 TRENDS IN THE ATTENTIVENESS OF EVALUATIONS TO COST ISSUES

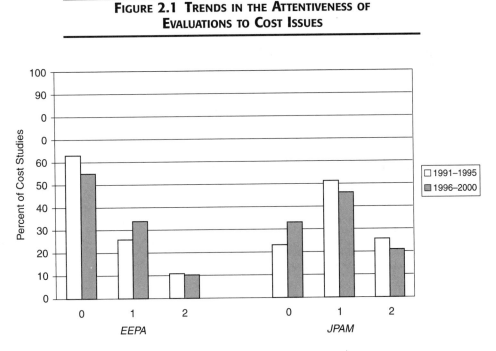

NOTES: 0 = no attention to cost, 1 = simple treatment with little or no analysis, 2 = some extended treatment of cost. *EEPA* includes volumes 12(1)-22(4). *JPAM* includes volumes 9(1)-19(4).

Figure 2.2 presents trends in the dimensions of quality found in the cost stud-ies published in *EEPA* and *JPAM* during the first and second halves of the 1990s. In most cases, an increase in the treatment of the five dimensions of quality can be observed. Of the cost evaluations published in *EEPA* during the 1990s, there was an increase in the percent that recognized multiple perspectives (coded "B"), considered costs over time (coded "C"), and compared the cost-effectiveness of mul-tiple courses of action (coded "D"). The percentage of cost studies that included difficult-to-value resources (coded "A") remained steady and the percentage that compared the costs and outcomes across multiple alternatives (coded "E") decreased across the first and second halves of the decade. The cost studies pub-lished in *JPAM* also showed improvement, sometimes dramatic, in terms of the quality dimensions addressed, with modest declines in just two areas: the inclu-sion of difficult-to-value resources and the extent to which studies compared the cost-effectiveness of multiple alternatives. Note that these are the same two dimen-sions for which *EEPA* remained steady or decreased.

In addition to analyzing the use of cost analysis in the evaluation studies published in these two journals, I kept track of the articles that addressed methodological issues related to cost analysis.[9] In *EEPA*, the number of such arti-

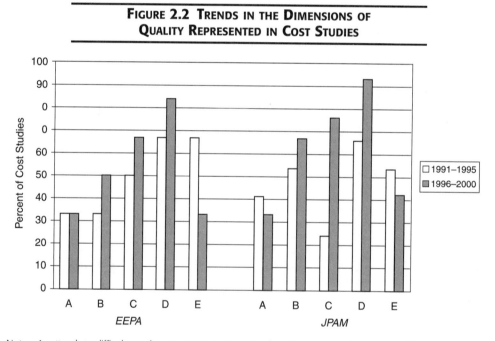

FIGURE 2.2 TRENDS IN THE DIMENSIONS OF QUALITY REPRESENTED IN COST STUDIES

Notes: A=attends to difficult-to-value resources, B=recognized multiple perspectives, C=considers costs over time, D=compares costs with measures of effectiveness, E=compares cost with effectiveness across multiple alternatives. *EEPA* includes volumes 12(1)-22(4). *JPAM* includes volumes 9(1)-19(4).

9 Since many if not most of the methodological discussions of cost analysis are published as books, this component of the analysis is somewhat limited. However, it does provide additional insight into the role and use of cost analysis in public policy research.

cles increased from zero during the first half of the decade to four during the second half. *JPAM* published four articles conceptually discussing cost analysis between 1991–1995, and three between 1996–2000. The increase in methodological discussions of cost analysis in *EEPA* may provide one explanation for the findings presented above. More in-depth discussion of the components and considerations that characterize high-quality cost analyses may result in better studies since the methodological articles promote a shared understanding of what counts as quality. On the other hand, these methodological discussions may inadvertently result in a decrease in the number of cost studies being published (particularly cost-effectiveness studies as seen in the decrease of those coded "E"), resulting either from tighter quality control on the part of journals (i.e., only the good studies are being published) or from fewer attempts on the part of researchers armed with a greater appreciation of the complex and demanding nature of the task.

CONTENT ANALYSIS OF EDUCATION COST STUDIES

The final step in this study was to explore the kinds of education policy issues most likely to be studied using cost analysis. I reviewed all of the cost evaluations identified in *EEPA* and *EER* and clustered them in terms of topical categories. As shown in Table 2.2, four such categories emerged. The most commonly addressed category included a variety of topics evaluating alternative financing strategies designed to increase educational quality, promote equity, or support school reform. A second category of topics addressed using cost analysis included studies evaluating popular school reform options such as comprehensive school reform models, year-round schooling options, early intervention services, and school and class size policies. Four of the cost analyses published in the education journals focused on policy issues related to private schools and choice plans, and a final set of three studies addressed policies related to standards and assessment.

Table 2.2 Education Policy Issues Studied Using Cost Analysis

Category	Examples of Topics	Number of Studies
Alternative financing strategies	To increase education quality To promote greater equity To support school reform plans To encourage decentralization	7
School reform options	Comprehensive models of school reform Year-round schooling Early intervention services Class size School size	6
Private schools and choice	Vouchers School choice Private schools Proprietary schools	4
Standards and assessment	Performance assessment Graduation requirements Standards	3

Summary and Discussion: Where Do We Go From Here?

The findings presented here are not inconsistent with what Monk and King (1993) found almost 10 years ago: education-policy evaluation pays substantially less attention to cost considerations than do other fields of public policy, but the nature of the studies that are conducted is not terribly different across the different policy arenas. The direct comparison with health policy is particularly interesting. While health-policy evaluations are the least likely to neglect cost altogether (perhaps due to pressures to at least mention this factor in the context of program/policy evaluation), the quality and sophistication of the studies that are conducted are not necessarily superior to those in the field of education policy. This finding is consistent with other reviews of cost analysis in the field of health policy (Gerard, 1992; Salkeld et al., 1995; Udvarhelyi et al., 1992).

In terms of changes over time, the trend analysis suggests very little change in the use of cost analysis during the decade of the 1990s. Serious attention to cost issues in public-policy evaluations published in reputable scholarly journals remained relatively steady with evidence of only modest declines. Education-policy research evidenced a slightly increasing tendency to mention cost in the context of evaluation studies, perhaps due to external pressures for greater accountability. Despite the fact that cost analyses did not become more widespread in policy evaluations published during the 1990s, the quality of the studies that were conducted tended to improve. This was the case both in the field of education as well as in the broader public-policy research community. The increase in methodological discussions of cost analysis in the field of education-policy may help to explain these longitudinal findings.

Finally, four broad education-policy categories emerged as most likely to be addressed using cost analysis: alternative financing strategies, school reform options, private schools and choice, and standards and assessment. Each of these categories includes a variety of specific policies observed in the education-policy journals.

So what does this comparative analysis tell us about the use of cost evaluation in education-policy research? Where do we go from here? One potentially productive line of discussion relates to thinking more about the kinds of cost studies that would be helpful to policymakers. I offer three criteria that education policy-researchers should consider. First, the analysis should address real policy trade-offs faced by education decision makers (e.g., higher teacher salaries, class size reduction, and comprehensive school reforms). Second, the interventions should have clear and measurable outcomes (e.g., achievement, attitudes, dropout rates, and earnings). Third, costs should be "unpacked" in a way that lays out the ingredients, values, and their distribution across different individuals and organizations so that decision makers can assess costs and effects relative to their local circumstances (see Rice, 1997). Further, education policy analysts should work with researchers in other fields of public policy to identify and overcome the hurdles that undermine the widespread use of this potentially valuable analytic tool.

While this comparative analysis sheds light on the status and evolution of the use of cost analysis in public-policy research, several limitations should be noted. First, the analysis is focused only on evaluations published in four scholarly journals and therefore is not representative of all of the evaluation work that is occurring, particularly work that is not shared through these types of forums (e.g., local evaluations not released to the public). Second, while the journals included in this analysis are well-respected outlets for the publication of cost evaluations, others also exist and could be included in this sort of analysis (e.g., *Journal of Education Finance*,

Education Economics, Journal of Human Resources, Health Economics). Third, this study focused on evaluations published over the five-year period between 1996 and 2000, with the longitudinal component including studies from 1991 to 2000. Different time frames could result in different findings. Finally, while this study identified the degree to which five dimensions of quality were addressed in published cost analyses, it did not evaluate the actual quality of the studies, i.e., how well these dimensions were executed. Rather, the benefit of the doubt was given to studies that made even limited efforts to recognize the various quality dimensions, resulting in a "best case" picture of the use of cost analysis.

REFERENCES

Barnett, W. S. (1993). Economic evaluation of home visiting programs. *The Future of Children, 3*(3), 93–112.

Berliner, D. C., and Biddle, B. J. (1995). The manufactured crisis: Myths, fraud, and the attack on America's public schools. Reading, MA: Addison Wesley.

Bracey, G. W. (1995). The fifth Bracey report on the condition of public education. *Phi Delta Kappan, 77*(2), 149–160.

Catterall, J. S. (1988). *Estimating the costs and benefits of large-scale assessments: Lessons from recent research.* Paper presented at the annual conference of the American Educational Research Association.

Gerard, K. (1992). Cost-utility in practice: A policymaker's guide to the state of the art. *Health Policy, 21,* 249–279.

Grissmer, D. W. (1998). *Education productivity.* Washington, DC: NEKIA Communications.

Grissmer, D. W., Flanagan, A., and Williamson, S. (1998). Does money matter for minority and disadvantaged students? In W. J. Fowler (Ed.), *Developments in school finance, 1997.* Washington, DC: U.S. Department of Education.

Haller, E. J. (1974). Cost analysis for educational program evaluation. In W. J. Popham (Ed.), *Evaluation in education: Current applications* (pp. 401–450). Berkeley, CA: McCutchan Publishing.

Hanushek, E. A. (with Benson, C. S., Freeman, R. B., Jamison, D. T., Levin, H. M., Maynard, R. A., Murnane, R. J., Rivkin, S. G., Sabot, R. H., Solmon, L. C., Summers, A. A., Welch, F., and Wolfe, B. L.). (1994). *Making schools work: Improving performance and controlling costs.* Washington, DC: The Brookings Institution.

Hanushek, E. A. (1996). Outcomes, costs, and incentives in schools. In E. A. Hanushek and D. W. Jorgenson (Eds.), *Improving America's schools: The role of incentives.* Washington, DC: National Academy Press.

Levin, H. M. (1983). *Cost-effectiveness: A primer.* Beverly Hills, CA: Sage.

Levin, H. M. (1991). Cost-effectiveness at quarter century. In M. W. McLaughlin and D. C. Phillips (Eds.), *Evaluation and education at quarter century* (pp.189–209). Chicago: University of Chicago Press.

Levin, H. M., and McEwan, P. J. (2001). *Cost-effectiveness analysis: Methods and applications* (2nd ed.). Thousand Oaks, CA: Sage.

Monk, D. H., and King, J. K. (1993). Cost analysis as a tool for education reform. In S. L. Jacobson and R. Berne (Eds.), *Reforming education: Yearbook of the American Education Finance Association.* Thousand Oaks, CA: Corwin.

National Research Council. (1999). *Making money matter: Financing America's schools.* Washington, DC: National Academy Press.

Rice, J. K. (1997). Cost analysis in education: Paradox and possibility. *Educational Evaluation and Policy Analysis, 19*(4), 309–317.

Rothstein, R., and Miles, K. H. (1995). Where's the money gone? Changes in the level and composition of education spending. Washington, DC: Economic Policy Institute.

Rothstein, R., and Mishel, L. (1997). Alternative options for deflating education expenditures over time. In W. J. Fowler (Ed.), *Developments in School Finance, 1996.* Washington, DC: U.S. Department of Education.

Salkeld, G., Davey, P., and Arnolda, G. (1995). A critical review of health-related economic evaluations in Australia: Implications for health policy. *Health Policy, 31*(2), 111–125.

Udvarhelyi, I. S., Colditz, G. A., Rai, A., and Epstein, A. M. (1992). Cost-effectiveness and cost-benefit analyses in the medical literature: Are the methods being used correctly? *Annals of Internal Medicine, 116,* 238–244.

3

ARE COST-EFFECTIVENESS METHODS USED CORRECTLY?

Patrick J. McEwan[*]

INTRODUCTION

Cost-effectiveness analysis (CEA) is a tool for comparing the costs and outcomes of educational alternatives. If properly conducted—and this paper describes what that may entail—CEA allows us to choose the most efficient alternatives for accomplishing particular objectives. That is, we can choose the alternatives that provide a given outcome for the lowest cost. Among educational economists, CEA is viewed as a necessary input to resource allocation decisions. Even among policymakers, there is recognition of the importance of making cost-effective decisions.

In light of this consensus, there are surprising contradictions in the cost-effectiveness literature. First, there seem to be relatively few systematic studies in education, especially relative to other fields of public policy (Levin, 1991; Levin and McEwan, 2001; Monk and King, 1993; Smith and Smith, 1985; also see Chapter 2). Even though the term "cost-effectiveness" is ubiquitous, it is mainly used as a rhetorical bludgeon to argue for or against policies (see Chapter 4). Second, there are few attempts to define methodological standards for a proper CEA in education, or to evaluate whether the extant literature adheres to these standards. As a consequence, researchers have few guideposts when conducting new research, and decision makers cannot determine how existing studies should inform policy. This paper is a basic attempt to address the second problem.

It proceeds in several steps. First, it defines a basic set of standards for CEA studies, focusing on the appropriateness of the costing methodology and the joint interpretation of costs and outcomes (relying on the concepts and definitions set forth in Chapter 1). Second, it assesses whether educational cost studies adhere to those standards. The paper concludes by assessing the relevance of the findings to educational policy.

---

[*] The author is grateful to Clive Belfield and Henry Levin for their comments.

ESTABLISHING METHODOLOGICAL STANDARDS

This section defines what constitutes a high-quality CEA, appealing to methodological writings in education and health. It then describes a simple coding form for evaluating whether quality standards are being met.

DEFINING A "GOOD" STUDY

A good cost-effectiveness study tells us which alternatives are the least costly means of accomplishing a particular educational objective. But how, exactly, should we obtain this information? I relied upon several sources for their answers. First, the textbooks of Drummond, O'Brien, Stoddart, and Torrance (1997, pp. 28–29) and Levin and McEwan (2001, pp. 228–230) present checklists for evaluating the quality of cost-effectiveness studies. Second, a national panel issued recommendations on the proper conduct of CEA in health and medicine (Weinstein, Siegel, Gold, Kamlet, and Russell, 1996). Third, Barnett's (1996b) monograph on the Perry Preschool Program is oft-cited as an exemplary cost-benefit study in education.

There is wide agreement on the procedures of a minimally competent study. These include: (1) identifying the alternatives; (2) establishing the effectiveness, benefits, or utility of alternatives; (3) establishing the costs of alternatives; (4) adjusting outcomes and costs for differential timing; (5) evaluating the distribution of outcomes and costs; (6) calculating and interpreting summary measures of cost-effectiveness; and (7) accounting for uncertainty.

IDENTIFYING THE ALTERNATIVES

At the outset, researchers should identify the alternatives that are being considered, including the exact nature and scope of activities that are contemplated. Without a clear description of alternatives, much of the subsequent analysis is problematic (Drummond et al., 1997, pp. 30–31). Most importantly, one cannot evaluate the costs and outcomes of alternatives that are vaguely described, or adequately judge whether evaluators have omitted costs or outcomes. Moreover, one cannot replicate such alternatives in other settings.

ESTABLISHING EFFECTIVENESS, BENEFITS, OR UTILITY

In a cost-effectiveness analysis, researchers must assess whether alternatives have a causal relation to measures of effectiveness. To do so, researchers choose among multiple research designs, including experimental, quasi-experimental, and non-experimental. If the resulting estimates have a causal interpretation, then they are said to possess internal validity. A vast literature enumerates potential threats to internal validity, and assesses whether evaluation designs can adequately rule them out (e.g., Campbell and Stanley, 1966; Cook and Campbell, 1979). Attempts to evaluate the quality of social science research typically focus on internal validity (Wortman, 1994).

In a cost-benefit analysis, researchers must express outcomes in monetary terms. In some cases, this is straightforward. For example, evaluation designs may be used to gauge whether an alternative produces increased earnings. In other cases, non-monetary outcomes—obtained from standard evaluation designs—can be readily converted to monetary terms (e.g., Barnett, 1996b). Increasingly, economists are applying alternative methods of measuring benefits (for descriptions, see Levin and McEwan, 2001). In contingent valuation, for example, researchers directly survey individuals on benefits received (Escobar, Barnett, and Keith, 1988). In revealed preference studies, researchers infer the magnitude of benefits by observing individual behavior in the marketplace (Black, 1999). Nonetheless, the latter methods are almost never applied in educational cost-benefit analysis.

In a cost-utility analysis, researchers must also measure individual preferences for diverse outcomes (i.e., is more mathematics achievement preferable to more reading achievement, and by how much?). There are a vast array of methods for doing so, and some controversy exists regarding their application. The methods have typically been developed and applied by researchers in decision analysis and health policy (e.g., Clemen, 1996; Drummond et al., 1997). To date, cost-utility analyses are almost nonexistent in education (for exceptions, see Fletcher, Hawley, and Piele, 1990; Lewis, Johnson, Erickson, and Bruininks, 1994).

ESTABLISHING THE COSTS

A good estimate of opportunity costs is the *sine qua non* of a cost study. It is usually obtained through a two-step procedure: (1) identifying a full range of cost ingredients and (2) valuing ingredients at their opportunity cost. When researchers do not apply the method—or apply it partially—cost estimates are often incorrect. One common error is the exclusion of important ingredients or categories of ingredients. For example, researchers sometimes neglect to identify capital ingredients (e.g., buildings and equipment), volunteer personnel, or donated materials. Another common error is to misvalue ingredients. When calculating the annual cost of durable assets like buildings, researchers may incorrectly use the entire purchase price of the building. The correct procedure would be to annualize the cost over the lifetime of the asset (see Drummond et al., 1997; Levin and McEwan, 2001). Similarly, researchers may neglect to value ingredients that do not appear in program budgets, such as volunteer personnel or donated materials.

ADJUSTING FOR DIFFERENTIAL TIMING

If one dollar of benefit is received now, it is more valuable than a dollar received 10 years in the future, if only because the dollar received sooner can be invested or used for other valuable pursuits. Yet, a simplistic comparison would presume that each dollar provided equivalent benefits. To make valid comparisons, the dollar received in the future should be discounted to its present value.[1] Similarly, costs and non-monetary outcomes received in the future should be discounted to their present values. By doing so, we account for a common preference among individuals: to receive desirable outcomes sooner rather than later.

EVALUATING DISTRIBUTIONAL CONSEQUENCES

Costs and outcomes are rarely distributed evenly across individuals. Some bear a greater burden of costs, and some may receive a disproportionate share of outcomes. This information can be of vital use in the interpretation and application of results (for examples of this, see Chapter 6). Thus, evaluators should attempt, when possible,

---

1   The procedures for discounting are well-described in most economic evaluation textbooks (e.g., Boardman, Greenberg, Vining, and Weimer, 1996; Drummond et al., 1997; Levin and McEwan, 2001).

to evaluate distributional consequences. The definition of the groups to consider may differ, depending on the context. It is common, however, to assess how costs and outcomes are distributed across the sponsors of alternatives, their clients (perhaps dividing by gender, race, or income), and society-at-large (or the "taxpayers").

CALCULATING SUMMARY MEASURES

Once costs and outcome measures are obtained, it is important to rigorously compare them. In a cost-effectiveness analysis, this entails the calculation of a cost-effectiveness ratio for each alternative. The ratio expresses the cost of obtaining one additional unit of effectiveness. Alternatives with the lowest ratios are deemed most cost-effective. Besides a ratio of costs to benefits, the cost-benefit analyst can also calculate the net present value or the internal rate of return. The relative merits of these measures are discussed elsewhere (e.g., Boardman et al., 1996).

ACCOUNTING FOR UNCERTAINTY

Even when alternatives are ranked according to their cost-effectiveness, the analysis is not complete. Rarely, if ever, are the costs and outcomes of alternatives measured with certainty. If they are measured incorrectly, then cost-effectiveness rankings could also be incorrect. Thus, evaluators should assess whether their conclusions are robust to existence of uncertainty. A common method for doing so is called sensitivity analysis. The evaluator identifies parameters for which there is uncertainty—such as the discount rate, the quantity and value of ingredients, and the estimate of effectiveness—and specifies a range of plausible values. Usually the middle value is set at the original estimate, and high and low estimates are based on more or less conservative assumptions. The evaluator calculates new cost-effectiveness ratios and observes whether the cost-effectiveness rankings of alternatives are altered. While there are other methods for assessing uncertainty—such as Monte Carlo analyses—there is widespread agreement that basic sensitivity analysis is essential.

ESTABLISHING CRITERIA

In order to determine whether cost studies adhere to these standards, I developed a coding form. It is divided into two parts: general and technical characteristics. General characteristics are largely self-explanatory; they include the type of study (cost-effectiveness, cost-benefit, or cost-utility), the year of publication, the institutional affiliation of the first author, the type of publication (e.g., education journal, book chapter, etc.), the level of schooling that is examined (preschool, K–12, etc.) and the region of the world where the study was conducted.

The technical characteristics—described in Table 3.1—are divided among the seven categories described in the last section. In several instances, the coding form calls for a qualitative evaluation of some aspect of the study. For example, one question addresses whether cost ingredients have been adequately identified and valued, with the categories defined as "fully," "partially," "poorly," or "unable to determine." In such cases, the coding form provides a more detailed characterization of each category. A "full" specification of ingredients implies that all relevant ingredients are specified and valued. A "partial" specification identifies and values most ingredients, but excludes some (e.g., donated ingredients or volunteers). It may also purport to have followed the ingredients method but provide insufficient

Table 3.1 Technical criteria used to evaluate studies

Criteria	Categories
How many alternatives are considered? Is each alternative described?	*Fully:* Provides a detailed description of specific objectives and strategies of alternative. *Partially:* Provides a general description of objectives and strategies of alternative. *Poorly:* Provides a cursory description, often using generic descriptors with minimal elaboration (e.g., "teacher training").
What is the source of data on outcomes?	*Experimental evaluation:* Randomized assignment to treatment and control groups *Quasi-experimental evaluation:* Matching assignment to treatment and comparison groups, or other quasi-experimental method. *Non-experimental evaluation:* Non-randomized assignment; statistical methods control for differences between treatment and comparison groups. *Meta-analysis* *Multiple methods* *Other*
Are the cost ingredients of each alernative identified and valued?	*Fully:* Identifies a complete list of cost ingredients for each alternative, including personnel, facilities, equipment, and materials. Uses market prices, when possible, to value each ingredient. When market prices are unavailable (e.g., donated ingredients), there is some attempt to impute shadow prices for ingredients. Costs are annualized when necessary (e.g., facilities). *Partially:* Identifies most ingredients, but omits key ingredients (e.g., facilities or volunteer personnel). Does not obtain credible values for some ingredients. Purports to have followed the ingredients method, but provides insufficient details for verification. *Poorly:* Does not follow the ingredients method (e.g., dividing budgeted program expenditures by the number of participants). *Unable to determine:* Insufficient information to determine what method was followed to obtain reported cost estimates.
Were costs and outcomes discounted for their uneven distribution across time?	*Costs and outcomes* *Only costs* *Only outcomes* *Neither* *Unable to determine* *Not applicable*
Is there an analysis of the distribution of costs and outcomes	*Costs and outcomes* *Only costs* *Only outcomes* *Neither*
Are summary measures calculated for each alternative?	*Ratios:* Cost-effectiveness, cost-benefit, or cost-utility ratios. *Other measures:* Net present value, internal rate of return, etc. *No measures*
Is there an analysis of uncertainty and its effects on conclusions?	*Limited sensitivity analysis:* Varies 1-2 parameters. *Extensive sensitivity analysis:* Varies more than 2 parameters. *Multiple methods* *No analysis*

details for verification. A poor cost analysis uses an ad hoc method of the author's devising. A final category is reserved for studies that simply provide insufficient details to identify and evaluate the costing method.

EVALUATING A SAMPLE OF STUDIES

This section describes the literature search procedures, the criteria used to include or exclude studies, and their general characteristics. It then assesses the extent to which the studies meet the standards of quality established in the previous section. Lastly, it compares these findings with methodological reviews in health care.

DEFINING THE SAMPLE

The cost-effectiveness literature in education is scattered across many disciplines and publications. Hence, I conducted a wide-ranging search in several steps.[2] First, I searched under "cost-effectiveness," "cost-benefit," and "cost-utility" in the ERIC database. Second, I searched under these terms in the ECONLIT database, further limiting the search with the term "education."[3] Third, I contacted scholars in the economics of education, inquiring about their work. It quickly became clear that most literature that purports to conduct a cost-effectiveness study, particularly in ERIC, does nothing of the sort. Thus, I immediately discarded studies that reported neither estimates of effectiveness or costs.

I then excluded four types of studies: (1) studies that only report estimates of costs, but not outcomes;[4] (2) studies that do not analyze at least one alternative related to formal education between the levels of preschool and postsecondary; (3) studies that replicate another study using the same or similar data;[5] and (4) "rate-of-return" studies.

Rate-of-return studies are a particular kind of cost-benefit analysis that seeks to weigh the benefits and costs from additional years of schooling. See Card (1999) and Psacharopoulos (1994) for reviews of the international literature. These studies are numerous, not least because they can be readily conducted with earnings data from a household survey or census. However, they rarely include estimates of the costs of schooling beyond the income forgone by individuals. When they do, it is often impossible to ascertain the methods and data used to calculate them. In all likelihood, these studies would dramatically alter the results. Hence, I do not consider them, although the reader should bear their exclusion in mind.

---

2 Most studies from this search are cited in Levin and McEwan (2001, Appendix B). Ongoing searches produced several additional references.

3 ERIC is a database that gathers a wide range of educational materials, including unpublished ones. ECONLIT mainly includes published works in economics.

4 This led to the exclusion of many cost studies that did not combine their estimates with data on effectiveness due to limited data. For example, see the cost evaluations of whole-school reforms by Barnett (1996a) and King (1994). Chapter 5 addresses the particular challenges involved in comparing the cost-effectiveness of whole-school reforms.

5 For example, I excluded early cost-benefit evaluations of the Perry School Program (e.g., Barnett, 1985), instead focusing on the most recent and comprehensive monograph (Barnett, 1996b).

The preceding search yielded a sample of 54 studies.[6] The general characteristics of the studies are described in Table 3.2. Cost-effectiveness analyses comprise the vast majority of studies, with a lesser proportion of cost-benefit studies. In contrast, the use of cost-utility analysis is almost nil in education. This contrasts sharply with health care, in which cost-utility analysis is more common (Drummond et al., 1997; Gerard, 1992).

The past three decades have witnessed a sharp rise in the number of studies conducted, with 65 percent of the present sample from the 1990s. To some extent, this

Table 3.2 General characteristics of studies

Characteristic	Percent of studies (N=54)
Type of study	
Cost-effectiveness	70
Cost-benefit	26
Cost-utility	4
Year	
1970–79	9
1980–89	26
1990–	65
Affiliation of first author	
University (education)	39
University (economics)	7
University (other)	7
Research firm	15
International organization	17
Other	3
Not determined	11
Place of publication	
Journal (education)	39
Journal (economics)	18
Journal (other)	6
Book or book chapter	20
Report	11
Unpublished paper	6
Level of schooling	
Pre-primary	13
K-8	48
Secondary	17
Postsecondary	7
More than one	11
Not determined	4
Region of world	
U.S.	59
Africa	11
Asia	17
Latin America	13

---

6 When a study includes more than one analysis—i.e., a cost-benefit and a cost-effectiveness analysis—I count each as a separate study. This occurred in three instances (Fletcher et al., 1990; Glewwe, 1999; Harbison and Hanushek, 1992).

may result from a failure to locate earlier studies, particularly working papers and reports. Even doubling the number of studies from the 1970s, however, would indicate a similar pattern of growth. Though causality is difficult to pinpoint, the period of growth does coincide with the publication of Levin's (1975; 1983) work on the methodology of educational cost-effectiveness analysis. Both sources are frequently cited by authors of the empirical studies in this sample.

Thirty-nine percent of studies were conducted in schools of education, followed by international and research organizations. It is surprisingly rare for affiliates of economics departments to work in this area. It is more common for economists to carry out traditional rate-of-return studies (which have been excluded from this sample). This pattern is certainly reflected in the publications of field journals like *Economics of Education Review* and *Education Economics*. In part, this may stem from the predilections of economists to work with readily available data sets. Nevertheless, this does little to explain why cost analysis is relatively more common in health economics (see Chapter 2).

While not reported in Table 3.2, it is worth noting that three individuals were the principal authors or co-authors of at least three studies apiece: W. Steven Barnett, Henry M. Levin, and Darrell R. Lewis. Together, their work accounts for 17 percent of the sample.

The venues for publication are mainly education journals, books, and, to a lesser extent, economics journals. About 41 percent of studies are focused on grades K–8, with the rest evenly distributed among other levels. A surprising amount of work— 41 percent—has been conducted in developing countries of Africa, Asia, and Latin America. To a great extent this occurred under the guise of international organizations such as the World Bank. For example, two of the most ambitious cost-effectiveness studies in the sample—conducted in Brazil and India—were directly sponsored by this institution (Harbison and Hanushek, 1992; World Bank, 1997).

EVALUATING PATTERNS OF QUALITY

The coding of technical characteristics is presented in Table 3.3.[7] It is common for studies to present excessively vague descriptions of the alternatives that are under consideration (28 percent provide a "poor" description). Most common in these cases is a general appellation like "textbooks" or "furniture." A similar percentage of studies (26 percent) provided only a partial description, omitting important information about the objectives and strategies of alternatives.

Non-experimental evaluation designs are the most common strategy for measuring the effectiveness of alternatives (57 percent). In general, multiple-regression analysis is used to estimate the marginal effect of a given treatment on an outcome variable, conditional on variables like the socio-economic status of students. However, there is a substantial amount of variation in the causal interpretations that authors give to their results. Many authors do not admit that non-experimental estimates of effectiveness might be subject to various threats to internal validity. In contrast, other authors carefully probe their data for evidence of bias and state causal interpretations with a dose of caution. Randomized experiments are used in only 15 percent of evaluations, notwithstanding their frequent emphasis in methodological writings in evaluation.

---

7   The original data are available upon request from the author.

Table 3.3 Technical characteristics of studies

Characteristic	Percent of studies (N=54)
Number of alternatives?	
1	20
2	33
3	17
4 or more	30
Alternatives are described?	
Fully	46
Partially	26
Poorly	28
Source of outcome data?	
Experimental	15
Quasi-experimental	9
Non-experimental	57
Meta-analysis	6
Multiple methods	9
Other method	4
Cost ingredients are described and valued?	
Fully	31
Partially	30
Poorly	28
Unable to determine	11
Time discounting used?	
Cost and outcomes	19
Only costs	2
Only outcomes	2
Neither	11
Unable to determine	6
Not applicable	61
Distributional analysis conducted?	
Costs and outcomes	15
Only costs	17
Only outcomes	13
Neither	56
Summary measures calculated?	
Ratios	57
Other measures	19
No measures	24
Uncertainty analysis conducted?	
Limited sensitivity analysis	26
Extensive sensitivity analysis	19
Other method	4
Multiple methods	2
No analysis	50

The cost components of evaluations often leave much to be desired. In 11 percent of studies, there was simply not enough information to determine what method, if any, the authors used to derive cost estimates. Another 28 percent pursued some type of "shortcut" method, often based on a simple analysis of the program budgets (but with no attention paid to actual resource use in the programs). Thirty percent of the studies applied a flawed version of the ingredients method. For example, several studies neglected to consider the costs of durable goods such as buildings or valued them inappropriately (e.g., neglecting to annualize the costs of long-lasting ingredients). Some of these studies reported so few details that it was difficult to verify whether the ingredients method was conscientiously applied. It is tempting to ascribe the latter shortcoming to the constraints of space, which precluded a detailed discussion of costing methodology. Nevertheless, the same studies often lavished attention on the estimation of outcomes, using sophisticated methods that were described at greater length. In all, 31 percent of studies fully applied the ingredients method.

When costs and outcomes are distributed over time, it is essential to discount them. In 61 percent of studies, this was unnecessary because costs and outcomes were confined to single year. The remaining studies were evenly split between those that adequately discounted costs and outcomes, and those that neglected some aspect of time discounting—either costs, outcomes, or both.

In 56 percent of studies, there was no analysis of how costs or outcomes were distributed across different constituencies. Twenty-four percent of studies did not calculate summary measures such as cost-effectiveness ratios, or net present value. Lastly, it was surprisingly rare for studies to account for uncertainty. In 50 percent of studies, there was simply no analysis of uncertainty. Another 26 percent conduct a basic sensitivity analysis that varied one or two parameters (e.g., the discount rate or period of amortization of capital). Surely there is a great need for sensitivity analysis in most of these studies, given that many attempts to value ingredients were based on rough estimates, rather than a detailed cost analysis.

Comparison with Health Care Research

There is already extensive evidence from cost studies in health care on whether a similar range of methodological standards are employed. In general, the results are consistent with those from education. Udvarhelyi, Colditz, Rai, and Epstein (1992) reviewed 77 cost-effectiveness and cost-benefit studies in health. When discounting of outcomes and costs was necessary, they found that 52 percent failed to do so. In 47 percent of studies, the authors did not report cost-benefit or cost-effectiveness ratios, and 70 percent did not conduct a sensitivity analysis.

In her review of 51 health cost-utility analyses, Gerard (1992) concluded that 69 percent included a comprehensive set of ingredients and 63 percent provided a clear description of methods used to cost ingredients. When discounting was required, 15 percent failed to do so. Only 37 percent of studies conducted an extensive sensitivity analysis. Overall, Gerard concluded that about half the studies should be deemed "limited" in their execution.

Finally, a review of health-related cost studies in Australia was similarly pessimistic (Salkeld, Davey, and Arnolda, 1995). Of 33 studies, the authors note that "only 55 percent gave an adequate description of how the costs were measured. . . . Certain costs such as capital and overheads were often omitted completely and inappropriately" (p. 117).

Conclusions

This paper reviewed the methodological quality of cost-effectiveness, cost-benefit, and cost-utility studies in education. Like similar reviews in health care, it found substantial room for improvement. Around two-thirds of studies did not fully apply an ingredients-based costing methodology. Many studies did not carefully describe the alternatives that are being assessed, or account for uncertainty in their conclusions. These findings beg a question: why should we care so much about the quality of cost-effectiveness studies and, particularly, cost estimates?

The simple answer is that a cost-effectiveness ratio has two components: a numerator (cost) and a denominator (effect). If either is estimated with error—or simply not estimated—then we cannot draw strong conclusions about the preferred allocation of resources. The literature in evaluation and economics assigns great importance to obtaining unbiased measures of effectiveness. This paper suggests that equal importance may not be accorded to costs. That is regrettable, because the attractiveness of many proposals for school reform hinge vitally on their cost-effectiveness. Let us briefly consider two examples: class size reduction and private school vouchers. In each case, there is a paucity of cost-effectiveness studies, or the existing literature has defects. The limitations restrict our ability to make reasonable decisions about the proper allocation of resources to these interventions.

CLASS SIZE REDUCTION

The effectiveness of class size reduction has been extensively studied with experimental and non-experimental designs (on the experimental literature, see Grissmer, 1999; Krueger, 1999; for a review of non-experimental literature, see Hanushek, 1997). Primarily on the strength of findings from the Tennessee STAR experiment, it has received vast resources in recent statewide plans such as California's (for a recent evaluation, see Stecher and Bohrnstedt, 2000). Nevertheless, the costs and cost-effectiveness of class size reduction are the subject of disproportionately few studies. Fifteen years ago, Levin, Glass, and Meister (1987) compared the cost-effectiveness of four educational interventions and found that class size reduction was not the most consistently cost-effective means of improving achievement. Since then, there have been very few attempts to analyze its costs or its cost-effectiveness (for a recent study that focuses exclusively on costs, see Brewer, Krop, Gill, and Reichardt, 1999).

This volume presents some new evidence on cost-effectiveness. Relying on recently-conducted research with nationwide assessments, David Grissmer suggests in Chapter 6 that class size is not the most cost-effective investment for a broad sample of students. However, class size reductions that are targeted at states with large class sizes and high proportions of disadvantaged students appear to be considerably more cost-effective.[8] Using different data and two different methods, Doug Harris finds in Chapter 9 that class size reduction is a less cost-effective policy than raising teacher salaries. Notwithstanding the growing evidence base, there is considerable scope for increasing the amount of cost-effectiveness research in this vital area.

PRIVATE-SCHOOL VOUCHERS

Besides class size, the merits of private schools are a frequent topic of educational debates. Many argue that private schools produce academic outcomes in a more cost-effective manner than public schools. This assertion lies at the heart of school voucher policies that would encourage parents to choose private schools instead of public alternatives. In fact, we have learned a great deal about the relative

---

8 For the original empirical study, see Grissmer, Flanagan, Kawata, and Williamson (2000).

Escobar, C. M., Barnett, W. S., and Keith, J. E. (1988). A contingent valuation approach to measuring the benefits of preschool education. *Educational Evaluation and Policy Analysis, 10*(1), 13–22.

*Fletcher, J. D., Hawley, D. E., and Piele, P. K. (1990). Costs, effects, and utility of microcomputer assisted instruction in the classroom. *American Educational Research Journal, 27*(4), 783–806.

*Franklin, G. S., and Sparkman, W. E. (1978). The cost-effectiveness of two program delivery systems for exceptional children. *Journal of Education Finance, 3,* 305–314.

*Fuller, B., Hua, H., and Snyder, C. W. (1994). When girls learn more than boys: The influence of time in school and pedagogy in Botswana. *Comparative Education Review, 38*(3), 347–376.

*Garms, W. I. (1971). A benefit-cost analysis of the Upward Bound program. *Journal of Human Resources, 6*(2), 206–220.

Gerard, K. (1992). Cost-utility in practice: A policymaker's guide to the state-of-the-art. *Health Policy, 21,* 249–279.

*Glewwe, P. (1999). *The economics of school quality investments in developing countries: An empirical study of Ghana.* London: St. Martins Press.

*Greenwald, R., Hedges, L. V., and Laine, R. D. (1996). The effect of school resources on student achievement. *Review of Educational Research, 66*(3), 361–396.

Grissmer, D. (1999). Class size effects: Assessing the evidence, its policy implications, and future research agenda. *Educational Evaluation and Policy Analysis, 21*(2), 231–248.

*Grissmer, D. W., Flanagan, A., Kawata, J., and Williamson, S. (2000). *Improving student achievement: What NAEP state test scores tell us.* Santa Monica, CA: RAND.

Hanushek, E. A. (1997). Assessing the effect of school resources on student performance: An update. *Educational Evaluation and Policy Analysis, 19*(2), 141–164.

*Harbison, R. W., and Hanushek, E. A. (1992). *Educational performance of the poor: Lessons from rural northeast Brazil.* Oxford: Oxford University Press.

*Hartman, W. T., and Fay, T. A. (1996). Cost-effectiveness of instructional support teams in Pennsylvania. *Journal of Education Finance, 21*(4), 555–580.

Hoxby, C. M. (1998). What do America's 'traditional' forms of school choice teach us about school choice reforms? *Federal Reserve Bank of New York Economic Policy Review, 4*(1), 47–59.

*Jimenez, E., Lockheed, M., and Wattanawaha, N. (1988). The relative efficiency of public and private schools: The case of Thailand. *World Bank Economic Review, 2*(2), 139–164.

*Jimenez, E., Lockheed, M. E., Luna, E., and Paqueo, V. (1991). School effects and costs for private and public schools in the Dominican Republic. *International Journal of Educational Research, 15,* 393–410.

*Karoly, L. A., Greenwood, P. W., Everingham, S. S., Hoube, J., Kilburn, M. R., Rydell, C. P., Sanders, M., and Chiesa, J. (1998). *Investing in our children.* Santa Monica, CA: RAND.

King, J. A. (1994). Meeting the educational needs of at-risk students: A cost analysis of three models. *Educational Evaluation and Policy Analysis, 16*(1), 1–19.

*Kingdon, G. (1996). The quality and efficiency of private and public education: A case-study of urban India. *Oxford Bulletin of Economics and Statistics, 58*(1), 57–82.

*Klein, S. P., Bohannan, H. M., Bell, R. M., Disney, J. A., Foch, C. B., and Graves, R. C. (1985). The cost and effectiveness of school-based preventive dental care. *American Journal of Public Health, 75*(4), 382–391.

*Knapp, T. R., and Knapp, L. T. (1990). A benefit-cost analysis of New York State's "Bundy Aid" program. *Economics of Education Review, 9*(1), 31–37.

Krueger, A. (1999). Experimental estimates of education production functions. *Quarterly Journal of Economics, 114*(2), 497–532.

*Krueger, A., and Whitmore, D. (2000). *The effect of attending a small class in the early grades on college-test taking and middle school test results: Evidence from Project STAR* (Working Paper No. 7656). Cambridge, MA: National Bureau of Economic Research.

*Levin, H. M. (1970). A cost-effectiveness analysis of teacher selection. *Journal of Human Resources, 5*(1), 24–33.

Levin, H. M. (1975). Cost-effectiveness in evaluation research. In M. Guttentag and E. Struening (Eds.), *Handbook of evaluation research* (Vol. 2). Beverly Hills, CA: Sage Publications.

Levin, H. M. (1983). *Cost-effectiveness: A primer.* Newbury Park, CA: Sage.

Levin, H. M. (1991). Cost-effectiveness at quarter century. In M. W. McLaughlin and D. C. Phillips (Eds.), *Evaluation and education at quarter century* (pp. 188–209). Chicago: University of Chicago Press.

Levin, H. M., and Driver, C. E. (1997). Costs of an educational voucher system. *Education Economics, 5*(3), 265–283.

*Levin, H. M., Glass, G. V., and Meister, G. R. (1987). Cost-effectiveness of computer-assisted instruction. *Evaluation Review, 11*(1), 50–72.

*Levin, H. M., Leitner, D., and Meister, G. R. (1986). *Cost-effectiveness of alternative approaches to computer-assisted instruction* (87–CERAS–1). Stanford, CA: Center for Educational Research at Stanford.

Levin, H. M., and McEwan, P. J. (2001). *Cost-effectiveness analysis: Methods and applications* (2nd ed.). Thousand Oaks, CA: Sage.

*Lewis, D. R. (1990). Estimating the economic worth of a 5th-year licensure program for teachers. *Educational Evaluation and Policy Analysis, 12*(1), 25–39.

*Lewis, D. R., Johnson, D. R., Erickson, R. N., and Bruininks, R. H. (1994). Multiattribute evaluation of program alternatives within special education. *Journal of Disability Policy Studies, 5*(1), 77–112.

*Lewis, D. R., Stockdill, S. J., and Turner, T. C. (1990). Cost-effectiveness of microcomputers in adult basic reading. *Adult Literacy and Basic Education, 14*(2), 136–149.

*Mayer, S. E., and Peterson, P. E. (1999). The costs and benefits of school reform. In S. E. Mayer and P. E. Peterson (Eds.), *Earning and learning: How schools matter* (pp. 341–354). Washington, DC and New York: Brookings Institution Press and Russell Sage Foundation.

*Mayo, J. K., McAnany, E. G., and Klees, S. J. (1975). The Mexican Telesecundaria: A cost-effectiveness analysis. *Instructional Science, 4*(3/4), 193–236.

McEwan, P. J. (2000). The potential impact of large-scale voucher programs. *Review of Educational Research, 70*(2), 103–149.

Monk, D. H., and King, J. A. (1993). Cost analysis as a tool for education reform. In S. L. Jacobson and R. Berne (Eds.), *Reforming education: The emerging systemic approach* (pp. 131–150). Thousand Oaks, CA: Corwin Press.

*Murphy, P. (1993). Costs of an alternative form of second-level education in Malawi. *Comparative Education Review, 37*(2), 107–122.   •

*Niemiec, R. P., Sikorski, M. F., and Walberg, H. J. (1989). Comparing the cost-effectiveness of tutoring and computer-based instruction. *Journal of Educational Computing Research, 5*(4), 395–407.

Psacharopoulos, G. (1994). Returns to investment in education: A global update. *World Development, 22*(9), 1325–1343.

*Psacharopoulos, G., and Loxley, W. (1985). *Diversified secondary education and development: Evidence from Colombia and Tanzania.* New York: Oxford University Press.

*Quinn, B., Van Mondfrans, A., and Worthen, B. R. (1984). Cost-effectiveness of two math programs as moderated by pupil SES. *Educational Evaluation and Policy Analysis, 6*(1), 39–52.

Rouse, C. E. (1998). Schools and student achievement: More evidence from the Milwaukee Parental Choice Program. *Federal Reserve Bank of New York Economic Policy Review, 4*(1), 61–76.

Salkeld, G., Davey, P., and Arnolda, G. (1995). A critical review of health-related economic evaluations in Australia: Implications for health policy. *Health Policy, 31,* 111–125.

*Schiefelbein, E., Wolff, L., and Schiefelbein, P. (1998). Cost-effectiveness of education policies in Latin America: A survey of expert opinion, unpublished manuscript.

Smith, N. L., and Smith, J. K. (1985). State-level evaluation uses of cost analysis: A national descriptive survey. In J. S. Catterall (Ed.), *Economic evaluation of public programs* (pp. 83–97). San Francisco: Jossey-Bass.

*Solmon, L. C. (1999). Afterword. In D. Mann, C. Shakeshaft, J. Becker, and R. Kottkamp (Eds.), *West Virginia story: Achievement gains from a statewide comprehensive instructional technology program* (pp. 43–50). Santa Monica, CA: Milken Family Foundation.

Stecher, B. M., and Bohrnstedt, G. W. (Eds.). (2000). Class size reduction in California: The 1998–99 evaluation findings. Sacramento, CA: California Department of Education.

*Stern, D., Dayton, C., Paik, I. W., and Weisberg, A. (1989). Benefits and costs of dropout prevention in a high school program combining academic and vocational education: third-year results from replications of the California Peninsula Academies. *Educational Evaluation and Policy Analysis, 11*(4), 405–416.

*Tan, J. P., Lane, J., and Coustere, P. (1997). Putting inputs to work in elementary schools: What can be done in the Philippines? *Economic Development and Cultural Change, 45*(4), 857–879.

*Tatto, M. T., Nielsen, D., and Cummings, W. (1991). *Comparing the effects and costs of different approaches for educating primary school teachers: The case of Sri Lanka* (BRIDGES Research Report Series No. 10). Cambridge, MA: Harvard University.

*Taylor, C., White, K. R., and Pezzino, J. (1984). Cost-effectiveness analysis of full-day versus half-day intervention programs for handicapped preschoolers. *Journal of the Division for Early Childhood*, 76–85.

*Tilson, T. D. (1991). *The cost-effectiveness of interactive radio instruction for improving primary school instruction in Honduras, Bolivia and Lesotho.* Paper presented at the Comparative and International Education Society, Pittsburgh.

Udvarhelyi, I. S., Colditz, G. A., Rai, A., and Epstein, A. M. (1992). Cost-effectiveness and cost-benefit analyses in the medical literature: Are the methods being used correctly? *Annals of Internal Medicine, 116*, 238–244.

*Warfield, M. E. (1994). A cost-effectiveness analysis of early intervention services in Massachusetts: implications for policy. *Educational Evaluation and Policy Analysis, 16*(1), 87–99.

Weinstein, M. C., Siegel, J. E., Gold, M. R., Kamlet, M. S., and Russell, L. B. (1996). Recommendations of the panel on cost-effectiveness in health and medicine. *Journal of the American Medical Association, 276*(15), 1253–1258.

*World Bank. (1997). *Primary education in India.* Washington, DC: Author.

Wortman, P. M. (1994). Judging research quality. In H. Cooper and L. V. Hedges (Eds.), *The Handbook of Research Synthesis* (pp. 97–109). New York: Russell Sage Foundation.

4

METHODOLOGICAL STRENGTH AND POLICY USEFULNESS OF COST-EFFECTIVENESS RESEARCH

*William H. Clune**

INTRODUCTION

This article is a review of educational research on the cost-effectiveness of educational interventions. Why educational researchers might be interested in cost-effectiveness is not difficult to understand. The educational system is under great pressure from society to improve the knowledge and skills of students. At the same time, resources are limited; and historically the education system has seemed more concerned about increasing available inputs than using resources in the most productive manner (Barnett, 1994).

Cost-effectiveness research is a method designed to compare the productivity or efficiency of alternative educational investments (or interventions) in terms of common measures of effectiveness (such as "effect size" on a standardized achievement test) and cost, expressed as the dollar value of resources used by the intervention (Levin, 1991). The effectiveness side of the method overlaps broadly with the field of evaluation and requires appropriate experimental or non-experimental designs as a means of identifying the value added by the intervention. Costs must be measured comprehensively; for example, they must include both volunteer time and the opportunity costs of any resources transferred from other activities. For this reason, an "ingredients" method usually is recommended for measuring costs rather than reliance on the official budget.

Unfortunately, many studies do not meet the requirements of valid cost-effectiveness research, thus possibly reaching invalid conclusions and misleading

* Many thanks to Jennilynn Lawrence who conducted the ERIC search and did much of the work involved in the ratings and to Patrick McEwan for helpful comments and editing. This article was prepared in cooperation with Henry Levin, and many points in the article were jointly discussed. However, Professor Levin did not approve the final draft, and may well disagree with at least some of its ratings, reasoning, and conclusions.

recommendations for educational policy (Levin, 1991). Major problems in measuring either effectiveness or costs can render a piece of research useless. On the other hand, valid and useful conclusions sometimes can be reached from research with major flaws.

This article investigates the appeal and limitations of research on cost-effectiveness by reporting the results of a survey of articles in the ERIC database, assessing the quality of the research design employed in these articles, and discussing criteria for evaluating the usefulness for policy of research with varying degrees of methodological strength.

RESEARCH METHOD

A search was conducted of the ERIC database for studies containing the words "cost-effectiveness." ERIC was chosen because it is a common research tool used by educational professionals and policymakers.[1] The initial search produced a list of 9015 titles. To limit the size of the task and focus on recent research, the search was then restricted to the years 1991–1996, producing a list of 1329 titles. Abstracts of the studies were downloaded and a classification made according to four categories of methodological rigor:

1. Rhetoric. Claims to show that an intervention is cost-effective but contains no data on either effects or costs.

2. Minimal attempt. Contains minimal data. May list costs or allege affordability. May claim feasibility and cite categories of effectiveness or other research on effectiveness.

3. Substantial attempt. Substantial data on cost and effectiveness but with serious flaws (e.g., budgetary costs rather than observed ingredient costs, subjective ratings of effectiveness, weak design for causal attribution, or lack of cost-effectiveness measures for alternative interventions).

4. Plausible study. Ingredients or resource approach to cost. Strong design on effectiveness, with comparison to alternatives.

The examination of the abstracts demonstrated a need for two adjustments. First, a large group of studies was deemed not relevant to this article's focus on educational productivity, because the effects examined did not include the outcomes of K–12 education. The 788 studies in this category concerned such topics as library science, school-lunch programs, school-building construction, medical school improvements, and computer hardware cost comparisons. Removal of these 788 studies reduced the sample of abstracts from 1329 to 541. Second, it was found that an intermediate category between three and four was needed—between substantial and plausible—

---

1   The ERIC database includes a wide range of sources in addition to articles published in journals; for example, unpublished papers, official reports, and reports of contract researchers. A substantial portion—far more than the published articles—consists of "gray" or "fugitive" research literature that never reaches journals and exists mainly on office desks. The quality of the research is not necessarily correlated with the journal/ non-journal distinction because of the presence of many casual journal articles and serious non-published research reports.

to handle studies which had strong data and design for either cost or effectiveness but not for both. Thus, category 4 became, in effect, a partially plausible study with strength in either cost or effectiveness, and a plausible study (still the top category) was rated as 5. After the initial classification of abstracts, a sample of the full studies from each category was obtained and reclassified with the same rating system.[2]

RESULTS

The number of abstracts and the percent of the total abstracts placed in each category are given in Table 4.1. It can be seen from Table 4.1 that, based on abstracts alone, the number of rhetorical and minimal studies outnumbered the more substantial pieces by a wide margin—83 percent to 17 percent—and that the number meeting the high standard of 4 or 5 was quite small—12 studies comprising 2 percent of the total.

Table 4.1 Ratings of Studies Mentioning Cost-Effectiveness in the ERIC Database, 1991–1996

Category	Number of abstracts (% of total abstracts)	Number of full studies sampled (% of abstracts sampled in each category)	Rating of full studies
1. Rhetoric	302 (56%)	15 (5%)	23
2. Minimal	147 (27%)	14 (10%)	16
3. Substantial	80 (15%)	15 (19%)	13
4. Partially plausible	7 (1%)	7 (100%)	4
5. Plausible	5 (1%)	5 (100%)	0
Total	541 (100%)	56 (10%)	56
Average rating		2.51	1.96

Table 4.1 also reports the number and percent of full studies from each category that were randomly sampled for the next stage of analysis. About 10 percent of the total sample was selected—56 full studies—with oversampling in the more rigorous

---

2 Each study was scored on the rating sheet shown in the Appendix (which is organized into the four original categories rather than the five categories reported). Almost always, the "checks" on rating sheets fell distinctly into one rating level or another (thus supporting the validity of the rating protocol). If a study received checks in the highest category on the rating sheet (4) for both effectiveness and cost, it was rated 5; if it received a check for one but not the other, it was rated 4. The abstracts were rated by one researcher, and the full articles by the author. Thus, differences in rating between the abstracts and the full articles may reflect either imperfect inter-rater reliability or differences between the content of the abstracts and articles, or both.

categories. A comparison of the ratings of the abstracts and full studies also appears in Table 4.1. The notable difference resulting from analyzing the full studies was the further diminishment of the higher ratings. Since all of the abstracts rated 4 or 5 were sampled and read in full, the inference is that less than 1 percent of the full group of abstracts deserve those scores (4 of 541). Also noteworthy is that the average rating fell 0.55 of a point, to a level just below 2 (minimal attempt). On the other hand, studies rated 3 or 2 remained reasonably common, making it important to assess the contribution of this kind of study to policy and practice, a task that will be undertaken below.

DISCUSSION: METHODOLOGICAL STRENGTH AND POLICY USEFULNESS

This part of the paper considers the question of whether and to what extent cost-effectiveness studies with weaker methodology can still be relied on by policymakers and practitioners, at least under restricted conditions. The rest of the article proceeds in three steps. First, it suggests that even studies meeting the most rigorous methodological standards still have limitations, or flaws, resulting in less than complete confidence in the results and restricting the conditions of application. Second, studies with stronger and weaker designs from the ERIC sample discussed in this article are selected for more extended discussion of policy usefulness. Third, a general approach for determining policy usefulness is recommended and applied to a study of school restructuring from the ERIC sample, followed by an overall conclusion.

LIMITATIONS OF EVEN THE BEST STUDIES

In an article assessing the status of cost-effectiveness research in education, Levin (1991) examines related aspects of the research that are worth discussing here: the quality and replicability of the programs on which the estimates of cost-effectiveness are based and the range of educational outcomes accounted for. My aim is to show that Levin's recommendations of best practice involve implicit tradeoffs among internal validity (the strength of causal inferences), external validity (the generalizability of the causal findings to other settings), and policy usefulness of the same kind that are required in assessing the value of methodologically weaker research.

One point made by Levin is that meta-analysis usually cannot be relied on to establish effect size because such analyses often include little information on cost ingredients, poor research designs, imperfectly implemented interventions, and an assortment of interventions in the same general category, not all of which are of interest to a particular policymaker (e.g., peer tutoring with and without any training of the tutors). For example, meta-analyses are based on the effects of many different types of programs and almost never give sufficient details on interventions and their ingredients to develop decent cost estimates (Levin and McEwan, 2001). Maintaining that policymakers are interested in highly reliable comparisons of specific policy alternatives, Levin recommends secondary analysis of data on specific, well-described programs implemented successfully in real school settings.

Levin's emphasis on the need for thoughtful review of the specifics of programs and the strength of research designs is well taken; but the idea of a single, clear standard of best practice is problematic. The inclusion of poorly implemented interventions is not always and obviously fatal or even inferior, depending on circumstances. On one end of the continuum, studies of high-quality, replicable interventions are always preferable for generalization over studies of "hot house" pilot programs (e.g., those benefiting from extraordinary skill and care). But high-quality, replicable programs may have hot house problems of their own. An argument for including weak interventions exists when the policymaker is not sure about the feasibility of high-quality interventions on a large scale and would prefer to use a lower estimate of program effectiveness. Replicability across any given range of attempts does not establish replicability on a larger scale. With whole-school restructuring, for example, there is an argument for including all interventions, well and poorly implemented, in calculations of the effect size, precisely because successful intervention may be difficult and reflect variations in school capacity.

In some ways, the question of including low-quality implementations is a classic tradeoff between internal validity (strength of the internal comparisons) and external validity (applicability to the messy world outside). For example, in a 1988 article, after careful selection of studies of well-implemented programs, Levin found that, while reducing class sizes had lower annual costs, cross-age peer tutoring was three to five times as cost-effective because of its larger effects (Levin, 1988). The finding is highly relevant because it means that for the same dollars used to reduce class size, policymakers could implement tutoring on a sufficient scale to purchase several times as much student achievement. On the other hand, the apparent fondness of policymakers for reductions in class size may be more logical than the difference in the ratios suggests. A policymaker might wonder about the relative robustness of peer tutoring compared with reductions in class size—tutoring programs seem tricky and reducing class size sounds easy (partly because the research reviewed did not discriminate between high- and low-quality reductions in class size). A policymaker might choose reducing class size because it does some good and sounds relatively easy to do. Policymakers might also be concerned about problems of scale. Reducing class size seems less challenging to implement on a large scale than tutoring. A cost-effectiveness ratio of 3–5 to 1 might or might not be enough to overcome these reservations, but that becomes a matter of judgment in context.

The second example of a tradeoff, rather than clear best practice, is the range of educational outcomes measured by the research. In the 1991 article, Levin discusses the longitudinal study of the Perry Preschool program study which found long-term positive effects of preschool on dropout rates, college attendance, and post-schooling earnings. These positive findings offset earlier findings about the lack of any permanent effect on raising IQ scores. In other research, Carnoy and Levin (1975) criticize studies of long-distance learning for cost-effectiveness estimates based on achievement in the subjects taught rather than the full range of outcomes expected in full-day resident schooling (such as social adjustment and networking). Both of these are serious criticisms, reminding us, for example, of the risks that may be involved in the heavy use of high-stakes testing on particular outcomes. But often the choice of which outcomes to measure is a difficult one with no clear answer. Levin himself points out that the whole field of cost-effectiveness research in education arose partly because the more powerful technique of cost-benefit analysis often is unavailable, especially in the early grades. Cost-benefit analysis translates program effects into the common denominator of dollars, for example, the effect of educational gains on earnings. Knowing the dollar return to gains in third-grade reading obtained through different levels of investment certainly would be relevant to policymakers (especially since higher gains are likely to be more and more expensive). The problem is that such research takes too long, and we may need to do the best we can with currently available test scores. Also, at a certain point, insisting on more and more outcomes seems to introduce a bias against change. If we assume that the existing practice may have multiple unknown long-range beneficial outcomes which the changed practice does not, all change would be suspect regardless of the size of demonstrated effects. For example, big gains in third grade reading might come at the expense of some other subject or skill; but such gains are extremely attractive partly because of the known multiple effects of early reading proficiency on later educational success.

My point in this section has been that choice of best practice in cost-effectiveness methodology often requires judgments about questions that cannot be answered by the research itself, such as the feasibility of interventions on a larger scale and the range of outcomes measured. In the next section, I pursue this theme by showing that the practical importance of methodological weaknesses in four less than ideal studies from the ERIC sample depends upon making similar judgments.

THE POLICY USEFULNESS OF METHODOLOGICALLY IMPERFECT RESEARCH FROM OUR SAMPLE

This section of the paper considers the policy usefulness of four research studies from the ERIC sample discussed earlier. The studies cover the full range of our ratings from a high of 4 (which were earned by only four studies) to 1.

Glantz, Goodson, and Layzer (1991), rated 4, was a study of the cost-effectiveness of a half-day pre-school intervention for children and their families, Project Giant Step. Children in the program were randomly selected and tested before and after the intervention, but there were no control groups. While recognizing the importance of measuring multiple outcomes, the study relied on a test of cognitive development to measure effectiveness. Gains on the test were compared to several external benchmarks for the age group. The gain size of 1.0 items per month for Project Giant Step children compared favorably to the 0.45 items in normal development and 0.61–0.67 items in other high-quality day-care programs enrolling a greater percentage of higher-income families.

On the cost side, the study recognized the presence of in-kind contributions in the form of rent-free property and volunteer time but decided to focus on budgetary costs because of the lack of good data on in-kind costs. The budgetary costs of Project Giant Step were found to be considerably higher than the average expenditures of high-quality, developmental day-care ($3.27–$5.77 per hour compared with $1.76–$2.65 per hour for the other programs) but about equal to the national expenditures for Head Start. The study reached two conclusions: (a) the intervention had relatively large effects and costs, (b) the cost-effectiveness ratio of Project Giant Step was higher than comparable high-quality day-care centers in the Northeast (for which effectiveness data were available using the same standardized assessment). The conclusion, that equal resources in the less costly program would purchase greater total aggregate development but lower development per child, seems valid within the limitations of the methodology. The more costly program would be preferable only if the high average outcomes were considered sufficiently important. Measuring only one outcome, cognitive development, is troublesome in the context of day care but is justified because it allows comparison with other programs measured for the same outcome and costs. Although there were no control groups, the external norms used for comparison seemed well chosen. Failure to measure non-budgetary costs leaves a gap in our knowledge, but the estimates seem reasonable for the budgetary costs of expanding the program on a modest scale.

Wilkinson, Mangino, and Ligon (1993), rated a 3, was a report of the Office of Research and Evaluation of the Austin, Texas, Independent School District (AISD), later delivered at the American Educational Research Association. This particular study compared the comparative cost-effectiveness of a set of instructional interventions (e.g., a computer lab, a science academy, Title I supplementary instruction) and a set of dropout prevention programs. Effects of the instructional programs were judged by achievement gains of students in the programs on a state test or the Iowa Tests of Basic Skills, compared with average gains in the district, controlling for available data on student demographics (e.g., poverty but not parental education). Effects of dropout programs were judged by the number of students dropping out. The study recognizes that the low costs of some dropout programs were due to the use of volunteers in these programs, but relied on the official budget as the only available, comparable information. Since there were no control groups or benchmarking to similar programs and no observation of costs beyond the official budget, the study was rated a 3. Conclusions from a methodology with these flaws are vulnerable to many plausible rival hypotheses, including systematic variations in unmeasured characteristics of the students served.

On the other hand, the availability of longitudinal data on student achievement and budgetary costs must count for something. One way to recognize the presence of valuable data, without overstating it, is to accept that conclusions based on large, or very large (even "sledgehammer") effects are less likely to have occurred through spurious correlations. Such reliance on effect size should be employed with caution. The biases of methodology of any study may be correlated with (and be largely responsible for) the size of observed effects. An excellent and unfortunately common example is failing to control for student characteristics. Student characteristics are a powerful determinant of achievement and other outcomes, and selective enrollment (intended or unintended) may explain the apparent effectiveness of programs. High achievement scores in magnet schools may be caused by selective enrollment rather than value-added by the school (Blank, 1990). In its achievement studies (as opposed to the dropout studies), the AISD paper avoided the most serious version of this flaw by using average gains for the same students, rather than average test scores, as the measure of effectiveness and by controlling for poverty. Pre-test scores do partially reflect other kinds of student characteristics other than poverty, such as mother's education. But differences across programs in the characteristics of students served may explain apparent program effectiveness even using gain scores and limited controls. For example, gains attributable to a school may decline with each significant control variable introduced (e.g., poverty, mother's education, English-language facility, race and ethnicity). Careful design and statistical controls in non-experimental designs are at best an imperfect approximation of randomization in true experiments. For this reason, it is always preferable to collect data on student characteristics—either initially or in a subsequent evaluation of a program chosen based on a study with imperfect design.

With those cautions in mind, at some point the size of the effects may outweigh the likely impact of the uncontrolled variables, depending on the overall quality of the design, and the AISD study had reasonable controls (consider that many school accountability measures are based on gains in test scores with no controls for student demographics). The differences in cost-effectiveness ratios observed in the AISD study were large. For the achievement programs, the cost per unit of an additional month of gain (compared to the average) ranged from $6 per student on the low side (a computer lab) to $400 and $500 dollars on the high side. There was some tendency for the higher cost programs to serve more students. The dropout programs ranged from under $100 to tens of thousands of dollars per dropout prevented. Recognizing the coarse nature of the data, the study presented its findings in terms of programs that were shown to have a positive effect vs. those not shown to have such an effect and programs that had high cost vs. those with low cost. The conclusions of cross-cutting themes reached by the study also lent some validity to the conclusions. Instructional programs which worked seemed to have high opportunity to learn (enriching academic content). Effective dropout programs kept students in class and used volunteers to reduce district costs.

Pringle and Rosenthal (1993), rated 2, assessed the costs of Chapter 1 migrant education summer services. The funding formula, based on enrollment, had the incentive effect of encouraging lower-cost, home-based instruction over higher-cost, campus-based instruction. The cost differentials were computed on the basis of much higher instructional time and student transportation costs of the campus programs. No data on educational effects were collected or available, but previous research suggested that campus-based instruction probably would have a greater impact on student learning. Independently of the method of service delivery, the study also found that the costs of serving currently migratory students were greater than former migrant children. The needs of current migrant children were greater (e.g., language difficulties) and more costly (e.g., more difficult coordination with the local school district). But there was no obvious correlation between method of service delivery and population served. Both campus and home instruction were useful to both groups under different circumstances. Home instruction, for example, often was the best way to reach pre-school children and to involve the whole family. Lacking a clear method of comparing cost-effectiveness, the study recommended only that Congress consider softening the strong incentive effect toward home instruction and providing extra money for currently migratory children. Thus, the study did discover a distributional impact with apparent educational significance, a finding which seemed sufficient to support a moderate shift in policy.

Nachtigal (1991) reviewed the relationship of school size, cost, and quality, and was rated as a 1. No original data on effects or costs were collected. The main thrust of the study was relying on published research to rebut the conventional claim that larger schools, such as those produced historically by the school consolidation movement, offer significant gains in cost-effectiveness. Early studies, in fact, did not take account of any educational effects and costs beyond the availability of specialized courses. More recent research showed that smaller schools allow students more access to education in the community, encourage a broader range of course taking (though also less specialization), encourage more extra-curricular activity, and, on the cost side, involve less transportation cost for the district and transportation time for the students (a factor which offsets the lower administrative costs of fewer, larger schools). Meanwhile, specialized courses can be made available by clusters of smaller schools on a regional basis. This kind of study, finding flaws in a conventional line of argument, cannot be the basis of any clear conclusions in favor of or against smaller schools. But there are some interesting points made about both cost and effectiveness that could serve to undermine any strong efficiency argument in favor of large schools which might exist in the professional culture of, say, school superintendents. Thus, even a study rated 1 can be relied on as a caution flag on reaching easy conclusions.

These four studies show that conclusions become decreasingly robust and generalizable in proportion to their lower ratings. The conclusions become more constrained in their relevance for policy: cautiously ignoring the problem of unmeasured outcomes and non-budgetary costs (Glantz et al.), choosing between programs with very large differences in cost-effectiveness ratios (Wilkinson et al.), choosing a program based on clear distributional effects (population served) rather than cost-effectiveness measures (Pringle and Rosenthal), and raising a caution about conventional wisdom (Nachtigal). The greatest drop-off in policy usefulness probably occurs below the "3" level (the Wilkinson et al. study) with the absence of good longitudinal data on effects and systematic data on budgetary or resource costs. Within these limitations, however, all studies can be seen as having some usefulness. Furthermore, in assessing the usefulness of the studies, we must rely on similar factors as are used in evaluating the strongest studies. A common theme is the size of the effects relative to the weaknesses of the design. Just as a 3–5 to 1 advantage in cost effectiveness may have been enough to overcome doubts about the large scale feasibility of cross-age tutoring compared with reductions in class size, large gains from Project Giant Step and certain programs in Austin, Texas, may validly argue for their expansion despite methodological weaknesses. One way to think about the question is whether the threats to internal validity from incomplete controls on student characteristics in the latter studies are substantially greater (or require a higher level of subsequent evaluation) than the threats to external validity of going to scale with cross-age tutoring. If the controls are weak an affirmative answer to this question is likely to be easier than if the controls are good but imperfect.

Problems of choosing outcome measures also are common, particularly the reliance on available common testing data and budgetary costs, when it is known that measuring a wider range of outcomes and costs might change the results. Even the lowest rated Nachtigal study scored points by citing research which included a wider range of educational outcomes. Notice also common problems of program scale and target group. The more expensive interventions in Austin, like the more expensive option of reducing class size, might well serve a greater number of total students.

POLICY USEFULNESS: A MULTI-FACTOR APPROACH APPLIED TO SCHOOL RESTRUCTURING

Previous sections of this paper established that choice of the strongest research design sometimes is not clear, involving tradeoffs among competing considerations, and that weaker research designs may nevertheless provide some useful information to policymakers. This section is an attempt to generalize on those lessons in a more systematic way.

In general it would seem that requiring a higher standard of methodology prior to implementing a program based on existing (flawed) research makes sense when: (1) the higher standard eliminates a serious risk of making a bad decision, (2) the costs of doing research under the higher standard are not excessive, and (3) the costs of implementing the new practice are high.[3]

---

3 Patrick McEwan suggests a possible fourth factor: the reinforcing effect of high standards on the quality of future research and the general lowering of standards resulting from bad practice.

The risk of a bad decision is affected by whether the known threats to validity of a particular research design are large or small in the particular research context. In studies of student achievement, baseline data is almost always necessary. For example, much research that compared student achievement in magnet schools and other schools was virtually useless in the absence of such longitudinal data because of the obvious risk that higher achieving students would selectively attend the magnets (Blank, 1990). Likewise, pilot interventions are always a dubious basis for large-scale implementation in part because the quality and quantity of resources invested in the pilot may not be available on a large scale and also may be difficult to measure accurately in the pilot (for example, special attention from expert consultants and selection of sites on the basis of enthusiasm and high capacity). Other threats to validity may be higher or lower depending on context. Reliance on budgetary costs as opposed to observed costs is especially risky where the non-budgetary costs may be substantial (Carnoy and Levin, 1975). The risks of making a bad decision are also affected by the size of the effects shown for the new policy compared to what is known about the effectiveness of the status quo.

The cost of a higher research standard (in effect, the cost of design improvements) is the second major factor to be considered in deciding whether to adopt improvements in a research design. Sometimes big improvements in design can be made for little or no cost; for example, keeping baseline data instead of discarding it, or improving the sample design without increasing sample size. On the other hand, design improvements may be very costly. For example, while baseline data on student achievement and budgetary data may be collected routinely by educational authorities, going the extra step to collect original data on cost ingredients or unmeasured student characteristics could be so expensive as to require a much greater reduction of the risk of a bad decision. Thus, a high cost of extra research could be justified where large, positive benefits have been shown in pilot studies, or where there is a major threat to the validity of budgetary data (like the known use of many volunteers).

The cost of making a change in policy or practice is the final factor in deciding whether to make improvements in the research. A higher cost of change justifies more investment in design and data. School restructuring with different costs is an example. If the marginal costs of implementation are low, immediate implementation may be just as acceptable as further research, given big effect sizes and no serious threat to validity in the preliminary research. Further research can then be conducted on the newly implemented programs. With higher costs of restructuring, greater additional research costs are justified before proceeding to large-scale adoption.

Let us now apply this three-factor analysis to a study of school restructuring that was part of our ERIC sample and was given a rating of 4 (Slavin et al., 1992), a report of the cost and effects of the Success for All program (SFA) in five schools, findings similar to later research on the same program in more schools (Barnett, 1996; King, 1994; Slavin et al., 1996). Student achievement was measured before and after each grade (1–3) in both treatment and what the paper refers to as "matched control students." Details of the matching procedure are not given, and readers are referred to another paper for more details of the research design. The later published research paper uses the language, "matched control schools," and refers to a Table showing the following characteristics of SFA schools: enrollment, percent free lunch, and percent ethnicity (African-American, Asian-American, Latino, white) (Slavin et al., 1996).

Costs were budgetary, including extra tutors, a full-time program facilitator, and full- or half-day Kindergarten. On the effects side, the SFA schools showed an effect size advantage from 0.57 to 1.00 over the controls, translating into an advantage of about one full grade level by third-grade. Effects were largest for the bottom 25 percent of the students. Only 3.9 percent of students in SFA schools were two years behind grade level in reading (a traditional measure of learning disabilities), contrasted with 11.7 percent in the control schools.

The study says that costs of the program were "high," but the cost of a fully funded program for the highest poverty school, aside from Kindergarten and pre-Kindergarten, were about $1000 per-pupil; and this amount could be covered by federal Title I money usually received by such schools. Also, fully funded schools had bigger effects than lower funded ones, particularly for the most disadvantaged students. Tutoring and family-support services were the most effective expenditures for these students. An important claim of the study was the measurement of savings from retention and reduction of assignments to special education. By keeping students up to grade level, the program was able to reduce placements in special education and use some special education teachers as tutors. Another interesting point was the favorable comparison of the cost-effectiveness of SFA with other interventions whose cost-effectiveness has been established by other research, such as reduction in class size, pre-school, instructional aides, and at least one form of computer-assisted instruction. Comparison with alternative Title I programs was not given and would have been desirable, especially the ones replaced (or restructured) by SFA. However, the matched control schools in the same city and with similar student demographics probably had some kind of whole-school Title I program, offering a control for the impact of some Title I alternatives.

The conclusion of the study, that SFA can produce big effects within typical budgets, seems valid within the limitations of methodology. Reading gains may have been overstated because alignment of the test instrument to the program goals (but not to the goals of the control group). The schools used for comparison to SFA may have had important unreported differences in student characteristics or characteristics of their Title I programming. The program schools themselves were pilot, or demonstration, sites, and hence may have received an unusual level of skilled technical assistance from university personnel. The study does not measure possible benefits lost from the reallocation of Title I and special education resources (other than to the extent that the comparison schools provide a baseline). Gains in reading scores for the students previously receiving services under these programs conceivably might have been produced at the cost of reducing other outcomes, such as social adjustment. Also, the study mentions that the family support team included social workers who were working in the school but does not tell us whether extra social workers were assigned to the school because of the program.

How can the three-factor analysis of policy usefulness help in deciding how much to rely on this study? Some may consider several of the threats to internal validity to be serious. In my opinion, the greatest threat is to external validity—reliance on data from pilot sites where distinctive resources may be responsible for the size of effects. This threat is always serious and is so in this context because school restructuring may be highly sensitive to the expertise of consultants and to selection of high-capacity schools. The only obvious solution is replication in a larger number of sites where the unique resources could not be concentrated, establishing a range of effect sizes and thus a more reliable estimate of average effect size. A published article reviewing a larger body of research describes a method of "multi-site replicated experiment" in which each grade-level cohort in each SFA and comparison school is considered a replication (Slavin et al., 1996).

In contrast, the other obvious threat to validity, reliance on budgetary as opposed to observed cost data, does not seem so serious in this context. Unlike the case of distance education critiqued by Carnoy and Levin (1975), as a program operating in regular public schools SFA does not seem likely to involve major off-budget costs. Given the small size of this threat to validity, and the high cost of research on observed costs, a full investigation of all cost ingredients probably is not necessary in every replication of restructuring. Rather, an appropriate response might be a spot-check on observed cost ingredients in a smaller number of schools to verify that the assumption of low off-budget costs does hold up empirically in a range of contexts.

Meanwhile, the cost of change does not seem too high because of the promise of big effects from the intervention, the absence of known effective alternatives, including the status quo, and the relatively low incremental cost of replication (assuming the availability of the normal $1000 per-pupil in Title I funds). A higher cost intervention might argue for some other way of controlling for the pilot effect, perhaps slower replication using local implementation teams trained by other teams instead of by the original university-based experts. In fact, the Success For All program seems to have followed the first path, with replication occurring as fast as good training would allow.

Here again, weakness of research design does not necessarily translate into a lack of value to policymakers. Policy conclusions do seem justified for interventions where the threats to validity are relatively low and the results strong.

Conclusion

This paper has reviewed the quality of cost-effectiveness research in a sample of recent articles drawn from ERIC, the educational database. The appropriate conclusion to be drawn about that quality depends on the standard applied. If we ask how good the studies are compared to the best possible, on a scale of 1–5 with five representing the best (plausible) and 1 representing the worst (rhetorical), the studies clustered toward the bottom rather than the top. Higher ratings were initially obtained based on abstracts, suggesting that close examination of full research studies usually results in a lower rating.

But there are less stringent standards for looking at the data. If we ask how useful the studies are to policymakers, keeping in mind that ranking policy options is the main purpose of cost-effectiveness analysis, the situation is more complex. Under the multi-dimensional approach suggested here, weaker designs may still produce useful results depending on the seriousness of the known threats to validity in context, the size of the effects shown by the research compared to the status quo (assuming they are unrelated to bias in research design), the costs of improving the design, and the costs of changing the status quo in the direction of the intervention.

Such a context-sensitive approach focusing on the net benefits of incremental improvements in research design, seems to fit the realities of most social science research on educational policy. Indeed, a comparative analysis looking at relative strengths and payoffs is probably the only possible approach where even the very best research has flaws and represents a choice among competing tradeoffs. Practical judgments of this nature seem to underlie a recent report evaluating research support for school reform models which found that only three of 24 popular models have strong evidence that they improve student achievement (including Success For All) (see Olson, 1999). Finally, the theory of cost-effectiveness itself, applied to cost effectiveness-research, argues for developing a sense of relative risks and rewards rather than a stark contrast between completely acceptable and completely unacceptable designs. Research, like the objects of its study, offers us more and less rather than all or nothing at all.

REFERENCES

Barnett, W. S. (1994). Obstacles and opportunities: Some simple economics of school finance reform. *Educational Policy, 8*(4), 436–452.

Barnett, W. S. (1996). Economics of school reform: Three promising models. In H. F. Ladd (Ed.), *Holding schools accountable: Performance-based reform in education.* Washington, DC: The Brookings Institution.

Blank, R. (1990). Educational effects of magnet high schools. In W. Clune and J. Witte (Eds.), *Choice and control in American education* (Vol. 2, pp. 77–109). London: The Falmer Press.

Carnoy, M., and Levin, H. M. (1975). Evaluation of educational media: Some issues. *Instructional Science, 4,* 385–406.

Glantz, F., Goodson, B., and Layzer, J. (1991). *Cost-effectiveness of early childhood programs: Low-income children: Findings from the evaluation of Project Giant Step.* Paper presented at the NAEYC Annual Conference, Denver, CO.

King, J. (1994). Meeting the educational needs of at-risk students: A cost analysis of three models. *Educational Evaluation and Policy Analysis, 16*(1), 1–19.

Levin, H. M. (1991). Cost-effectiveness at quarter century. In M. W. McLaughlin and D. C. Phillips (Eds.), *Evaluation and education at quarter century* (pp. 189–209). Chicago: University of Chicago Press.

Levin, H. M. (1988). Cost-effectiveness and educational policy. *Educational Evaluation and Policy Analysis, 10*(1), 51–69.

Levin, H. M., and McEwan, P. J. (2001). *Cost-effectiveness analysis: Methods and applications* (2nd ed.). Thousand Oaks, CA: Sage.

Nachtigal, P. (1991). Remapping the terrain: School size, cost, and quality. In *Source book on school and district size, cost, and quality.* Mid-continent Regional Educational Laboratory.

Olson, L. (1999, February 17). Researchers rate whole-school reform models. *Education Week, 18*(23), 1, 14–15.

Pringle, B., and Rosenthal, E. (1993). *An analysis of the costs of Chapter 1 Migrant Education Program Summer Services.* Washington, DC: Policy Studies Associates, Inc.

Slavin, R., Dolan, L., Madden, N., Karweit, N., and Wasick, B. (1992). *Success for All: Policy implications* (Report No. 35). Center for Research on Effective Schooling for Disadvantaged Students. Johns Hopkins University.

Slavin, R., Madden, N., Dolan, L., Wasick, B., Ross, S., Smith, L., and Dianda, M. (1996). Success for All: A summary of research. *Journal for Students Placed at Risk, 1*(1), 41–76.

Wilkinson, D., Mangino, E., Ligon, G. (1993). *What works, and can we afford it? Program effectiveness in AISD, 1991–92*. Austin, TX: Austin Independent School District, Department of Management Information, Office of Research and Evaluation.

APPENDIX

1. *Rhetoric*
   Language claiming cost-effectiveness
   No data on either costs or effectiveness
   Other
2. *Minimal attempt*
   Some data on costs
   Some data on effectiveness
   List of costs
   Claim of affordability
   Claim of feasibility
   Categories of effectiveness
   Other research on effectiveness
   Other
3. *Substantial attempt*
   Substantial data on cost
   Substantial data on effectiveness
   Serious flaws
   Budgetary costs only
   Subjective effectiveness
   Weak design for effectiveness
   No comparison to alternatives
   Other
4. *Plausible study*
   Ingredients or resource costs
   Strong design on effectiveness
   Comparison to alternatives
   Other

KEY ISSUES IN CONDUCTING RESEARCH

5

ISSUES IN DESIGNING COST-EFFECTIVENESS COMPARISONS OF WHOLE-SCHOOL REFORMS

Henry M. Levin

INTRODUCTION

The deep concerns about U.S. education, and particularly the education of students in at-risk situations, have led to searches for comprehensive new models of school reform. Previous attempts at reform focused on innovations in particular parts of the school such as its curriculum, its instructional strategies, its organization, its staff development, its use of educational technology, and so on. What has distinguished the new breed of school reform has been its emphasis on transforming the school in its entirety including all of the above dimensions and more. The underlying notion is that nothing short of a new school environment encompassing all school organization and practices can achieve major educational breakthroughs. Much of this focus has been on changing the culture of the school, including the beliefs, expectations, and images of what are appropriate educator, family, and student roles, even while instituting new practices that promise stronger educational results (Finnan and Levin, 2000).

By the year 2000 there were dozens of such movements. Among the best known were the Coalition of Essential Schools of Theodore Sizer, the School Development Project of James Comer, the Success for All endeavor of Robert Slavin, and the Accelerated Schools Project of Henry Levin. In addition, there were the Core Knowledge Project of E. D. Hirsch, the Padaeia Project of Mortimer Adler, the Effective Schools movement of Larry Lezotte, and seven initial projects of the New American Schools Development Corporation (now called New American Schools [NAS] with an expansion to more projects). Even this list is far from complete, but it provides a bewildering array of choices available to school districts and schools that wish to remake education.[1]

---

1 A more complete list with details on each model is available in the *Catalog of School Reform Models* compiled by the Northwest Regional Educational Laboratory: <www.nwrel.org/scpd/catalog>.

The central question that arises is how school systems can choose among these different approaches. One general policy tool for comparing social interventions is to evaluate them according to their costs and effects or costs and benefits. Cost-effectiveness analysis compares interventions with common goals to ascertain which have the strongest results relative to their costs. Cost-benefit analysis compares interventions with similar or different goals to see which have the largest benefits relative to costs, under the assumption that benefits can be measured monetarily. In principal, comprehensive school reforms could be evaluated for their costs and effectiveness or costs and benefits and compared with each other to see which ones are most promising. In reality, some may work better in certain contexts and for certain populations than others, so such comparisons would need to be done for particular settings. But, the overall notion of applying a policy tool like cost-effectiveness analysis to school reforms would seem to be a high priority.

The initial goal of this endeavor was to construct cost-effectiveness comparisons of some of the existing whole-school interventions on the basis of available data. For reasons that will become clear later, existing data are not adequate to make these comparisons. In short, school reform evaluations differ so much in evaluation methods, sampling, measurement of outputs, and perspectives of evaluators that the results are not scientifically valid for making objective comparisons despite comparative claims on behalf of different models. Further, the costs of replicating the school reforms have not been estimated in a consistent or defensible manner that provides any precision. With few exceptions available, cost data are inconsistent, incomplete, rarely based upon careful and systematic methods, and confuse reallocation of resources as costless. Accordingly, this paper is devoted to the issues surrounding cost-effectiveness studies of whole-school reform rather than comparative analysis of results. It is hoped that the discussion and guidelines will ultimately lead to valid cost-effectiveness comparisons.

CHALLENGES OF WHOLE-SCHOOL REFORM FOR EVALUATION

Up until about 1980 the traditional approach to improving schools was to identify school challenges individually and address them idiosyncratically. Most U.S. schools adopted new curriculum packages in different subjects, technology infusions, reductions in class size, new approaches to instruction such as cooperative learning or project learning, new organizational innovations such as block scheduling, and so on. These interventions were typically done on a piecemeal basis as issues were identified that required a response. Some schools experienced five or more different "reforms" in a single year and many more times over a decade. The larger features of the school typically remained intact as reforms were simply grafted onto existing institutions and their dominant practices. Over time schools would give up on specific reforms and replace them with others, often inserting each superficially in a school environment that was unreceptive. In most cases there was little change in the long-term as these individual reforms failed to modify school operations in any substantial way (Cuban, 1993).

In the 1980's the focus of reform began to shift from idiosyncratic and piecemeal attempts at reform to addressing the school as a whole. Much of this was galvanized by the work of Ron Edmonds (1979) in his attempt to capitalize on ways in which effective and ineffective schools differed. Reformers such as James Comer, Ted Sizer, Larry Lezotte, Carl Glickman, Robert Slavin, Henry Levin, and others developed models for school change that addressed wholesale the entire school rather than adding new appendages here and there. This became known as whole school reform or comprehensive school reform. By the 1990's it had become a prominent trend with the New American Schools Development Corporation (NASDC) seeking "break the mold" models for schools; publishing of major works on whole school change (e.g., Fullan, 1991; Hargreaves, Lieberman, Fullan, and Hopkins, 1998); and the establishment of federal legislation for Comprehensive School Reform Development (CSRD).

To understand the challenges that comprehensive school reform has raised for cost-effectiveness analysis, one must visit briefly the previous studies of cost-effectiveness analyses in education. Cost-effectiveness comparisons require that the alternatives being considered have common objectives so that their results can be readily compared. Costs also need to be measured in a uniform way, relying on the ingredients or resource method (Levin and McEwan, 2001). With common metrics for the cost and effectiveness components, it is possible to compare cost-effectiveness across alternatives for achieving the same objectives.

By adding modest interventions such as a new curriculum or instructional approach at a cost of less than $100 or so per student out of a total school budget of $5,000 to $10,000 per student, the task is simplified. That is, the overall school is left intact, and it is only necessary to isolate costs and effectiveness of the specific change. Costs are usually an add-on that can be identified by stipulating the additional resources that are needed. Effectiveness can be measured by the changes in results that are induced by the intervention.

Interventions that were evaluated comprised programs such as computer-assisted instruction, a different curriculum in a specific subject, smaller classes, longer school days, peer tutoring, and so on (Levin, 1991; Levin, Glass, and Meister, 1987). Measures of effectiveness established whether each of these types of interventions, when added to a regular school program, had an impact on student achievement and the magnitude of that impact. Cost measures examined only the marginal or additional costs of these interventions to the school, not the overall costs of school operations. Results were converted into units of effectiveness for a given cost and compared across alternatives.

In these cases the intervention could be readily identified as an "add-on" to the school program, and its costs and effectiveness could be measured somewhat independently of the existing program. Of course, some "add-ons" might work better at some sites with some types of students and existing programs than at other sites. But, even this could be taken account of by looking for statistical interactions between these specifics and the effectiveness of an intervention (Summers and Wolfe, 1977). At the same time it was relatively easy to separate out the added ingredients or resources that a school needed to implement each of the programs. And, effectiveness could be limited to one or two specific program outcomes when the interventions were compared for reaching a common goal; e.g. reading programs (Levin and McEwan, 2001, Chap. 6).

But, with whole-school reform there is a transformation from a traditional school to a restructured one with a potential impact on all of the goals of the school, not just one or two. At the same time there are both reallocations of existing resources and added resources that are pertinent to whole-school reform. These facts create an enormously greater challenge in doing a cost-effectiveness (or even just an effectiveness) comparison among different whole-school programs. Indeed, it is these types of methodological issues that are the subject of this paper.

A related challenge is that a focus on a single output such as reading or mathematics (or even both considered together) is an inadequate basis for considering the productivity of a school. Any formulation that considers only these outputs will fall prey to considering only a portion of outcomes that the schools produce. This will mean that major outputs will be unaccounted for. Thus, a comparison between two whole-school interventions that focus only on a single output or dual outputs will not monitor what is happening to other outputs. Certainly, by shifting resources from the production of unmeasured outputs to measured ones, it is possible to obtain more of the measured ones. But, this is only a partial measure of the total output of the school as it would be for any multi-product firm.

Consider that even a short list of what schools are expected to produce is formidable. It would include raising proficiencies in many subjects including reading, writing, speaking, mathematics, science, social studies, art, and physical education, as well as a large number of social values and behaviors. With respect to the latter, schools emphasize working cooperatively with others, following rules, accepting constructive criticism, planning a project, setting goals, seeking out necessary information, resolving conflict appropriately, and respecting differing viewpoints, to name just a few that come to mind. Inkeles (1966) suggests many more that schools are expected to provide to create competent adults.

In this situation it is possible to increase one output without improving productivity by neglecting other outputs. For example, if resources that were previously devoted to other outputs are focused more intensively on mathematics, it is possible to improve mathematics achievement without improving overall school effectiveness that takes account of other outputs. Allocating more of the school's personnel and greater instructional time to mathematics at the expense of other subjects and social behaviors and attitudes can improve mathematics achievement. As long as all school outputs are monitored, this shift in resource allocation will be reflected in shifts in the levels of outputs that are produced with a rise in mathematics achievement balanced by reductions in the attainment of other school goals. But, as we will see below, many studies focus on only one or two school objectives, such as reading or mathematics or graduation rates, rather than the plethora of outcomes that schools are expected to produce. The result is that it may be impossible to determine what is being given up among other outputs to obtain given increases in the output under scrutiny. For example, Bowles and Gintis (2000) provide cogent evidence that non-cognitive aspects of schooling that are not even measured in school accountability systems may be the dominant determinants of education's effect on earnings rather than cognitive aspects measured by tests.[2]

Whole-school reform is an attempt to alter the organization of schools, the use of resources, decision-making and information flows (Levin, 1997). To the degree that it is done largely within existing resources, when evaluations are based upon a single objective or narrow range of objectives, resources are likely to be reallocated from existing uses to those most closely aligned with those objectives. Thus, unless there

---

2   Some reformers suggest increasing the time devoted to mathematics or reading as if it is a costless reallocation. Where does this time come from, and what activities are sacrificed? Over the years a number of subjects, such as geography, have disappeared from U.S. schools. Does it matter if most Americans confuse Australia with Austria or do not know the continents or locations of nations?

is a way to assess the impact of the reform on all outcomes—or at least all major outcomes—any attempt to limit effectiveness studies to a single objective will be suspect as an overall assessment of effectiveness of the reform model. As we will see below, this also raises challenges for the measurement of costs, because reallocations of an existing budget may not be costless in an economic sense. In the next two sections we will review the implications of this background for measuring both effectiveness and costs.

Measuring Effectiveness

Ideally, we would like to obtain comparable data on school effectiveness to compare among school reform models. These can be combined with comparable data on costs to ascertain the cost-effectiveness of each of the approaches. Slavin and Fashola (1998) and Herman (1999) have published comparisons of effectiveness. In this section, we will argue that such comparisons—in the absence of methodological, sampling, and other adjustments—are invalid.[3] The lack of comparison validity is not due to subtle issues. It is due to fundamental differences among designs and procedures that can account for different evaluation results beyond differences in the impacts of the models themselves.[4] Each of these differences in treatment of the studies will be addressed below. Due to lack of space and an attempt to provide an overview, I will summarize these concerns with brief references to particular studies.

In particular I will address four issues that must be considered in doing a comparative cost-effectiveness analysis. The first addresses the issue of whether the overall evaluation approach is valid and how the particular choice of evaluation method may affect the magnitude of reported effectiveness. Second, there is the issue of how representative are the schools that are sampled for evaluations. Third is the issue of multiple products and how they will be accounted for. Fourth is the matter of potential bias in evaluations done by school reform sponsors or their representatives relative to independent evaluations. Each will be taken in turn.

---

3 It is important that I stipulate that I was the founder and director of one of the school reform models, the Accelerated Schools Project. I should add that I admire all of the reform efforts referred to in this paper, although each is based on different premises on the purpose of and strategy for school change. Slavin and Fashola (1998) and Herman (1999), the authors of the effectiveness comparisons of the different models, have been associated with Success for All and Roots and Wings, although Herman's study was done as an employee of the American Institutes of Research. It is also important to note that there are far more evaluations of Success for All than of the other reforms because of Robert Slavin's concern with demonstrating effectiveness of educational practices. In this respect we owe Slavin an important debt. The downside of that largesse is that the evaluations of Success for All provide many of the examples of issues that are raised in this paper.

4 An overview of some of these issues is found in Hunter and Schmidt (1994). As an illustration, Lipsey (1999, p. 627) finds that a significant portion of the variation in effect sizes is due to evaluation method in his meta-analysis of programs to reduce recidivism among juvenile offenders.

MODELS OF EVALUATION

A major issue is whether the evaluation model is an adequate one by which to obtain valid results. There are two primary approaches used in the literature and an eclectic third category.

EXPERIMENTAL

The pure experimental model requires schools to be randomly assigned to treatment and control groups (Boruch, 1997). If the treatment and control groups are large enough, comparability in school features is assured so that any difference between the two groups after implementation of the treatment could be attributed to the treatment. This type of approach is not easily applied to whole-school reform since all of the reforms require that schools select the specific reform that is adopted (typically approval by 80 percent or more of the teachers) rather than the reform being assigned to the school. In some cases this process of "informed consent" is breached as specific reforms are pushed on schools by school districts (Datnow, 2000). But, all of the major comprehensive school reforms attempt to ensure an active process of informed choice and buy-in. Once schools select or "buy-in" to a specific reform, they are usually accepted by the sponsor of the reform.

The only experimental studies that I could find were those undertaken by Thomas Cook and his colleagues.[5] Cook, Hunt, and Murphy (2000) compared 10 inner-city Chicago schools using the School Development Program or Comer model with nine comparison schools over a four-year period. The Comer schools and the comparison schools were selected randomly from a population of low-achieving Chicago schools, all that had volunteered to adopt the reform. The evaluators found small achievement advantages for the Comer Schools relative to the control schools (about 3 percent over three to four years) as well as advantages in student behavior and attitudes. Cook et al. (1999) also used the experimental methodology to study academic and other outcomes in a randomized study of 23 middle schools in an urban county in Maryland. Differences were found in favor of Comer schools in psychological and social outcomes, but not student achievement.

QUASI-EXPERIMENTS

Quasi-experiments represent attempts to emulate experimental conditions as closely as possible, in the absence of random assignment (Cook and Campbell, 1979a,b).[6] The typical quasi-experimental design attempts to compare units receiving the intervention with similar units that are not receiving the intervention. Statistical adjustments are often used to attempt to adjust for differences between intervention groups and the comparison ones that could affect outcomes. Robert Slavin and colleagues have carried out a large number of studies, where compari-

---

5 Slavin and Madden (1999) erroneously refer to evaluations of Success for All as experiments even though they do not use random assignment as the basis for comparison.

6 Almost all evaluations of whole-school reforms fit the quasi-experimental category. As Cook and Campbell (1979a,b) point out, there are many threats to the validity of such evaluations, so the reader should be aware that the fact that certain results are claimed in an evaluation (even what appears to be a sophisticated one) may not be substantiated.

son and intervention schools are assigned directly by the evaluators rather than randomly (Slavin and Madden, 1999, 2000). They conclude that their Success for All and Roots and Wings models show very substantial gains in student achievement relative to the comparison schools. The Center for Policy Research in Education (CPRE) evaluated schools from the America's Choice model in three cities, using as comparison schools that had not adopted the model in these cities (Supovitz, Poglinco, and Snyder, 2001). Statistical controls were provided for demographics and other factors that might affect achievement. They found small achievement advantages for the America's Choice schools at most grade levels for the first year of implementation. Ross and colleagues (1999) evaluated achievement gains of whole-school reforms by comparing a large number of schools undertaking whole-school reform in Memphis with a "matched" group of schools not undertaking the reforms. They also compared the achievement effects of the different reform models and found substantial achievement gains of those schools participating in the whole-school reforms relative to the comparison schools, using a value-added model.[7]

Millsap et al. (2000) found no difference in achievement between 12 Comer schools in Detroit and a set of matched, comparison schools, although they did find that those schools with the best implementation of the reform did have better achievement than the comparison group. In a similar type of study no overall difference in achievement was found between 12 Core Knowledge Schools and matched comparison schools, but an effect was observed for Core Knowledge Schools with a high level of implementation (Stringfield, Datnow, Borman, and Rachuba, 1998). In a study of five Core Knowledge Schools in Maryland, researchers found mixed results in comparing achievement in schools with the intervention and comparison schools (Mac Iver, Stringfield, and McHugh, 2000).

A different quasi-experimental design is that of interrupted or discontinuous time series (McCain and McCleary, 1979). In that case the pattern of achievement for a particular sample of schools is evaluated over time, for several years prior to the reform and several years following it to test whether the pattern was altered following the intervention. Statistical adjustments are made for other changes in the school over that period such as changes in socio-economic or racial composition of students. The Manpower Development Research Corporation used this technique to evaluate third-grade achievement for a national sample of eight Accelerated Schools with about 3,000 students in the study (Bloom et al., 2001; Doolittle, 2001). The improvement in mathematics and reading achievement by the fifth year of implementation was 7–8 percentiles.

OTHER METHODS

Several other methods have been used to evaluate whole-school reforms. The Rand Corporation has examined the degree to which such schools have outpaced the average achievement gains of the districts where they are situated (Berends, Kirby, Naftel, and McKelvey, 2001, pp. 130–32). This is a fairly common approach in which the district is viewed as the comparison standard where all schools in the district are assumed to be subject to the same non-reform influences. Correlational

---

7 See Sanders and Horn (1995) for a presentation of the value-added model.

approaches have also been used in which statistical models are designed to isolate the effects of a reform intervention from other factors which may influence achievement such as school resources and student characteristics.

Perhaps the weakest design is that of year-to-year achievement gains for individual schools without comparison data. This is the typical format used by school districts to report progress. Even with gains of reforming schools, the question is whether those gains are greater than those for comparable non-reforming schools. An equally serious challenge is the long-term reliability of such short-term, measured gains. Recent studies have found that a high proportion of achievement change from one year to the next is transitory and due to idiosyncratic factors (Kane and Staiger, 2001). This means that gains from year-to-year may not be "permanent," but due to temporary circumstances, such as an especially strong or weak student cohort or a disruptive period when testing was done. Kane and Staiger estimate that less than half of the average achievement gain in reading between fourth and fifth grades (the grades for which they tested the relationship) showed persistent differences between schools.

What is noteworthy is how many different methodologies are used and the variants of each in terms of details, such as sampling and measurement issues, that we will refer to below. Even within these evaluation methodologies there can be substantial differences in their implementation that can affect results. As we have noted, the choice of comparison schools in quasi-experimental studies is often arbitrary. With the exception of the studies by Cook and his colleagues (1999, 2000), comparison schools are not randomly chosen. For example, Supovitz et al. (2001) chose as comparison schools those schools not carrying out the America's Choice reform in the three districts that were studied. Evaluations of Success for All (Slavin and Madden, 1999) provide few specific details on how comparison schools are chosen other than an attempt to provide a demographic match.

Since all of the major whole-school reforms require buy-in with support from 80 percent or more of their teachers or school staff, it is likely that those with stronger leadership and committed staff will undertake the reform. *Prima facie* this suggests that one is comparing energized schools ready to undertake reform with ones that are not rather than comparing schools that are comparable in every way except for the nature of their programs. This is likely to lead to overstatement of the measured effectiveness of the reform.[8] But, differences in the rigor of the "buy-in" requirements among models will create differences in this bias with the models that demand greatest commitment in buy-in creating greater selection bias in favor of success. At the same time the standards for choosing comparison schools may differ substantially, resulting in estimated effects conditioned upon the readiness, leadership, and enthusiasm of schools undertaking reform versus the lassitude of the comparison school determining outcomes rather than the impacts of the reform models themselves.[9]

---

8 Even random assignment among "bought-in" schools might not provide appropriate comparisons if the schools that are randomly rejected for school reform experience a "letdown" because of the rejection (Fetterman, 1982).

9 Although all of the models seem to set similar criteria in their printed materials, the verification of buy-in varies profoundly from model-to-model and, perhaps, even school-to-school within models (Datnow, 2000).

SAMPLING OF SCHOOLS

One of the great challenges in education is replication. Even when an educational intervention has been shown to have strong effects at a demonstration site, it is rare that it is replicated at other sites with similar results. Indeed, the history of educational reform is more a testimonial to constancy and resistance to change than to change itself (Cuban, 1993; Sarason, 1982). From a policy perspective one is concerned not with the results from experimental, demonstration, or exemplary sites, but with the potential effect of expansion of initially successful sites to new sites and scaling up from a few to many. This means that evaluations for cost-effectiveness purposes should be based not upon initial results at a relatively small number of sites that have received special attention and nurturing, but replication under the ordinary conditions that will be found as expansion takes place. Too often educational evaluations are done in laboratory settings or in ones where university support and scrutiny are provided, factors that are unlikely to be pertinent in subsequent replications under ordinary conditions. Obviously, the first proto-types and initial replications will have the most assistance, attentive evaluations, and publicity. It is incorrect to assume that subsequent applications of the approach will be equally effective.[10]

Few evaluations of educational interventions can be found that reflect what happens under the most routine replications. It is widely recognized that published evaluations overstate the average or typical effects of interventions because poorly performing sites will not be evaluated and evaluations showing poor results will not be reported or published (Begg, 1994; Glass, McGaw, and Smith, 1981). Some authors even recommend eliminating from consideration evaluations of those sites that do not implement a model "correctly."[11] But, sites that implement the models well are not typical of the average implementation, and high implementation may also be related to strong leadership, staff comraderie, and staff talent, factors that are independent of the model.[12]

Thus, a first concern with respect to a cost-effectiveness evaluation is whether the study of effectiveness has been done on a typical replication that is reproducible from site-to-site under "ordinary" circumstances. Obviously, the most appropriate estimate of effectiveness would be to evaluate the full population of replicated sites or a representative sample of adequate size. As we will show below, results may be

---

10 For example, Lipsey (1999) found a very substantial difference in effect sizes in favor of demonstration programs over replication programs.

11 For example, Slavin and Madden (2000) suggest that instances of poor evaluation results for the Success for All model are a result of poor implementation rather than flaws in the model. But, this raises questions of whether the implementation process accompanying a reform is an integral part of it or is independent of it. Clearly the truth lies somewhere between these two extremes. The Rand Corporation analysis of New American Schools attempted to measure the degree of implementation of different models rather than an absolute measure (Berends et al., 2001, pp. 11–78). Surprisingly, the Rand study found no linkage between the degree of implementation and school performance among the 163 New American Schools for which data were available (p. 128). If a decision-maker asks the question, what is the expected effectiveness of a particular model under "typical" conditions, the probability of poor implementation should be included in the overall assessment of effects. Suchman (1971) has provided one of the best conceptual discussions distinguishing between the failure of theory versus the failure of program implementation.

radically different from study-to-study of the same school reform models, at least in part from sample selection.

There are at least three issues with regard to sampling bias. First, is the bias that we mentioned above, that only the most energized schools anxious to change will "buy in" to the reforms, making them unrepresentative of other schools that might be similar in demography, size, and location. This bias boosts the apparent effectiveness of all of the models requiring buy-in. But differences in the rigor and verification process of adoption criteria will create differences in the degree of bias among the different school models. Those models that set and enforce the most stringent criteria for staff participation in the adoption process will likely have schools that are more highly motivated and prepared to implement reforms than those that do not, independently of whatever reform is being implemented (Datnow, 2000).

Second, there is a question of whether the schools in the evaluation samples are representative of all schools participating in the school reforms, or only ones with good implementation, or samples of convenience (where data are available or results are promising). Only Cook and colleagues (1999, 2000) have made an attempt at random assignment of schools, and only within two specific localities, even though the model that they evaluated has been implemented nationally. Although the MDRC study of Accelerated Schools (Bloom et al., 2001; Doolittle, 2001) represents an attempt to study a national sample of implementing schools with eight years of data, data availability itself affected the nature of the sample. The recent study of America's Choice schools is based upon schools in the three school districts with the largest adoptions of its schools, suggesting atypical district support for its model relative to the typical situation. Although there are many more evaluations of Success for All than of other models, there is no information that suggests that an attempt has been made to get representative sites.

These sampling issues undermine attempts to predict the effectiveness of each reform model for future schools that might consider adoption. The buy-in requirements mean that the results cannot be extrapolated to other schools that have not gone through a similar buy-in. Further, the bias towards evaluation reporting only for schools with high implementation will tend to overstate results for more typical situations. Also, it is likely that schools selected for evaluation are those benefiting from favorable conditions such as strong district support, and this bias may differ from study to study. This means that even if the evaluation models used in all studies were similar, differences in sampling would threaten valid comparisons. And, the overall results across studies can not be generalized to the overall population of schools, even those with similar demographics or locations. It is noteworthy that the Rand study of comprehensive school reform models sponsored by New American Schools found that slightly fewer than half of the reforming schools had achievement gains greater than the averages for their districts, about what chance would predict (Berends et al., 2001, p. 131). All of the models report far greater success in their own evaluations based—in part—on different samples from those used by Rand.

---

12 In many cases, if not most, it may be impossible to know if a chosen school will provide good implementation. Therefore, the decision-maker is more likely to ask the question, if schools adopt a particular model, what is the likely outcome (not if they adopt a likely model and succeed at implementation).

A third way in which sampling will vary will be among the types of students who are evaluated. Different studies eliminate different types of students from the testing base, such as those with learning disabilities or in bilingual programs. Typically, evaluations of whole-school reforms focus only on students who were in the school continuously over the evaluation period. But, the most educationally needy and disadvantaged students have high mobility rates and are found in schools with high student turnover. For example, Kerbow (1996) found that in the typical Chicago elementary school, only half of the students were still enrolled at the school after three years. Restricting the evaluations to students who remain at a single school site restricts the evaluation to those students in stable situations who generally have higher achievement, irrespective of the reform model (Kerbow, 1996; Rumberger, 2001). Further, such children have an additional advantage because they are exposed to the reform for the entire duration of the period of evaluation. In contrast, students with high mobility spend less time in a particular school and have less exposure to the reform, often being churned among many different schools over a one- or two-year period. At the very least, studies that eliminate mobile students should report that their results apply only to stable students who have had continuous exposure to the reforms, not to all students attending the schools that are evaluated. Unfortunately, such studies tend to generalize their interpretations to all students.

But, in addition, the variance in treatment of student mobility among studies contributes to their non-comparability. For example, evaluations of Success for All have largely been limited to those students who attend the same school continuously for all of the years in which the school is evaluated, as many as five years. Such studies can say little about the effects of the reform on the many students—typically with lower achievement levels and lower achievement growth—who move to other schools (Kerbow, 1996, p. 16). The studies by Cook et al. (1999, 2000) and Millsap et al. (2000) of Comer schools and of Core Knowledge schools by Stringfield, Datnow, et al. (1998) also restrict themselves to students attending their schools for the duration of the program treatment and evaluation. In contrast, the evaluation of Accelerated Schools (Bloom et al., 2001; Doolittle, 2001) includes all students in the school at the time of the third-grade testing. It was estimated that about half had not received three years of exposure to the Accelerated Schools model and one-third had not even received two years of exposure (Bloom et al. 2001, p. 98). Obviously, a comparison of stable students who have been exposed continuously to a reform with one that also includes students who have not had that advantage will bias the result in favor of the reforms that eliminate mobile students from the evaluation. The evaluation of America's Choice by Supovitz et al. (2001) takes a middle position by including all students in the three districts for which there were longitudinal test scores. That is, students who moved to other schools in the district were included, but not those who moved to or from other districts. Studies that limit their analysis only to students who were attending the school for the duration of the evaluation period will show higher achievement effects than those that include all students in the analysis. This difference in student sampling undermines comparability of results.

Measuring School Outputs

A particularly difficult challenge is that of multiple outputs. Different school reforms have different foci. For example, the School Development Project, the Coalition of Essential Schools, Different Ways of Knowing, and the Accelerated Schools

Project all require schools to set their own priorities and address them. Such schools may focus on different subjects, student involvement in projects, and a range of other goals that are likely to vary from school to school. The School Development Project attempts to focus on the integration of families into a school community, while the Accelerated Schools Project and Coalition for Essential Schools focus on the development of a learning community with a specific philosophy based upon constructivist learning theory. Different Ways of Knowing utilizes the arts to connect all subjects. In contrast, Reading Recovery and Success for All focus primarily on early-childhood reading proficiency with explicit strategies and materials. Core Knowledge emphasizes mastery of a specific knowledge base and use of a particular curriculum.

There is absolutely nothing wrong with a school-wide strategy to improve student proficiency in single subjects. However, it is inappropriate to compare effectiveness in only one or two subjects among different school reform models, when some focus only on that subject and others focus more broadly on a variety of outcomes. And, indeed, this is the dilemma. Schools are multi-product firms with multiple goals. School reforms that focus only on one dimension can show superior results by concentrating their efforts on that goal. But, an evaluation on a single dimension is biased against those reforms that focus on improvements in multiple outcomes. Such a comparison also violates the assumption in cost-effectiveness analysis that only interventions with common goals should be directly compared—and all major goals must be included in the evaluations.

Beyond this the case of multiple outputs also raises the question of how to value effectiveness. For example, if one alternative does better on reading and the other on mathematics in the simplest case of two outputs, how does one determine the comparative effectiveness of the two alternatives? The standard approach is to place values on each of the two outputs using utility scales or other devices (Levin and McEwan 2001, pp. 189–216). Of course, one could weight each of the results equally (e.g., equivalent effect sizes in each subject are given equivalent weight). But, there is no reason *a priori* to provide equal weights to equivalent effect sizes across many subjects and other measures of student behavior. Although music and art are extremely important subjects in the curriculum, it is not clear how society should value them in comparison with reading, science, mathematics, social studies, writing, and the other academic subjects. It is possible that music and art should be considered more important than some of these other subjects because of their intrinsic value as well as the contributions that they can make to cultivating creative talents.[13] But, what is clear from this example is the complexity of the challenge of combining school results for different outcomes into an overall rating of effectiveness. There exist "solutions" to this problem, but they are highly subjective and based upon assumptions for ascertaining social value that are arbitrary (Levin and McEwan 2001, pp. 189–216).

How particular outcomes are measured is also an important criterion in comparing alternatives. When measuring change in academic achievement, it is common to use "effect size" as the criterion (McGaw, 1994). The advantage of using effect size is that it is a common measure that can be calculated for different tests that ostensi-

---

13 For example, Different Ways of Knowing of the Galef Foundation is a reform that uses the arts as an integrative strategy for other subjects. See <www.dwoknet.galef.org>.

bly measure achievement in the same domain. Thus, even though different schools and school districts utilize different testing instruments constructed by different test publishers, one can calculate the change in achievement between two periods and divide it by the standard deviation of the test to get an effect size. Presumably the effect size is a common metric that allows comparison of effectiveness.[14]

However, each test instrument measures its domain in different ways. For example, fourth-grade mathematics tests may differ in the weight given different types of mathematics operations, applications, concepts, and word problems. Some tests will rely more heavily on math facts. At the opposite extreme, some will emphasize concepts and solution of word problems. The same populations will obtain different results on different tests, depending on the composition of what is being tested and how it is tested. Thus, although it may appear to be intuitively plausible that test results can be compared in terms of a common metric, effect size, different tests represent different measurement systems. Some are considered to be more difficult than others because they have more complex calculations, harder problems, or rely more heavily on speedy solutions under rigorous timing restrictions. To some degree each test is measuring a different version of the same domain, and its results are not strictly comparable with the results of other tests, even though one can mechanically compute effect sizes for each.

A related problem is the issue of whether one uses a broad, spectrum test or one that is tailored to the curriculum that a reform represents. If a school reform model uses a prescriptive approach to curriculum content and instructional strategies, it will seem natural to align it with a specific test that measures the success of that approach. Thus, the criterion of effectiveness will match the intervention closely. But, where the school reform model leaves a large range of discretion for schools to construct their own curriculum content and instructional strategies, it is unlikely that one test instrument will match closely the goals of schools using that model. Further, school districts and states mandate many different tests, none of which may align perfectly with each subject area as represented among the school reform models that embrace all of the different subjects and school activities.

The result is that effectiveness measured by a test that is aligned with the specific curriculum content that is taught and the instructional strategies that are used is likely to be greater than on a broader criterion. In general, this means that school reforms that use aligned tests to measure results will show better results than when measured against more general testing systems. As an example, a Success for All school was matched with a comparison school to assess the gain in reading over an academic year. On the aligned tests used by Success for All, there was a statistically significant difference in reading in favor of the Success for All school. But, when the Tennessee Assessment Series was used to make the comparisons, there were no statistically significant differences between the Success for All and the comparison school in reading or any other subject (Ross and Smith, 1994).

---

14 Olejnik and Algina (2000) provide a cogent presentation on the limits of using measures of effect sizes for comparative studies. They conclude that: ". . . measures of effect size are affected by the research design used" (p. 280). Their cautions on the variability of effect size that is based upon differences in evaluation methods rather than differences in "true" effects is much more extensive than the measurement issue raised here. Also see Lipsey (1999) and Hunter and Schmidt (1994).

Several of the school reform movements, for example, the Coalition of Essential Schools and Accelerated Schools, place an emphasis on student performance on real-world or authentic tasks rather than on test scores which are usually far removed from those tasks. For example, instead of a test of knowledge of chemistry, a performance evaluation might require the student to analyze a "mystery" substance for its elemental components, testing the student's abilities to use logic, intuition, knowledge, and laboratory procedures to accomplish a real-world challenge. An evaluation of a student's mastery of a Shakespearean tragedy might entail the writing of a short work embodying the style of that form of work with a presentation before the class and a demonstration of how it meets the criteria as well as knowledgeable responses to questioning.

Consider the comparison for effectiveness of a school reform that is focused on performance assessment with one focused on criteria that are directly measurable by a standardized test. The standardized test will be far more closely aligned with the latter than the former. And, what appears to be a neutral measure of assessment—a chemistry test or English test or history test or mathematics test—will not be neutral at all. For the test-driven curriculum, students will be repeatedly tested in the standardized format with both testing experience and curriculum goals contributing to performance on that type of measure. In the school emphasizing performance assessment, both the goals and the students' experiences will not match up well to standardized tests. The result is that comparisons of effectiveness of school reforms will be problematic when a single set of standardized tests is used to assess reforms whose goals differ so substantially from reform to reform.

THIRD-PARTY EVALUATIONS

A particularly challenging aspect of the existing evaluations of effectiveness of whole-school reforms is that most have been done by the sponsors of the reforms. Almost three decades ago James Q. Wilson (1973) set out two laws that he believed apply to all cases of social science evaluation of public policy:

First Law: All policy interventions in social problems produce the intended effect—if the research is carried out by those implementing the policy or their friends.

Second Law: No policy intervention in social problems produces the intended effect—if the research is carried out by independent third parties, especially those skeptical of the policy.

Wilson is not accusing developers or their friends of fudging the data to support effectiveness claims, but simply stating that different standards of evidence and method selected by evaluators who are assessing their own interventions can have this effect. There are many areas for judgment-calls in evaluation. In general, the sponsors or their colleagues accept conditions, methods, and measures that are more favorable to their interventions than they would if they were evaluating competing models. Scriven (1976) has written comprehensively and perceptively on evaluation bias.

We define third-party evaluations as those meeting two conditions. First, the evaluations are carried out by independent evaluators who have virtually no personal or institutional links to the sponsors of the reform. Second, they are not funded directly by the reform sponsors or developers. Using these criteria, Cook, Hunt, and Murphy (2000), Cook et al. (1999), and Millsap et al. (2000) have carried out third-party studies of the Comer model. The Manpower Development Research Corporation has carried out a third-party study of Accelerated Schools (Doolittle, 2001). The Center for Social Organization of Schools at Johns Hopkins University (Stringfield, Datnow, et al., 1998; MacIver et al., 2000) completed third-party evaluations of Core Knowledge schools; and Supovitz and colleagues (2001) at the Center for Policy Research in Education undertook a third-party evaluation of America's Choice.[15] The Rand Corporation has carried out third-party evaluations of the New American Schools models.[16]

Most evaluations of whole-school reforms have been carried out by the sponsors of the reforms rather than by third parties.[17] Even attempts to summarize results across the different reforms have been carried out primarily by those associated with specific reforms. For example, a highly-publicized, "third-party" review of evidence on effectiveness of school reform models was carried out under the aegis of the American Institutes of Research (Herman, 1999). But, the director of the study had recently shifted employment from an organization sponsoring one of the reforms and had collaborated previously in a laudatory evaluation of that reform (Stringfield, Millsap, and Herman, 1998).[18]

As the literature predicts, third-party evaluations tend to find more modest effectiveness results than the assessment results of studies of the sponsors of those reforms.[19] For example, the Rand evaluation of New American Schools found that fewer than half of the schools showed achievement gains in reading or mathematics that were greater than those of the districts in which they were located. Bear in mind that by chance about half will be above the district average. The contrast between the assessments reported by the sponsors of the models and the Rand result is striking. For example, the summary of evaluation results for Success for All and Roots and Wings (Roots and Wings is an expanded model including other subjects

---

15 The study of America's Choice was funded by that organization, so it does not meet the condition of independent funding.

16 There has been considerable controversy over what is a third-party evaluation, particularly for Success for All/Roots and Wings as reflected in the exchange between critic Pogrow (2000) and the founders of Success for All, Slavin and Madden (2000). Slavin and Madden assert that anyone not situated in their foundation or at their center at Johns Hopkins University is a third party even if they are or have been closely associated with their organizations as former employees, collaborators or consultants. Most of the Success for All evaluations have been done by persons who have been associated with the organizations of the founder in one or more significant respects.

17 In my view, studies undertaken by school districts of their schools may be biased in either direction depending upon their point-of-view on a reform. This certainly seems to be a point of contention surrounding the evaluation of the whole-school reforms in Memphis which resulted in a report prepared for its school board recommending the abandonment of all such reforms (Calaway, 2001).

18 Perhaps unsurprisingly the review concluded that Success for All was one of only three models that had considerable evidence of results, a finding similar to the reviews by the author's former colleagues Slavin and Fashola (1998).

19 For example, Cooper, Charlton, Valentine, and Muhlenbruck (2000) found that in a meta-evaluation of summer-school effectiveness, the internal evaluations produced effect sizes about twice as large as external evaluations.

as well as reading) reports consistent and overwhelming evidence of effectiveness, primarily on the basis of the sponsor's own evaluations (Slavin and Madden, 1999). In contrast, the Rand evaluation (Berends et al., 2001) found that fewer than half of the Roots and Wings schools had achievement gains greater than their districts. Although America's Choice showed significant gains in reading and mathematics relative to comparison schools in three school districts, the Rand evaluation of its New American Schools found that only slightly more than half did better than their districts in mathematics and only a quarter of the schools in reading.

In a study of achievement using the value-added approach, the first wave of reforming schools in Memphis had much better results than a matched group of non-reforming schools (Ross et al., 1999).[20] But, a more recent report sponsored by the Memphis School District that evaluated all of the schools engaged in reform, including ones that started later, found virtually no achievement effectiveness among the reform models (Calaway, 2001).

This contrast provides a good example of the dilemma of attempting to compare differences in reform models. For the same set of school reforms and the same settings, the results differ markedly. Why? The two studies differ remarkably in their samples, time frames, and methods, all matters of judgment or choice in the evaluation process. Moreover, the potential orientations of the two evaluation groups are different. The Ross et al. (1999) study, with three of its co-authors associated with one of the models and its principal author also affiliated with the New American Schools evaluations, has made choices that are more likely to favor findings of effectiveness. For example, by including only the first wave of schools that volunteered for school reform, the sample is likely to have an upward bias relative to the later schools that were required to adopt a reform under an imposed deadline. In contrast, the study by the Memphis City Schools (Calaway, 2001) was prepared for a school-board meeting in which the new Superintendent was prepared to recommend the dropping of all school reforms promoted by the previous Superintendent. The result is that even schools that had barely begun to engage in the reform process and that had been pressured to adopt a reform were evaluated along with those that had actually implemented the reforms.

INCOMPARABILITY OF EFFECTIVENESS REPORTS

In summary, evaluations designed to estimate the effectiveness of the different school reform models are premised on choices of samples, measurements, methods of evaluation, and interpretations that differ markedly among evaluations. In particular, evaluations of sponsors tend to select "successful" schools and ignore those where the results are not salubrious and to select outcome measures that are aligned with their own purposes as well as methods of analysis (e.g., in choice of comparison schools) that tend to favor their reforms. Third-party evaluations may sample differently, use outcome measures that are broader, and employ methods that are not necessarily favorable or sensitive to specific reform efforts. Among both first-party

---

20 Three of the five co-authors were affiliated with Success for All/Roots and Wings which was found to have the largest average effect size across subjects. Slavin and Madden (2000) have argued that the two outsiders make this a third-party study.

and third-party evaluations, inconsistencies in evaluation procedures from study to study are likely to account for much of the observed difference in outcomes. A reasonable conclusion is that the body of effectiveness results that is presently available is based upon such different samples, methods, and measurements that direct comparison is inappropriate and can be very misleading. More contentious is that even within a single method the evaluations of sponsors tend to overstate the effectiveness that might be expected in a random replication.

COMPARING COST DATA

Two main issues emerge in considering the measurement of costs as one applies cost-effectiveness analysis to whole-school reforms. First, how should the cost methodology be chosen and applied, and second, how should reallocations be treated? Sadly, neither the appropriate cost methodology has been used, nor have reallocations of resources been treated appropriately in cost analysis of whole-school reforms.

APPLYING THE COST METHODOLOGY

As described above, the concept and procedures for measuring costs are fairly straightforward, certainly in comparison with those for measuring effectiveness (Levin and McEwan, 2001). The problem is that they have rarely been followed in education, and the advent of whole-school reform has not changed this situation (Levin, 2001). Cost analysis begins with the recognition that resources have value in alternative use, whether paid for or donated, and the most valuable alternative use determines the cost value of the resource. Thus, an exhaustive search must be undertaken to specify all of the resources or ingredients that are necessary for the intervention. Again, the concern is to estimate the cost of a typical replication. Often the initial implementations of a model receive considerably more personnel attention and other resources as the sponsors of the intervention go to heroic measures and draw upon developmental resources to make their intervention work. And, often these extra resources are not accounted for because they were thought to be incidental or not absolutely necessary to the design of the intervention. Nevertheless, they must be assumed to contribute to the effectiveness unless it can be shown that a "slimmed-down" version gets equal effects. So, one must be careful not to combine the effectiveness of the initial version with the costs of a slimmed-down one. Whatever ingredients were associated with the particular version whose effectiveness is being assessed provide a proper basis for the cost estimate.

Determining accurately the required ingredients is best done by drawing upon multiple sources of information. Initially, it is best to review reports and other documents which describe the development of the intervention and its requirements. This scrutiny will sensitize the analysis to the types of ingredients that are necessary and will enable the drafting of a preliminary list. Such a list must specify the ingredients in sufficient detail so that later the costs of each can be specified. Thus, knowing that a full-time teacher or half-time administrator is necessary is not adequate without some detail on the qualifications required for these positions.

A second source is that of direct observation of a replication at a representative site or a random selection of sites. This can be used to verify ingredients and their descriptions and qualifications. But, in addition, the direct observations are used to identify other resources that might be used such as personnel, facilities, equipment, materials, services, insurance, or other costs that might not have been identified or were not identifiable from the initial documents. This phase is combined with information from a third source, that of interviews with both key personnel and those involved in daily operations. As observations are made, it is important to ask different personnel about their functions, what other personnel are required (since some may be part-time, occasional, and away from the site), what outside services are used, which particular facilities are necessary to the intervention and so on. When a final list of ingredients is drawn up from the three sources (documents, observations, and interviews), it is also useful to verify its accuracy with someone who has authoritative knowledge about the intervention. It is also important to ascertain if these are the ingredients for replication.

The ingredient information is usually arrayed on a financial spreadsheet according to major categories of personnel, facilities, equipment, materials, and miscellaneous. Each of these can be divided into sub-categories. At this point it is necessary to estimate the cost-values of the ingredients. One possibility is to estimate the local costs at the site or sites being scrutinized. But, the problem with this is that such costs may be idiosyncratic to the sites and not generalizable to other sites. For example, in areas of high real-estate costs, facilities may cost considerably more than in areas of lower cost. The costs of educational personnel will tend to be higher in areas with a higher cost of living and higher salaries generally. Of course, at any specific local site, costs should be estimated for that site. But, when making overall cost-effectiveness comparisons, it is usually better to get a "standard cost" meaning the average cost for a particular geographical area. These standard costs can be applied to all of the interventions that will be compared for cost-effectiveness.

Methods for estimating costs of ingredients are found in Levin and McEwan (2001). However, it must be kept in mind that any resources that have value in alternative uses represent a cost, even if the resource is donated. The issue of who pays for a resource is separate from whether a cost is incurred. The same is true for a subsidized ingredient such as a facility that is paid for by another level of government. The cost is the value of the facility over the life of the intervention. That and other costs can be allocated to different constituencies or entities that bear the cost (Levin and McEwan, 2001, pp. 80–81).

Costs must then be determined for each alternative and compared with the effectiveness of each alternative. For educational interventions, the cost per student is often taken as the criterion and compared with average achievement gain per student. However, this mitigates against projects that have a large fixed cost such as ones that require a substantial investment in capital equipment that can accommodate a very broad range of enrollments. At lower enrollments the cost per student will be high because the fixed costs must be divided among very small numbers. However, with larger enrollments the fixed costs do not rise commensurately so that average cost per student drops. Therefore, the comparison of costs must be sensitive to different levels of scale rather than relying on a single enrollment level to estimate costs.

TWO EARLY COST STUDIES

Two early attempts to measure the costs of whole-school reforms are worthy of mention. King (1994) attempted to estimate the costs of three different approaches: Success for All (Slavin et al., 1990), the School Development Program (Comer, 1988), and Accelerated Schools (Hopfenberg et al., 1993). It is important to bear in mind the different foci of these reforms. The first of these is a highly prescribed approach to preventing failure in early childhood reading. The second applies a child development process and community involvement to the entire school program. The third represents an effort to transform schools and classrooms by replacing remediation with educational enrichment usually provided to gifted and talented students. King uses an appropriate conceptual framework in selecting the ingredients approach in which she intends to specify the resources used in each intervention and place cost-values on them for purposes of comparison. However, she does not gather the ingredients directly from field implementation of the models, but relies instead on general descriptions of the models that do not provide any detail from actual experience. It would have been preferable if ingredients had been derived from the actual replications of the models, given the many replications for all three models at the time of her research, rather than from general descriptions of the models. Using the ingredients framework as a guideline, she found substantial differences in costs among the three models. Accelerated Schools had the lowest cost per student, Success for All had the highest cost, and the School Development Program was intermediate between the two. No attempt was made to measure effectiveness.

In a more recent study Barnett (1996) made an attempt to compare both costs and effectiveness of the same three models. Although his study is more comprehensive than King's, he also had difficulty in providing data on costs and effectiveness. For reasons set out above, he is able to accomplish more on the cost side than on the effectiveness side. Using the ingredients approach and somewhat more extensive documentation than that available to King (because of the later date of his research), Barnett was able to make estimates of costs for each model. He, too, relied extensively on documents that suggested the cost elements rather than collecting data directly from school sites. The preferred method is to base costs on measures derived directly of the actual ingredients used in an intervention (Levin and McEwan, 2001, pp. 53–57). Barnett also finds that Success for All shows the highest cost per student and Accelerated Schools shows the lowest costs with the School Development Project occupying the middle position. Barnett makes an attempt to determine the effectiveness of the interventions, but finds that the available data are insufficient to make direct comparisons. He concludes that all are effective, but cannot draw more precise conclusions.

Both the King and Barnett studies are pioneering in making attempts to cope with the tremendous complexities of doing cost-effectiveness comparisons among whole-school change projects. Nevertheless, their studies fall short of providing comprehensive cost-effectiveness results because of the inadequacy of existing data and other obstacles which will be developed in the next sections.

When Resources are Reallocated

In some cases a whole-school reform will require considerable additional resources beyond those already deployed to meet its goals. Specific personnel, facilities, and equipment or additional personnel time will be required. But, instead of financing these with additional funds, existing resources are reallocated from other uses. For example, a school may be expected to give up other programs and activities to finance the ingredients needed for the reform. To the naïve observer the reform may appear to be costless. This assertion assumes that the resources had no productive use whatsoever before they were reallocated. That is, they were allocated from producing nothing for the school to producing a valuable outcome. Thus, they are simply being redeployed to make the school more efficient and productive.

In order for reallocation to be costless, it must be shown that there is no loss of other valued outcomes; that is that the resources that are being reallocated represent a deadweight loss in their existing use, producing nothing of value. Even if they are being used inefficiently, the only gain from reallocation would be the difference in shifting them from a lower valued output to a higher valued one. But, without a complete mapping and measurement of all valued outputs in assessing effectiveness, it will be impossible to ascertain the cost. When something of value is sacrificed, there is an economic cost. Accordingly, the true cost of the school reform is not only any additional resources that are added, but also the value of all resources that are reallocated from unmeasured outputs to the measured ones. Only if one can show that none of the other outputs are affected by the reallocation can one claim that it is costless. More likely the resources were at least somewhat productive in their initial use. Whether the shift has made them more productive in their new use depends on their relative efficiency in producing the "old" versus the "new" outputs as well as the relative value assigned at the margin to units of each of the outputs. As a practical matter, taking resources from one activity (e.g, music or social studies or special education) may solve the challenge of financing new programs. But, to assert that there is no cost is incorrect.

Consider a shift in teachers and teacher time from one subject to another. The cost is the value of what is given up in productivity in the other subject. If time devoted to reading is increased by one hour at the expense of one hour of mathematics, it is likely that mathematics performance of students will be affected. Thus, the redeployment of resources in this case is not costless, and to make up any loss in mathematics achievement would likely require replacement of the reallocated resources. [21]

This means that a cost-effectiveness analysis of school reforms that focus on only a single or a limited set of outcomes by reallocating resources must undertake one of two tasks. First, it can choose to specify the major outcomes of the school, whether they are addressed by the reform or not, and measure the changes in all outputs resulting from the intervention to ascertain the impact on both the outputs of focus and those from which resources have been reallocated.[22] A more modest approach would be limited to measuring changes only in those outputs that would appear to be affected by the reallocation to assess how they are affected along with those to which the resources are addressed. This more limited undertaking would require identifying the source of the reallocations and including those outputs in the analysis. But, simply assuming that reallocation is costless and that nothing is given up in that process is inappropriate without direct verification.

---

[21] This was suggested in one study by the observation that a comparison school had greater gains in mathematics relative to a school that had increased reading time and redeployed its remedial resources for reading (Jones, Gottfredson, and Gottfredson 1997).

[22] This matches the problem on the output side of valuing total output when it is divided among many non-commensurate dimensions. See Levin and McEwan (2001, Chap. 8).

AVAILABLE DATA ON COSTS

If the data for making comparisons in effectiveness of whole-school reform models is wanting, it is almost non-existent for costs. There are virtually no systematic studies of costs using the ingredients or resource method other than the attempts by King (1994) and Barnett (1996). Typically, the costs that are presented are limited to the costs paid to the sponsor of the model for adoption and technical assistance. For example, the New American School's "price list" for 2001–02 for the school reform models that it represents vary from about $45,000 a year to about $100,000 for schools with about 500 students.[23] This would appear to be about $90 a year to $200 a year per student. The comparison of models by Herman (1999, p. 4) reports values in this range, but much lower if "current staff are reassigned."

But, for almost all of the models the costs for contracting with the developer are the part of the iceberg that is visible. Below the surface there are costs of additional personnel to implement the models such as coaches, teachers, coordinators, and, perhaps, materials and travel. For example, the Accelerated Schools Project requires a quarter-time external coach and internal facilitator for each school, and most of the other models require a full-time coordinator. Success for All requires teachers who will serve as tutors for at least 30 percent of first-graders with 8–11 students per teacher, a minimum of three full-time, additional teachers and a full-time coordinator of family support. These five positions with fringe benefits have an additional cost of $250,000 to $300,000. Odden, Archibald, and Tychsen (2000) suggest that another model, Modern Red Schoolhouse, is even more costly, although the details of the methodology and their application in particular settings (as opposed to theoretical costs) is not identified.

Many of the developers argue that all of these costs can be covered from federal grants such as Title I or through other reallocations. This is a view that is reinforced by a noted expert in financing education, Alan Odden (Odden and Archibald, 2001; Odden, Archibald, and Tychsen 2000). But, virtually no attempt is made to consider what is being sacrificed when resources are shifted from one use to another. The result is that these reallocations are treated as costless. And, available data on the cost of the reforms—as many schools find out later—are much higher in terms of their resource requirements than the cost information provided by the reforms when schools do not wish to sacrifice other programs.[24]

The cost of an intervention must be based upon the value of all of the resources that are required to replicate it. Once the costs are determined, it will be necessary to figure out how to fund it. Reallocation of resources is a method of financing, but it is not cost-free as some advocates have claimed. The appropriation of all Title I funds for a school reform program devoted to one or two subjects entails sacrifices of other beneficial uses of those funds for such purposes as screening and interven-

---

23 Success for All is a reading program. It charges about $75,000 to $85,000 a year in the initial year and twice that if Math Wings (a math program) is added as part of Roots and Wings, or about $150,000 a year. This is about $300 a year per student for contracting with the developer, but not including any costs for additional resources at the school site.

24 In the course of writing this paper I came across an attempt to do a cost-effectiveness analysis of the persisting effects of Success for All (Borman and Hewes, 2001). Although I admire

tion programs for students' health needs, psychological services, after-school programs, and academic activities that may be of equal or greater benefit to students.

SOME CONCLUSIONS AND RECOMMENDATIONS

The bottom line is that available data are not sufficient to make cost-effectiveness comparisons among the different whole-school reform models. The effectiveness results are not based upon a standard sampling strategy among schools. Measures of outcomes favor some models over others and are particularly deficient where reforms are focusing on more than one or two outcomes. Evaluation models differ substantially in both their design and the quality of their implementation. And, cost data are not based upon a rigorous methodology for identifying the actual resources required for replication and obtaining accurate estimates of their costs. In particular, the recommendations to reallocate resources tend to hide the true cost of the reforms because they ignore what is being given up when resources are reallocated.

This raises the question of what needs to be done to obtain comparability for cost-effectiveness purposes.

1. Combine for comparison those groups of reforms with similar goals rather than imposing the same outcome criterion for all models. If reforms aim to increase student discourse, problem-solving, research, and artistic endeavors, limiting outcome measures to standardized tests of reading and mathematics will be inappropriate.

2. Include in the sample a population representative of all attempts to replicate the model or some other consistent criterion rather than permitting evaluators (especially first-party evaluators or reform sponsors) to select their samples on the basis of convenience or ostensible success.

3. Use a similar set of methodologies in making comparisons, not only in evaluation design, but such details as how comparison schools are selected in the event of quasi-experimental designs using comparison schools.

4. Employ a rigorous and systematic methodological approach to cost-estimation based upon the state-of-the-art.

---

this as a first effort, it suffers from the flaw of both "costless" reallocation and of not considering the costs of resources provided by other agencies such as social workers. In addition, it is inconsistent in comparing its figures with the putative, full-cost of class size reduction and pre-school programs since all of these could also "reduce" costs through reallocation of resources or through obtaining resources from external sources. Perhaps the largest bias is introduced by charging the full cost of class size reduction to reading, rather than recognizing that class size reductions also improve mathematics (as in the Tennessee experiment) and other subjects and activities. Previous studies have charged one-third of the cost of class-size reduction to the improvement of reading. When this assumption is made the paper's cost-effectiveness estimate for class size reduction is superior to that of Success For All by about 2.5 to 1. For examples of class-size reduction through redeployment of teachers (in one case in a Success for All school), see Miles and Darling-Hammond (1998).

5. Employ third-party evaluators who are both disinterested in the outcomes and are funded by organizations other than an individual reform sponsor.

Above all, the audiences for such evaluations should be made aware of the flaws in existing comparisons and claims of superiority of one model over another. Although the challenges of obtaining truly comparable cost-effectiveness comparisons are great, it is clear that the knowledge-base can be improved considerably. At the present time, those who use evaluations of whole-school reforms for making adoption decisions should augment the evaluations with other data including those that can be derived from school visits and other measures of school success and resource requirements rather than limiting their perspectives to existing evaluation reports.[25]

REFERENCES

Barnett, W. S. (1996). Economics of school reform: Three promising models. In H. F. Ladd (Ed.), *Holding schools accountable* (pp. 299–326). Washington, DC: The Brookings Institution.

Begg, C. B. (1994). Publication bias. In H. Cooper and L. V. Hedges (Eds.), *Handbook of research synthesis* (pp. 399–410). New York: Russell Sage Foundation.

Berends, M., Kirby, S. N., Naftel, S., and McKelvey, C. (2001). *Implementation and performance in New American Schools.* Santa Monica, CA: RAND.

Bloom, H., Ham, S., Kagehiro, S., Melton, L., O'Brien, J., Rock, J., and Doolittle, F. (2001). *Evaluating the Accelerated Schools Program: A look at its early implementation and impact on student achievement in eight schools.* New York: Manpower Development Research Corporation.

Borman, G. D., and Hewes, G. M. (2001). *The long-term effects and cost-effectiveness of Success for All.* Available: www.successforall.net/resource/researchpub.htm.

Boruch, R. (1997). *Randomized experiments for planning and evaluation.* Thousand Oaks, CA: Sage Publications.

Bowles, S. and Gintis, H. (2000). Does schooling raise earnings by making people smarter? In K. Arrow, S. Bowles, and S. Durlauf (Eds.), *Meritocracy and economic inequality* (pp. 118–36). Princeton: Princeton University Press.

Calaway, F. (2001). *Evaluation of the comprehensive school reform models in the Memphis City Schools.* Memphis: Memphis City Schools, Office of Research and Evaluation.

Comer, J. (1988). Educating poor minority children. *Scientific American, 259*(5), 42–48.

Cook, T. D., and Campbell, D. T. (1979a). *Quasi-experimentation: Design and analysis for field studies.* Chicago: Rand McNally.

Cook, T. D., and Campbell, D. T. (1979b) *Quasi-experimentation: Design and analysis issues for field settings.* Boston: Houghton-Mifflin.

---

25 For example, some of the reform models have persistent, high turnover among teachers. This imposes a cost on schools and on districts for teacher selection, training, and personnel accounting that is not captured by typical cost studies. These costs are especially high at a time of teacher shortages.

Cook, T. D., Farah-Naaz, H., Phillips, M., Settersten, R. A., Shagle, S. C., and Degir-mencioglu, S. M. (1999). Comer's School Development Program in Prince George's County, Maryland: A theory-based evaluation. *American Educational Research Journal, 36*(3), 543–597.

Cook, T. D., Hunt, H. D., and Murphy, R. F. (2000). Comer's School Development Program in Chicago: A theory-based evaluation. *American Educational Research Journal, 37*(2), 535–597.

Cooper, H., Charlton, K., Valentine, J., and Muhlenbruck, L. (2000). *Making the most of summer school* (Monographs Series of the Society for Research in Child Development). Malden, MA: Blackwell.

Cuban, L. (1993). *How teachers taught* (2nd ed.). New York: Teachers College Press.

Datnow, A. (2000). Power and politics in the adoption of school reform models. *Educational Evaluation and Policy Analysis, 22*(4), 357–369.

Doolittle, F. (2001). *Using interrupted time-series analysis to measure the impacts of Accelerated Schools on the performance of elementary school students.* Paper presented at the Annual Meeting of the American Educational Research Association, Seattle.

Edmonds, R. (1979). Effective schools for the urban poor. *Educational Leadership, 37,* 15–24.

Fetterman, D. M. (1982). Ibsen's Baths: Reactivity and insensitivity. *Educational Evaluation and Policy Analysis, 4*(3), 261–279.

Finnan, C., and Levin, H. (2000). Changing school cultures. In H. Altrichter and J. Elliott (Eds.), *Images of educational change* (pp. 87–99). Philadelphia: Open University Press.

Fullan, M. (1991). *The new meaning of educational change.* New York: Teachers College Press.

Glass, G. V., McGaw, B., and Smith, M. L. (1981). *Meta-analysis in social research.* Beverly Hills, CA: Sage.

Hargreaves, A., Lieberman, A., Fullan, M., and Hopkins, D. (Eds.). (1998). *International handbook of educational change.* Boston: Kluwer Academic Publishers.

Herman, R. (1999). *An educator's guide to schoolwide reform.* Arlington, VA: Educational Research Service.

Hopfenberg, W., Levin, H., Chase, C., Christensen, S. G., Moore, M., Soler, P., Brunner, I., Keller, B., and Rodriguez, G. (1993). *The Accelerated Schools resource guide.* San Francisco: Jossey-Bass.

Hunter, J. E., and Schmidt, F. L. (1994). Correcting for sources of artificial variation across studies. In H. Cooper and L. V. Hedges (Eds.), *Handbook of research synthesis.* New York: Russell Sage Foundation.

Inkeles, A. (1966). The socialization of competence. *Harvard Educational Review, 36*(3), 265–283.

Jones, E., Gottfredson, G., and Gottfredson, D. (1997). Success for some: An evaluation of the Success for All program. *Evaluation Review, 21*(6), 599–607.

Kane, T. J., and Staiger, D. O. (2001). *Improving school accountability measures* (Working Paper No. 8156). Cambridge, MA: National Bureau of Economic Research.

Kerbow, D. (1996). *Patterns of urban student mobility and local school reform* (Technical Report No. 5). Baltimore, MD: Center for Research on Education of Students Placed At Risk, Johns Hopkins University.

King, J. (1994) Meeting the needs of at-risk students: A cost analysis of three models. *Educational Evaluation and Policy Analysis, 16*(1), 1–19.

Levin, H. (2001). Waiting for Godot: Cost-effectiveness analysis in education. In R. J. Light (Ed.), *Evaluation findings that surprise* (Vol. 90, pp. 55–68, New Directions for Evaluation). San Francisco: Jossey-Bass.

Levin, H. (1997). Raising school productivity: An X-efficiency approach. *Economics of Education Review, 16*(3), 303–310.

Levin, H. (1991). Cost-effectiveness at quarter century. In M. W. McLaughlin and D. C. Phillips (Eds.), *Evaluation and education at quarter century* (pp. 189–209, 90th Yearbook of the National Society for the Study of Education). Chicago: University of Chicago Press.

Levin, H. M. and McEwan, P. J. (2001). *Cost-effectiveness analysis: Methods and applications* (2nd ed.). Thousand Oaks, CA: Sage.

Levin, H., Glass, G., and Meister, G. (1987). Cost-effectiveness of computer-assisted instruction. *Evaluation Review, 11*(1), 50–72.

Lipsey, M. W. (1999). Can rehabilitative programs reduce the recidivism of juvenile offenders? *The Virginia Journal of Social Policy and the Law, 6*(3), 611–641.

MacIver, M., Stringfield, S., and McHugh, B. (2000). *Core knowledge curriculum: Five-year analysis of implementation and effects in five Maryland schools* (Report No. 50). Baltimore: Center for Research on the Education of Students Placed at Risk, Johns Hopkins University.

McCain, L. J. and McCleary, R. (1979). The statistical analysis of the simple interrupted time-series quasi-experiment. In T. D. Cook and D. T. Campbell (Eds.), *Quasi-experimentation: Design and analysis issues for field settings* (pp. 233–294). Boston: Houghton Mifflin.

McGaw, B. (1994). Meta-analysis. In T. Husen and T. N. Postlethwaite (Eds.), *The International Encyclopedia of Education* (Vol. 7, 2nd ed., pp. 3775–3784). New York: Pergamon.

Miles, K. H. and Darling-Hammond, L. (1998). Rethinking the allocation of teaching resources: Some lessons from high performing schools. *Educational Evaluation and Policy Analysis, 20*(1), pp. 9–30.

Millsap, M. A., Chase, A., Obeidallah, D., Perez-Smith, A., Brigham, N., and Johnston, K. (2000). *Evaluation of Detroit's Comer Schools and families initiative* (Final Report). Cambridge, MA: Abt Associates Inc.

Odden, A., and Archibald, S. (2001). *Reallocating resources.* Thousand Oaks, CA: Corwin Press.

Odden, A., Archibald, S., and Tychsen, A. (2000). Can Wisconsin schools afford comprehensive school reform? *Journal of Education Finance, 25*(3), 323–342.

Olejnik, S., and Algina, J. (2000). Measures of effect size for comparative studies: Applications, interpretations, and limitations. *Contemporary Educational Psychology, 25*, 241–286.

Pogrow, S. (2000). Success for All does not produce success for students. *Phi Delta Kappan, 82*(1), 67–81.

Ross, S., and Smith, L. (1994). Effects of the Success for All model on kindergarten through second-grade reading achievement, teachers' adjustment, and classroom-school climate at an inner-city school. *Elementary School Journal, 95*, 121–138.

Ross, S. M., Wang, L. W., Sanders, W. L., Wright, S. P., and Stringfield, S. (1999). *Two- and three- year achievement results on the Tennessee value-added assessment system for restructuring schools in Memphis.* Memphis: University of Memphis, Center for Research in Educational Policy.

Rumberger, R. W. (2001). *Mobility and student outcomes.* Arlington, VA: Education Research Service.

Sanders, W., and Horn, S. (1995). The Tennessee value-added assessment system (TVAAS): Mixed model methodology in educational assessment. In A. Shinkfield and D. Stufflebeam (Eds.), *Teacher evaluation: Guide to effective practice* (pp. 337–350). Boston: Kluwer Academic Publishers.

Sarason, S. (1982). *The culture of the school and the problem of change* (2nd ed.). Boston: Allyn and Bacon.

Scriven, M. (1976). Evaluation bias and its control. In G. V. Glass (Ed.), *Evaluation studies review annual* (Vol. 1, pp. 119–139). Beverly Hills, CA: Sage Publications.

Slavin, R. E., and Madden, N. A. (2000). Research on achievement outcomes of Success for All: A summary and response to critics. *Phi Delta Kappan, 82*(1), 38–40.

Slavin, R. E., and Madden, N. A. (1999). *Success for All/Roots and Wings: Summary of research on achievement outcomes* (Report No. 41). Baltimore: Center for Research on the Education of Students Placed at Risk, Johns Hopkins University.

Slavin, R. E., Madden, N., Karweit, N., Livermon, B., and Dolan, L. (1990). Success for All: First-year outcomes of a comprehensive plan for reforming urban education. *American Educational Research Journal, 27,* 255–278.

Slavin, R. E., and Fashola, L. S. (1998). *Show me the evidence!* Thousand Oaks, CA: Corwin Press.

Stringfield, S., Datnow, A., Borman, G., and Rachuba, L. (1998). *National evaluation of core knowledge sequence implementation: Final report.* Baltimore: Center for Social Organization of Schools, Johns Hopkins University.

Stringfield, S., Millsap, M. A., and Herman, R. (1998). Using "promising programs" to improve educational processes and student outcomes. In A. Hargreaves, A. Lieberman, M. Fullan, and D. Hopkins (Eds.), *International handbook of educational change* (Part two, pp. 1314–1338). Boston: Kluwer Academic Publishers.

Suchman, E. (1971). Evaluation of educational programs. In F. Caro (Ed.), *Readings in evaluation research* (pp. 43–48). New York: Russell Sage Foundation.

Summers, A., and Wolfe, B. (1977). Do schools make a difference? *American Economic Review, 67*(4), 639–651.

Supovitz, J. A., Poglinco, S. M., and Snyder, B. A. (2001) *Moving mountains: Successes and challenges of the America's Choice comprehensive school reform design.* Philadelphia: Center for Policy Research in Education (CPRE), University of Pennsylvania.

Wilson, J. (1973). On Pettigrew and Armor: An afterword. *The Public Interest, 30,* 132–134.

6

COST-EFFECTIVENESS AND COST-BENEFIT ANALYSIS: THE EFFECT OF TARGETING INTERVENTIONS

*David Grissmer**

INTRODUCTION

Levin and McEwan (2001) provide a comprehensive approach to cost-effectiveness or cost-benefit analysis in educational research. This paper will focus on a complicating, but important, issue in such analysis. Interventions may have differential effects on different kinds of students, possibly in a systematic way related to the amount of prior family and school investment. Previous studies measuring the effectiveness of interventions have not systematically tested for differential effects. However, the importance of differential effects and measurements of differential effects has been noted in many studies dating as early as the 1970s (Levin, 1970; Quinn, Van Mondfrans, and Worthen, 1984; Snow, 1986). While these early studies identify SES or race/ethnicity as a moderating variable, they do not suggest a broad, systematic relationship that identifies the characteristics of students that might be expected to have differential effects.

Grissmer, Flanagan, and Williamson (1998) and Grissmer, Flanagan, Kawata, and Williamson (2000) suggested that the empirical evidence supports the hypothesis that additional educational resources have much stronger effects on minority and low-income students than on more advantaged, non-minority students. We suggest here that this systematic relationship may derive simply from the greater prior private and public human capital investment made in more advantaged, non-minority children, so that current investment in interventions represents a greater portion of total human capital investment for minority and low-income children than for more advantaged, non-minority children. Another way of stating this is that human capital investments have diminishing returns.

* This research has been supported by the Center for Research on Educational Diversity and Excellence (CREDE), a research center funded by the Office of Research and improvement in the Department of Education and a grant from the Office of program Evaluation Services in the Department of Education.

If this hypothesis is true, there are some implications for doing cost-effectiveness or cost-benefit analysis. Levin and McEwan (2001) suggest three approaches to dealing with differential effects. The first approach ignores the differential effects and proceeds with a single cost-effectiveness measure. The second option is to estimate cost-effectiveness measures for each group having a differential effect. The third approach is to develop weights or utilities to combine the separate measures for each group—essentially assigning a utility or social priority to each group.

The first option, the most commonly utilized, has very limited generalizability, and can also be quite misleading. The estimate from the first option would only be useful where the set of students that form the generalizable population matches the intervention group and no flexibility exists to apply interventions to subsets of the generalizable population. Routinely publishing such single estimates without tests for differential effects can lead to false elimination of what may be highly cost-effective options for population subsets. Since this has been the common practice, much of the literature may be misleading if differential effects are commonly present. In citing previous literature, it would be important to determine if differential effects were tested before concluding that certain interventions were more or less cost-effective than others.

The second alternative essentially expands the alternatives to be evaluated from a column of alternatives to a matrix with each alternative defined with respect to specific types of students. Such an approach places greater demand on the design and analysis of interventions often requiring larger samples and more detailed evaluation. However, the key advantage of such an approach is that one can generalize the results of an intervention with more confidence to a wide range of populations, and design targeted interventions that may be even more cost-effective than the original intervention.

The third approach using weighted estimates based on utilities assigned to each subgroup seems impractical since it implicitly involves political choices in assigning utilities, and these political choices may not generalize to interventions under different political regimes. Essentially a new set of utilities would be needed for each regime.

In this paper we will utilize two recent cost-effectiveness analyses and one cost-benefit analysis that measured differential effects to illustrate analyses using the second alternative. We first utilize recent experimental and quasi-experimental research on class size that obtains differential effects on minority and disadvantaged students (Finn and Achilles, 1999; Krueger, 1999, Molnar et al., 1999). The second example is drawn from research using the National Assessment of Educational Progress (NAEP) that suggests larger effects for pupil/teacher reductions and public pre-kindergarten programs in states with higher proportions of disadvantaged students (Grissmer et al., 2000). The third example is drawn from research on nurse-visiting programs for teen mothers where benefits exceeded costs for a lower functioning population of mothers, but not for a higher functioning population (Karoly et al., 1998).

After describing the results of these analyses, we discuss in the final sections the possible origins of such differential effects and strategies for spending public resources on children more cost-effectively.

COST-EFFECTIVENESS OF CLASS SIZE
REDUCTIONS VERSUS TEACHER AIDES

The multi-district Tennessee STAR experiment randomly assigned a single cohort of kindergarten students in 79 participating schools to three treatment groups: large classes (approximately 22–24 students) with or without an aide and small classes (approximately 15–16 students). Those students entering at kindergarten were scheduled to maintain their treatment through first, second, and third grade.

The beginning sample of participating students was over 6,000 students. The students in the experiment had a greater minority and free lunch proportion than in Tennessee or the U.S.[1] Finn and Achilles (1999) restate the measured achievement differences for the Tennessee experiment between those in large and small classes at each K–3 grade in each subject tested. The results show these class size reductions had statistically significant effects in each K–3 grade and all subjects tested showing higher achievement by 0.15–0.25 standard deviations. However, the Finn and Achilles sample contained some students who had not been in small classes all four years. Krueger (1999) and Nye, Hedges, and Konstantopoulos (1999) estimate the effects for students in small classes all four years and obtain higher effects—between 0.25 and 0.4 standard deviation (see Grissmer, 1999 for a discussion and comparison of the various results). Both Krueger and Finn and Achilles show positive, but statistically insignificant effects, from teacher aides.

Finn and Achilles report minority effects that are approximately double those for white students in Grades K–3. Krueger (1999) also reports larger effects for minority students. Estimated short-term effects for minority students from four years in small classes would be 0.3 standard deviations or greater, with effects for remaining students closer to 0.2 standard deviations or greater. In a Wisconsin quasi-experiment, Molnar et al. (1999) show that minority students have significantly larger effects than non-minority students. Current analysis also indicates that free-lunch students have larger short-term effects than their counterparts. Estimates from Krueger (1999) for free-lunch and non-free-lunch students are 0.27 and 0.21, respectively.

The Tennessee experiment provided compelling results on the effects of class size reductions and teacher aides. While there were the usual implementation issues and sample attrition, extensive analysis of the data has mostly ruled out these flaws as a source of bias (Grissmer, 1999). Given such results, it is surprising that a cost-effectiveness analysis of class size reductions vs. teacher aides has not been done using this data until recently. Grissmer et al. (2000) presented an analysis as part of a more comprehensive cost-effectiveness analysis of educational spending alternatives.

The estimate of cost-effectiveness for reductions in class size used a conservative 0.30 standard deviation for the effects of class size reductions from 24 to 16. The estimates for the effects of teacher aides in a large classroom are generally positive, but not statistically significant and highly variable (Krueger, 1999). Depending on equations utilized and the grade analyzed, the effect varies from zero to 33 percent of the class size effect. The estimates use a liberal estimate of 25 percent of the class size effect or 0.075 standard deviation.

The experiment was implemented in 79 separate schools with some schools having multiple classrooms with each intervention. Levin and McEwan (2001) recommend an ingredients approach to costing interventions. This approach involves

---

1   The experimental sample contained approximately 33 percent minority students and over 50 percent to 60 percent of all students were eligible for free or reduced-price lunch, compared to 23 percent minority students and about 43 percent free or reduced-price lunch for Tennessee students in 1986. The sample was also quite different than U.S. students where approximately 30 percent were minority students and 37 percent were eligible for free and reduced-price lunch in 1990.

identifying the inputs required to implement the intervention and developing the cost of each input. This approach works well for costing specific, local interventions where all inputs can be identified, and longer term adjustments in expenditures are not a significant factor in costs. It works less well when the intervention is implemented widely in many or all schools or school districts in a state, or where longer term adjustments can add significantly to short-term costs.[2] The actual costs to individual schools were not captured in the Tennessee experiment. Here we develop a cost estimate using nation-wide expenditure data and a series of assumptions that is less refined than an ingredients approach.[3] We assume that smaller classes from 24 to 16 students per class increased the number of teachers by 50 percent in K–3. We assume that K–3 teachers are 4/13 (13 being the total number of grades in K–12) of total K–12 classroom teachers, and that classroom instructional related costs (teacher salary, tuition assistance, instructional supplies and purchased instructional services) consume about 65 percent of the total budget.[4] Then the estimated percentage increase in expenditures from the Tennessee class size reduction is $(0.50)(4/13)(0.65)=0.10$ or ten percent of the budget for regular students. The per-pupil expenditure in 1993–94 in Tennessee for regular students was approximately $4400, so the added per-pupil expenditure is estimated at $(0.10)(\$4400)= \$440$ per-pupil. The cost per 0.10 standard deviation gain (the actual gain is estimated at 0.30) is then around $150 per-pupil in additional expenditures.

---

2 The problem with widespread implementation is that costs are likely to vary across sites and cost data from individual sites is rarely available. The second problem is that the short-term and long-term costs of implementing an intervention often differ, and the ingredients approach essentially provides a short-term cost estimate. Alternative estimates use state-wide averages for the costs of inputs or using a regression-based approach that estimates the marginal costs of smaller class size based on actual expenditures across schools/districts with differing class size. Such an approach can theoretically capture long term-costs as well as the average costs across schools or districts based on actual implementation. In general, estimates using each method for which data is available should be done and analyzed to determine if significant differences exist and why.

3 In this case, an ingredients approach might be difficult as well since there was no time for new construction, and classroom space was carved from existing or unused space. In a short-term experiment, this might be possible, but over a longer term some new construction may take place. Also in many cases additional teachers were not hired, but were transferred from administrative positions. Thus an ingredients approach would have to make assumptions about what school districts would do in the long run in response to permanent class size reductions. See Levin, Glass and Meister (1987) for costing of class size reductions based on an ingredients approach.

4 Table 163 in the Digest of Educational Statistics provides 1993–94 expenditures for classroom instruction ($141.6 billion) and total expenditures ($265.3 billion). We have included capital outlays ($23.7 billion) and interest on debt ($5.3 billion) to allow for classroom construction costs, but excluded "other current expenditures" related to adult education ($4.7 billion). This provides an estimate of $(141.4+23.7+5.3)/(265.3–4.7 \text{ billion})=0.65$. Arguably one should include operation and maintenance ($23.9) that would bring the total to 0.75. However, some slack classroom capacity exists and operation and maintenance costs should not rise proportionately even if all new construction is required.

Adding teacher aides would increase "teachers" by 100 percent in K–3. We assume that the costs of a full-time aide to be 40 percent of a classroom teacher.[5] No new classrooms are needed for aides, so we assume that instructional expenditures are only .60 percent of total expenditures. Then the estimated increase in per-pupil expenditures is $(1.0)(0.40)(4/13)(0.60)=.074$ or 7.4 percent of expenditures. The cost in per-pupil expenditures is ($4400)*(0.074) or $325 per-pupil with an estimated gain from a full-time aide of 0.075 standard deviation. So the cost per 0.10 standard deviation of gain is $(325)(0.10)/0.075 = \$430$ per-pupil, compared to $150 per-pupil for class size reductions. It is doubtful any set of changed assumptions could make aides nearly as cost-effective as class size reductions for students with these characteristics.

If we assume that the cost of class size reductions is similar in schools with high and low minority populations, then the differential achievement effects for minority students will make cost-effectiveness estimates for class size reductions different for schools with high minority populations. No separate estimates of the effects of teacher aides by race are available. Table 6.1 summarizes the cost-effectiveness estimates for schools with different minority populations. The Tennessee experimental sample was about 33 percent minority. So estimates are available for both interventions for this case. The remaining estimates for class size reduction assume that minority effects are 50 percent larger than non-minority effects (Krueger, 1999).

Table 6.1 Estimated Costs in Expenditures Per-pupil to Raise Achievement Scores by 0.10 Standard Deviation

	Minority percentage in school			
	0	33	67	100
Teacher aides	NA	$430	NA	NA
Class size reductions	$169	$150	$131	$112

COST-EFFECTIVENESS OF ALTERNATIVE STATE EDUCATIONAL EXPENDITURES

States have a large variance in the level of per-pupil expenditure and in the way in which those expenditures are utilized. They also have a large variance in test scores as measured by the seven-state National Assessment of Educational Progress Tests given to fourth and eighth graders in math and reading across states from 1990–1996 (Shaughnessy, Nelson, and Norris, 1998; Miller, Nelson, and Naifeh, 1995; Reese, Miller, Mazzeo, and Dossey, 1997; Campbell, Donahue, Reese, and Phillips, 1996). These scores are the only tests with representative sampling of students within each

---

5   In the Tennessee experiment all aides were full-time. Almost 90 percent of aides had a high-school diploma, but only about 17 percent had a post-secondary degree (Finn, Gerber, Farber, and Achilles, 1999). The costs of aides was not collected in the experiment. The median wage of teacher aides was $16,400 in 1999, and elementary teachers $39,600 (see the 1999 National Employment and Wage Estimates, Bureau of Labor Statistics). Current data from North Carolina shows full-time aides have average salaries in 2000 of about $17,000 and teachers $41,000. In North Carolina, aides and teachers have equivalent benefits.

state, and thus the only comparable scores across states. Approximately 2500 students per state take each test.

Grissmer et al. (2000) used this data to test hypotheses concerning the marginal costs and effects of various utilization of resources. Surprisingly, most of the variance in educational spending across the states can be traced to a few resource-intensive variables. Table 6.2 shows the results of a regression analysis using about 12 years of state-expenditure data. Differences in per-pupil expenditure across states were regressed on average teacher salary, pupil/teacher ratio, public pre-kindergarten participation, the reported adequacy of teaching resources by teachers, per-pupil transportation expenses, and the incidence of special education and Limited English Proficiency students.

Table 6.2 Regression of State Per-pupil Expenditures (in Thousands of 1993–4 School Year Dollars) on Educational Policy/Characteristics Over a 12-Year Period

Variables	Coefficient	T-statistic
Teacher salary ('000)	0.1480	12.7
Pupil/teacher ratio	−0.1960	−7.1
Teacher resources—some	0.0056	1.8
Teacher resources—most	0.0051	1.5
Pre-kindergarten	0.0120	2.7
Per-pupil transportation costs	0.0040	4.2
Limited English Proficiency (%)	0.0040	0.3
Individualized learning (%)	0.0160	1.2

Source: Grissmer et al. (2000, Table 8.1)

The regression accounts for 95 percent of the variance across states in per-pupil expenditures indicating that most expenditures in education can be captured by these few variables. States either pay teachers higher salaries, hire more teachers to lower class size, provide teachers more resources, provide an extra grade of schooling at pre-kindergarten, or spend more because of higher transportation and special education costs.

The coefficients can be interpreted as the marginal cost per-pupil of changing the policy/educational characteristics based on the experience across states of providing these different policies/characteristics. These marginal estimates theoretically include all the long-term costs associated with each action. For instance, raising teacher salaries by $1000 per-teacher probably implies salary increases for non-teaching professional staff and perhaps even support staff. The pupil-teacher ratio coefficient should reflect the full costs of providing classroom capacity and increased salary costs due to higher demand for teachers.[6]

The coefficients all show the expected sign and nearly all the resource variables are significant at the 10 percent level or better. The results would indicate that raising teacher salaries by $1000 per-teacher would raise per-pupil expenditures by $148

---

6 The per-pupil expenditures include capital outlays and interest on debt theoretically allowing inclusion of the long-term costs of additional classrooms due to lower pupil/teacher ratio.

per-pupil. Lowering pupil/teacher ratio by one student would cost an additional $196 per-pupil. Increasing by one percentage point-teachers reported adequacy of resources from each category into the highest category would cost an additional $5.00–$6.00 per-pupil. Increasing by one percentage point the percentage of children in public pre-kindergarten would cost an additional $12 per-pupil.

An alternate set of equations focused on explaining achievement across states on the seven NAEP tests using these major resource variables. These equations also included an extensive set of family characteristics in order to separate the school and family effects. The analysis showed statistically significant positive effects for higher per-pupil spending. However, the results suggest that it is as important how the money is spent as the level of spending. When the major variables that account for the variance in spending across states are included with family variables, the results show positive, significant effects on achievement from lower pupil/teacher ratios in lower grades, higher levels of participation in public pre-kindergarten, teachers reporting more adequate levels of resources and smaller proportion of inexperienced teachers. Higher average-teacher-salary-levels did not show statistically significant effects.

Table 6.3 summarizes the effects from the analysis of the marginal effects of different educational expenditures on achievement as well as the marginal costs of changing these expenditures. Table 6.4 converts these results into comparable cost-effectiveness ratios. Using the data in Table 6.3, we calculate the additional cost per-pupil (state wide) for each expenditure to achieve average score gains of 0.10 standard deviation. These results would indicate that additional resources put into teacher resources and public pre-kindergarten would be more cost-effective than lowering class size in all grades and raising teacher salaries.

However, including interaction terms shows that the effects on achievement of pupil/teacher ratios are stronger if done at lower grades and that both lower pupil/teacher ratios and public pre-kindergarten participation are stronger for states

Table 6.3 Marginal Cost and Achievement Gains for Each Resource

Cost Regression	Cost per-pupil ($)	Achievement Regression	Effect size range
Cost per-pupil to raise per-pupil expenditures by $1000 per-pupil	1000.00	Score gain from general increase of $100 per-pupil	0.042–0.098
Cost per-pupil to lower pupil/teacher ratio by one student (K–12)	196.00	Score gain from lowering pupil/teacher ratio by one student	0.019–0.026
Cost per-pupil to raise average teacher salary by $1000	148.00	Score gain from raising teacher salary by $1000	0.000–0.005
Cost per-pupil to shift teacher's responses by one percentage point from lowest to highest adequacy leve of resources	5.10	Score gain from shifting teacher responses one percentage point from lowest to highest category	0.002–0.003
Cost per-pupil to shift teacher's responses by one percentage point from middle to highest adequacy level of resources	5.60	Score gain from shifting teacher responses one percentage point from middle to highest category	0.002–0.003
Cost per-pupil to increase public pre-k participation by one percentage point	12.00	Score gain from increasing public Pre-K by one percentage point	0.003–0.005

Source: Grissmer et al. (2000, Table 8.2)

Table 6.4 Estimates of Additional Per-pupil Expenditures in Each Resource Category to Raise Average Scores by 0.10 Standard Deviation

Resource	Cost per-pupil per 0.10 gain
Per-pupil expenditure	$1020–2380
Pupil-teacher ratio (K–12)	$750–1030
Teacher salary	>$2980
Teacher resources—low to adequate	$170–260
Teacher resources—medium to adequate	$190–280
Public pre-kindergarten	$240–400

Source: Grissmer et al. (2000, Table 8.3)

with a higher proportion of disadvantaged students. It was also found that lowering pupil/teacher ratios had a marginally decreasing effect so that states that start from high pupil/teacher levels would see more achievement effect than states that currently have low pupil/teacher levels. The effects of increasing public pre-kindergarten participation by 10 percentage points were found to be 0.11 standard deviation in states with the highest proportion of disadvantaged students, 0.05 standard deviation in states with average number of disadvantaged students and no effect in states with the smallest proportion of disadvantaged students.

Table 6.5 summarizes the cost-effectiveness measures that include the effect of targeting resources to different grades, toward states with different proportions of disadvantaged students and the current levels of pupil/teacher ratio is taken into account. The estimates show that the expenditures with more favorable cost-effectiveness ratios include targeted pupil-teacher reductions to states with high proportions of disadvantaged students and current high levels of pupil/teacher ratios, providing public pre-kindergarten in states with high proportions of disadvantaged students and providing teacher- more resources in all states.

Table 6.5 Estimates of Additional Per-pupil Ependitures to Achieve 0.10 Gain in Achievement for States with Different SES and Initial Pupil-Teacher Ratio for Regular Students

Type of expenditure	Proportion of disadvantaged students		
	High	Medium	Low
Lower pupil-teacher ratio in grades 1–4 from 26 to 23	$110	$180	$260
Lower pupil-teacher ratio in grades 1–4 from 23 to 20	$140	$300	$600
Lower pupil-teacher ratio in grades 1–4 from 20 to 17	$200	>$1000	>$1000
Lower pupil-teacher ratio in grades 1–4 from 17 to 14	$450	>$1000	>$1000
Raise public pre-kindergarten participation	$120	$320	>$1000
Provide teachers in the most inadequate category with more resources	$90	$90	$90
Provide teachers in the typical resource category with more resources	$110	$110	$110

Source: Grissmer et al. (2000, Table 8.5)

Taking into account targeting of expenditures by grade, by state characteristics, and by current levels of pupil/teacher ratio leads to a different identification of which programs are cost-effective. Estimates for across-the-board pupil/teacher reductions in all grades and states were $750 to $1030 to achieve a 0.10 gain, but targeted reductions to states with high pupil/teacher ratios and high proportions of disadvantaged students were $110. Similarly the estimates for universal public pre-kindergarten were $240 to $400, but targeted programs to states with high proportions of disadvantaged students were $120.

This data suggests that targeting of expenditures not only by program or policy but by types of students may be critical to obtain efficiency in educational expenditures. It also suggests that cost-effectiveness analysis must focus on defining alternatives that include the possibility of differential effects by type of student.

COST-BENEFIT ANALYSIS OF NURSE VISITING PROGRAMS

Karoly et al. (1998) present a cost-benefit analysis of a home-visiting program for teen mothers based on a randomized design. The intervention consisted of monthly visits during pregnancy and for two years after birth by a trained nurse. The nurses provided parent education, social support for the mother, and referrals to social services. Two target populations of mothers received the intervention and corresponding control groups did not receive the intervention. The two target populations were chosen on the basis of criteria that attempted to determine a group of higher-risk mothers and lower-risk mothers. The higher risk group consisted of single mothers with lower SES status, and the lower-risk group of two parent families with higher SES characteristics.

The mothers and children were followed to age 15. The measures used to track outcomes included IQ measures, special education placement, grade retention, health utilization and criminal activity of the children, and the mother's education, employment and welfare utilization, subsequent births and healthcare utilization and costs. The expenditures included in the benefits were only those accruing to the government and included tax revenues generated by employment, welfare expenditures, health and education expenditures and criminal justice system costs. The estimated benefits were conservative since it did not include expected benefits generated after the children were age 15.

The results showed that the net present value of cost (using a 4 percent real discount rate) was approximately $6000 per child, but the benefits were quite different for higher- and lower-risk families. For higher-risk mothers, the net present value of benefits were estimated at nearly $25,000 with about 80 percent of the benefit arising from the mother's increased employment and reduction in welfare. The benefits attributable to the child were mainly from reduced criminal justice expenditures. In this case the benefits exceeded the program costs by a significant margin.

The results for the lower-risk mothers were quite different. While the costs were still approximately $6000, the estimated benefits were less than $4000. The lower-risk mothers showed much less savings from welfare utilization and smaller increased tax contributions. The difference is mainly attributable to the fact that lower risk mothers in both treatment and control groups utilized welfare much less frequently than did higher-risk mothers, and there were smaller differences in employment among the lower-risk mothers. In this case, benefits did not exceed costs.

This analysis underscores the need to design programs that are appropriate to specific populations. In the lower-risk group, welfare utilization was at much lower levels, and employment at much higher levels, so the intervention was not effective in either reducing welfare utilization from these already lower levels, or boosting employment from their higher levels.

The Critical Role of Targeting

One hypothesis about why interventions would differentially impact minority or disadvantaged children is the inequality in resources available to such children. Governments at all levels spent over 500 billion dollars in 1995 directed toward children of ages 0–18 (Office of Science and Technology, 1997).[7] Approximately two-thirds of this is for direct K–12 educational expenditures, while the remaining amount is directed primarily toward family assistance of various types and criminal justice system expenditures for juveniles. Besides government expenditures, families spend approximately 600 billion annually on children between ages 0–18.[8] Even modest increases in efficiency in this spending would have a significant payoff.

This public and private investment is disproportionately targeted toward higher SES children. Private spending per-child depends on the level of family income with children in higher-income families receiving significantly more expenditures. Public expenditures per-pupil on K–12 education also show higher amounts for children from higher SES families.[9] Only public spending on family assistance is primarily directed toward lower SES families. The net result of both private and public spending on children is still a significant gap in net spending on lower SES children. Thus, additional spending at the margin might provide a greater percentage increase in resources to lower SES children, and might be expected to have a larger impact.

If we assume that targeting is an important component of achieving efficiency in expenditures toward children, the question arises as to the best method to identify children who would show the largest impact from targeted funds. This question is intimately connected to who controls and allocates funds and whether funds are fungible across types of programs.

Rothstein (2000) raises an important issue in this regard, namely whether expenditures directed toward families may be more efficient at the margin than funds directed toward schools. Until recently, the federal government maintained the primary policymaking and funding role with respect to family programs, while the state and local government maintained a similar role for educational expenditures. Now for the first time all of these programs are primarily the responsibility of the states. The states now have the pivotal role in policymaking with respect to both family and school expenditures for at-risk children. States would be expected to take different approaches to begin to integrate the policymaking across school and family programs.

For instance, some states are moving responsibility and providing more fungible funding across programs to lower levels. In at least one case—North Carolina—some of these expenditures are being combined and provided not to direct governmental agencies, but to local county-level quasi non-profit/governmental entities. These

---

7   This estimate does not include the forgone taxes from child deductions, day care and other deductible items related to children, nor does it include housing subsidies.

8   This amount is estimated assuming the cost of raising a child to age 18 to be approximately $150,000 and assuming approximately 70 million children between 0–18. (United States Department of Agriculture, 1997).

9   Per-pupil expenditures (cost of living adjusted) across states varied from approximately $4000 to $9000 per-pupil in 1993–1994 with poorer states spending less. In addition to between-state disparities, there are disparities within state school district expenditures

entities have broad authority with fungible funds to allocate across a broad range of services that reflect the needs of the specific locale. Local entities may have significant competitive advantages in efficiently allocating funds to help at-risk children. The children/families and schools in different locales may have distinctly different needs, and local entities can probably better identify these needs, and if funds are somewhat fungible, a more efficient mix of programs may be funded. For instance, health care or after-school care or teen pregnancy prevention may each be severe problems in some communities, but not others.

Besides better identification of needs, local authority may have an even more important advantage. It is still hard to identify at-risk children based solely on family characteristics. For instance, only approximately one-half of children in the lowest quartile of income score in the lowest quartile of achievement.[10] Moreover, the literature on risk and resiliency shows that about one-half of children from the poorest family environments will become adults with jobs and families, and without severe dysfunction.[11] This literature tells us that determining which children are at-risk is a difficult undertaking. Often children in the same family environments will have quite different outcomes, so some children in a family are at-risk, while others are not.

Children near the bottom of the achievement score distribution are best identified by multiple risk indicators. It is the combination of low parental education, low income, large family size and living in a single parent that are much better predictors of risk. An indication of this is that most—but not all—children of unmarried teen parents have among the poorest educational outcomes. These children are most likely to be at multiple risk: living with one parent, in families with low income and low parental education, and often in larger families. Funding of national and state programs such as AFDC, food stamps, Medicaid, Title I and housing programs are usually allocated based on a simple income measure. Since income alone is a poor predictor of at-risk children, these programs are likely to be less efficiently targeted than programs that can take into account a more comprehensive set of measures available at local levels.[12] In addition, it is often indicators not available to any government- such as mental health and addiction conditions in parents—that better predict at-risk children and can only be known in the local environment.

While local entities comprised of professionals may have the most potential for the efficient allocation of funds, there can be inefficiency at this level also. Local

---

between wealthy and poorer districts. A few states have nearly equalized expenditures across districts after successful litigation (Carr and Fuhrman, 1999). However, most states still have significant variation in per-pupil expenditures across districts (Parrish and Hikido, 1998). Variation across states accounts for about two-thirds of the total variation, while within-state variation accounts for only one-third of the variation (Evans, Murray, and Schwab, 1999).

10 This result is obtained from tabulations of the National Educational Longitudinal Survey (NELS) eighth-grade sample given in 1988.

11 See Rutter (1988) and Masten (1994) for introductions to the rich literature on risk and resiliency in children.

12 A second reason why these programs may be inefficient is that the political process inevitably widens the target group to include higher income levels.

politics can certainly introduce inefficiency into the process. The reason for the North Carolina Smart Start program being governed by a quasi-public/private entity may be to avoid this kind of inefficiency. Some locales may not have the kind of multi-faceted expertise to make efficient judgments. State politics can certainly still make inefficient allocations across locales. However, the difficulty of efficiently identifying which children are at-risk makes local control potentially the most efficient allocator.

CONCLUDING OBSERVATIONS

The effects of interventions into families and schools can vary widely across types of families, children and students. The variation in effects probably arises from the current significant inequality in resources available to families and children in our society. Families and children with the most resources may be impacted less by additional resources than families and children with the lowest level of resources.

These variations mean that the same intervention can have a range of cost-effectiveness or cost-benefit measures depending on the population served. Recent empirical evidence suggests that these differences may be large, and that analysis involving costs, effectiveness and/or benefits needs to focus on defining alternatives in more precise ways that include particular characteristics of the applicable population. Targeting of expenditures and interventions toward specific populations can increase its efficiency markedly, so targeting becomes an integral part of defining and carrying out analyses involving costs, effectiveness and/or benefits.

Identifying efficient programs then requires designing and matching particular interventions to families and/or children. Today, targeting of this kind usually relies on a simple poverty or income measure to allocate funds. However, empirical evidence suggests that poverty measures alone do not target funds effectively because multiple factors usually are implicated in poor outcomes for children. Moreover, many of the measures that identify families and children at greatest risk, and those who would have the larger effects from intervention, are usually only observable at the local level. Thus research needs to focus on identifying the combination of measures that identify high-risk children and matching particular interventions to such children in cost-effective ways. It has been suggested that this process of identification and matching of programs to families and children is best done at the local level where the best indicators are available. However, funding at the local level would also need to be fungible across a wide variety of services to make the matches efficient.

REFERENCES

Campbell, J. R., Donahue, P. L., Reese, C. M., and Phillips, G. W. (1996). *NAEP 1994 reading report card for the nations and the states: Findings from the National Assessment of Educational Progress and Trail State Assessment.* Washington, DC: National Center for Education Statistics.

Carr, M., and Fuhrman, S. H. (1999). The politics of school finance in the 1990s. In H. F. Ladd, R. Chalk, and J. S. Hansen (Eds.), *Equity and adequacy in education finance.* Washington, DC: National Academy Press.

Evans, W. N., Murray, S. E., and Schwab, R. M. (1999). The impact of court mandated school finance reform. In H. F. Ladd, R. Chalk, and J. S. Hansen (Eds.), *Equity and adequacy in education finance.* Washington, DC: National Academy Press.

Finn, J. D., Gerber, S. B., Farber, S. L., and Achilles, C. (1999). *Teacher aides: An alternative to small classes?* Paper presented at the Conference on Class Size.

Finn, J., and Achilles, C. (1999). Tennessee's class size study: Findings, implications, and misconceptions. *Educational Evaluation and Policy Analysis, 21*(2), 97–110.

Grissmer, D. (1999). Class size effects: Assessing the evidence, its policy implications, and future research agenda. *Educational Evaluation and Policy Analysis, 21*(2), 231–248.

Grissmer, D. W., Flanagan, A., Kawata, J., and Williamson, S. (2000). *Improving student achievement: What NAEP state test scores tell us.* Santa Monica, CA: RAND.

Grissmer, D., Flanagan, A., and Williamson, S. (1998). Does money matter for minority and disadvantaged students: Assessing the new empirical evidence. In W. Fowler (Ed.), *Developments in school finance: 1997* (NCES 98–212). Washington, DC: U.S. Department of Education.

Karoly, L. A., Greenwood, P. W., Everingham, S. S., Hoube, J., Kilburn, M. R., Rydell, C. P., Sanders, M., and Chiesa, J. (1998). *Investing in our children.* Santa Monica, CA: RAND.

Krueger, A. B. (1999). Experimental estimates of education production functions. *Quarterly Journal of Economics, 114*(2), 497–532.

Levin, H. M. (1970). A cost-effectiveness analysis of teacher selection. *Journal of Human Resources, 5*(1), 24–33.

Levin, H. M., Glass, G. V., and Meister, G. R. (1987). Cost-effectiveness of computer-assisted instruction. *Evaluation Review, 11*(1), 50–72.

Levin, H. M., and McEwan, P. J. (2001). *Cost-effectiveness analysis: Methods and applications* (2nd ed.). Thousand Oaks, CA: Sage.

Masten, A. S. (1994). Resilience in individual development: Successful adaptation despite risk and adversity. In M. C. Wang and E. W. Gordon (Eds.), *Educational resilience in inner city America: Challenges and prospects.* Hillsdale: Lawrernce Erblaum Associates.

Miller, K. E., Nelson, J. E., and Naifeh, M. (1995). *Cross-state data compendium for the NAEP 1994 grade 4 reading assessment.* Washington, DC: National Center for Education Statistics.

Molnar, A., Smith, P., Zahorik, J., Palmer, A., Halbach, A., and Ehrle, K. (1999). Evaluating the SAGE program: A pilot program in targeted pupil-teacher reduction in Wisconsin. *Educational Evaluation and Policy Analysis, 21*(2), 165–177.

Nye, B., Hedges, L. V., and Konstantopoulos, S. (1999). The long-term effects of small classes: A five-year follow-up of the Tennessee class size experiment. *Educational Evaluation and Policy Analysis, 21*(2), 127–142.

Office of Science and Technology Policy. (1997). *Investing in our future: A national research initiative for America's children for the 21st century.* Washington, DC: The White House.

Parrish T. B., and Hikido, C. S. (1998). *Inequalities in public school revenues* (NCES 98–210). Washington, DC: U.S. Department of Education.

Quinn, B., Van Mondfrans, A., and Worthen, B. R. (1984). Cost-effectiveness of two math programs as moderated by pupil SES. *Educational Evaluation and Policy Analysis, 6*(1), 39–52.

Reese, C. M., Miller, K. E., Mazzeo, J., and Dossey, J. A. (1997). *NAEP 1996 mathematics report card for the nation and the states.* Washington, DC: National Center for Education Statistics.

Rothstein, R. (2000). Improving the efficiency of public expenditures directed toward children. In *Improving educational achievement: A volume exploring the role of investments in schools and other supports and services for families and communities.* Washington, DC: Center for Educational Policy.

Rutter, M. (Ed.). (1988). *Studies in psychosocial risk: The power of longitudinal data.* Cambridge: Cambridge University Press.

Shaughnessy, C. A., Nelson, J., and Norris, N. (1998). *NAEP 1996 mathematics cross state data compendium for the grade 4 and grade 8 assessment* (NCES–98–481). Washington, DC: U.S. Department of Education.

Snow, R. E. (1986). Individual differences and the design of education programs. *American Psychologist, 41,* 1029–1039.

U.S. Department of Agriculture. (1997). *Estimates of the costs of raising children.* Washington, DC: Author.

7

COMPARING THE COSTS OF PUBLIC AND PRIVATE SCHOOLS IN DEVELOPING COUNTRIES

Mun C. Tsang

INTRODUCTION

Many important decisions in education are concerned with the costs of education. Information on costs, for example, is necessary to find out how many resources are needed to operate an educational program, to ascertain the financial feasibility of an education project, to monitor resource allocation over time, to diagnose the status of health of the education system, and to assess efficiency in resource utilization in educational institutions. Cost analysis can be applied to a variety of issues and settings to contribute to informed decision-making in education (Tsang, 1997a). A fitting example of its application is the comparison of the costs of public and private schools.

The relative merits or demerits of public versus private schooling have been a subject of intense debate in both developing (Cuellar, 2001; Jimenez and Lockheed, 1995; McEwan, 2001; Tsang, in press) and advanced industrialized countries (Belfield, 2001; Levin, 2000; Peterson, Myers, Howell, and Mayer, 1999; Rangazas, 1997). Proponents of private schooling, for example, argue that it could address the unmet demand of parents for additional schooling for their children because of limited capacity in the public sector, expand the choice in schooling to meet the varied educational preferences of parents, and enhance efficiency in the utilization of scarce national resources through market-based competition in education. They point out that alternatives to traditional government schools could be created to serve children from marginalized backgrounds so that such children are not trapped in low-performing government schools. Opponents to private schooling, on the other hand, question the presumed efficiency-advantage of private schools, and raise serious concerns about the negative effects of private schooling on social equity and social cohesion. While improving the educational opportunity of children from marginalized backgrounds is a desirable goal, alternatives to government schools may attract the most motivated families, leaving government schools to deal with the less motivated ones.

Comparing the costs of public and private schools could contribute to an informed debate. First, a careful estimation of costs will show all the resources required to provide alternative programs to meet unfulfilled educational demand or to serve population groups with particular educational needs. For example, the analysis may show that public and private schools have different amounts of donated inputs not reflected in their operational costs; it can show what the per-student cost of private schools would be if they were required to provide special education programs as a condition for receiving government subsidy; and it can clarify how much it actually costs parents to send their children to private schools. Second, a policy in favor of private schooling may increase the reliance on family financing of education; and the economic burden on families may vary by socio-economic background. Thus, a shift in the mix of public and private schooling can have significant equity-related implications. Third, an analysis of the per-student costs of public and private schools will improve our understanding of the determinants of education costs and show whether or not there are systematic differences in the operation of the two types of schools. Fourth, information on costs is necessary for assessing the validity of claims on the relative cost-effectiveness of public and private schooling.

Earlier studies of the relative merits of public and private schooling tend to focus on school effectiveness, with little analysis of costs (Coleman, Hoffer, and Kilgore, 1982; Willms, 1983). In recent years, studies on the relative costs and relative cost-effectiveness of public and private schools have begun to emerge to fill this obvious gap in the research literature (Jimenez and Lockheed, 1995; McEwan and Carnoy, 2000; Tsang and Taoklam, 1992). This is certainly an encouraging development. However, a careful examination of published studies so far indicates that there are significant conceptual and methodological deficiencies in the analysis of the costs of public and private schools, and that these deficiencies could lead to misleading policies regarding public versus private schooling. For example, some studies underestimate the total education cost by either ignoring household resources devoted to schooling or not including education inputs donated by parents or community sources (Jimenez and Lockheed, 1995). To the extent that private schools rely more on private resources or donations, these studies will under-estimate the cost of private schools relative to public schools and over-estimate the cost-effectiveness of private schools relative to public schools, other things being equal. Also, some cost-effectiveness studies focus more on collecting and analyzing information on effectiveness with little corresponding effort on the cost component, thus resulting in very crude or incomplete estimates of costs. But strong statements are made about the relative cost-effectiveness of public and private schooling (Jimenez, Lockheed, and Wattanawaha, 1988). Moreover, some studies ignore institutional diversity among public and private schools and compare the average unit costs of public schools and private schools. To the extent that different schools can operate in different social settings (e.g., urban vs. rural) or cater to different clienteles (e.g., children from poor vs. wealthy backgrounds), they may not be realistic schooling alternatives. Hence, a comparison of average unit costs of the two aggregate groups is not meaningful.

This is an article on properly comparing the costs of public and private schools and the implications for educational policy. This discussion is based on a conceptual and methodological discussion of cost analysis and a review of studies on primary and secondary schools in developing countries. Through actual examples in developing countries, the article explains the potential pitfalls of improper cost comparison in the public debate over the relative merits of public and private schooling, especially with respect to the cherished goals of expanded access, increased social equity, and improved efficiency. The article focuses on primary and secondary schools because privatization is generally less of an issue at the post-secondary level. To limit the scope of the review, only studies on developing countries are considered. But many of the issues raised here could also be relevant for advanced industrialized countries.[1] The rest of the article is divided into three sections. Section 2 presents a concise summary of the conceptual and methodological issues in cost comparison. Section 3 compares private educational resources for public and private schools while Section 4 compares their institutional costs. The last section discusses the implications for educational policy by highlighting cost issues involved in current educational initiatives in developing countries.

CONCEPTUAL AND METHODOLOGICAL ISSUES IN COST COMPARISON

CONCEPTUAL ISSUES

The costs of education refer to the resources used in the production of education services. They include not only public expenditures on education, but also household spending on education, donations to educational institutions from private sources, and the economic value of foregone opportunities of education (Levin and McEwan, 2001). A comparison of the costs of public and private schooling thus has to take account of the direct and indirect resources from various sources. The inclusion of household education spending and contributions is particularly relevant in many developing countries in which educational financing depends to a significant degree on private sources (Tsang, 1994).

The costs of public and private schools are often compared at the school level, because of interests in relative efficiency and operational characteristics at the institutional level. For analytical purposes, costs at the school level can be divided into two groups: institutional costs and private resources (Tsang, 1995a). Institutional costs refer to costs incurred by the school on its production of educational services; they are usually divided into recurrent and capital categories for accounting purposes. Recurrent costs are costs of inputs that are expended in a period of one year; they consist of the costs of school personnel and non-personnel items. Capital costs are costs of inputs that last for more than one year; they include the costs of buildings, equipment, and land.

Private resources at the school level refer to resources provided by households, individuals, and the community to support the production of educational services at the school. Private resources for education can be classified into three categories: direct private costs, private contributions, and indirect private costs. Direct private costs refer to household educational expenditure related to a child's schooling, including tuition spending and non-tuition spending (such as spending on other school fees, textbooks and supplementary study guides, uniform, writing supplies, school bag, transportation, and boarding). Private contributions refer to donations, in cash and/or in kind, from parents, individuals, or community organizations to a school. Indirect private costs refer to the economic value of the foregone opportunities of schooling. While private resources can be reported in monetary value, their magnitude could be better assessed by comparison with government spending on education.

The institutional costs of public schools are supported by government educational spending, fee-related spending by households, and private contributions to school.

---

1 See Chapters 2 and 3 in this volume.

Government educational spending usually constitutes the largest share of these costs. For private schools, fee-related spending by households is often the major source of support for institutional costs, while private contributions and government subsidies can also be significant in some instances. For both public and private schools, total cost at the school level equals the sum of institutional costs, non-fee-related direct private costs, and indirect private costs. It is important to point out that institutional cost does not represent the total cost at the school level and that households and the local community could be the major financing source for institutional cost.

There are educational resources incurred above the school level, such as the costs of operating educational bureaucracies at the local, provincial/state, and central/federal levels. Such costs are usually small compared to school-level costs, on a per-student basis. A shift in the mix of public and private schools may entail a change in the educational costs above the school level.

The costs of public and private schools are often compared on a unit basis, particularly in terms of costs per student. It is useful to distinguish between two types of unit costs, average cost per student and marginal cost per student, which are often used in different decision contexts. Average cost per student is defined as total cost divided by total student enrollment. This measure can be used to find out, for example, whether a system of public schools is more expensive to operate than a system of private schools. Marginal cost per student is defined as the additional cost of serving one more student; it is used to estimate the additional cost associated with the expansion of a system of schools at the margin. If there is slack (e.g., excess capacity) in an existing school system, additional students can be served at relatively lower costs; marginal cost will be less than average cost. In some situations, marginal cost could be higher than average cost; for example, when serving additional students increases the demand for teachers and then compensation for teachers. Thus, at a given scale of operation, marginal cost could be different from average cost. In choosing between these two measures of unit cost, the analyst has to be clear whether the decision is about comparing system averages or comparing changes at the margin.

The comparison of the relative unit costs of public and private schools is complicated by the possibility that unit costs may change with the scale of operation. The changing relationship could be represented by a cost function, which could be a flat line, a U-shape curve, or some other curve. If the cost function is not flat (a very likely situation in reality), the relative cost ratio may change when the scale of operation changes. Public and private schools may have the same cost function but they could be at different points of the scale of operation, or they may have different cost functions.

Pertinent to the above discussion of changing unit costs are two different concepts of efficiency: technical efficiency and economic efficiency. Technical efficiency is enhanced when more output is produced with a given mix of inputs. Thus, when there is slack in the existing schools (public or private), technical efficiency will be improved by more fully utilizing the existing inputs. On the other hand, producing more output through changing the mix of inputs enhances economic efficiency. For example, supporters of private schooling argue that private schools can be economically more efficient than public schools since the former have more freedom in choosing the right mix of inputs while the latter are constrained by powerful interest groups (such as teachers unions) and can not easily choose the right mix of inputs. In short, in comparing the costs of public and private schools, the cost analyst has to determine: (1) what is the decision context; (2) what is the appropriate unit-cost measure; and (3) how to measure the unit cost properly.

METHODOLOGICAL ISSUES

Experience has shown that cost comparison of schools in developing countries should be cognizant of a number of methodological issues (Tsang, 1995a).[2] First, private resources could be a very substantial source for financing schools, including public ones. They have to be carefully estimated.

Second, how school revenue from households (in addition to the amount of revenue) is utilized could have an impact on school output. In some countries, such revenue is an important source of funding for quality-related school inputs (such as textbooks and instructional materials). Thus, it is useful to examine the pattern of resource utilization at school.

Third, good and relevant data may not be readily available. With respect to data problems, there are at least three distinct issues: (1) information on some relevant costs may not be available and this could lead to underestimation of cost; (2) the quality of available information is poor and the resulting cost estimates are unreliable; and (3) the use of school revenue data instead of school cost data could be associated with significant measurement error. Information on private schools is generally more difficult to obtain than that for government schools and this may result in an under-estimation of the costs of private schooling. Because of a lack of school-level information on institutional cost, some studies resort to using total government spending on public education to estimate the per-student cost of public schooling.

Fourth, there are substantial diversities among developing nations and the cost analyst should be cautious in generalizing the findings from these countries and in drawing lessons from cross-national studies.

Fifth, related to the previous point, public and private schools may mean different things in different countries. Even within a country, there could be a range of private schools as well as a range of public schools; and these schools could operate in different settings (e.g., urban and rural). Cost analysis should clarify the nature of these schools and their setting and to perform appropriate comparisons.

Sixth, cost comparison without considering effectiveness is as problematic as effectiveness comparison without considering costs.[3]

The next two sections present a review of educational cost studies in developing countries, with a focus on primary and secondary education. Section 3 compares the two types of schools in terms of private resources and Section 4 compares the institutional costs of these schools. This discussion is based on studies and reviews in the past two decades published in English. While specific findings will obviously be influenced by the studies and countries covered, the purpose here is to try to find some general lessons in properly comparing the costs of public and private schools in these countries.

---

2 To some extent, many of these observations are also relevant to advanced industrialized countries.

3 Analytically, a cost function relates schooling output to cost. It could be empirically estimated with cost and output information.

Comparing Private Resources in Public and Private Schools

The improper estimation of private resources is a common problem in cost comparison between public and private schools. The deficiency may consist in either underestimating or in not estimating the amount of private resources. In many instances, this deficiency is related to the lack of good information.[4]

The estimation problem is not serious if private resources are relatively small and there is no significant difference between public and private schools. However, as the empirical studies reviewed here show, private resources can be significant compared to public educational spending and that they can be very different for public and private schools

Table 7.1 shows the magnitude of private resources to public education in developing countries in Asia, Latin America and the Caribbean, and Africa.[5] The great majority of the studies in Table 7.1 focus on direct private costs, with few studies also considering private contributions and indirect private costs. To assess the magnitude of private resources, two measures are used: private resources as a percentage of public recurrent educational spending, and private resources as a percentage of total public educational spending (which includes both recurrent and capital spending). Both measures could be estimated at the primary, secondary, and all-education levels. It should be pointed out that the studies were not based on a uniform estimation procedure; some studies relied on a sample of schools in a city, a province, or a country while others employed information from a socio-economic survey of households. Caution must be exercised in comparing the findings across national settings. The studies also used data over different time periods; and the magnitude of private resources could change over time within a country (e.g., because a change in government financing policy for schools). Nevertheless, taken together, these studies demonstrate the magnitude of and the large variation in private resources to education both within and across developing countries.

---

4 Understandably, information on private spending on education is not as easily available as that on public spending on education. Earlier research studies on education costs rarely undertook household surveys to estimate private costs because such surveys could be expensive to undertake (Tsang, 1988). But in more recent years, government agencies in developing countries have started collecting information on household educational spending as part of their periodic socio-economic survey of households. For example, the World Bank has a LSMS (Living Standards Measurement Study) database on a number of countries that contains information on household educational spending. However, such surveys rarely provide information on private contributions to schools and on indirect private costs. Private contributions to schools could be estimated by collecting information from schools themselves. This strategy will not work for private schools if the school principal is reluctant to provide such information.

5 Developing nations vary in what schools they consider to be part of the public system. It is a common practice across countries that schools funded and managed by the government are considered public schools (the "traditional" public schools). However, schools with significant government subsidies, but managed by non-government agencies (such as the church), are put under the public sector in some countries (Tsang, Fryer, and Arevalos, in press) and in the private sector in some other countries (McEwan and Carnoy, 2000). Table 7.1 refers to schools that are considered public in their own context.

Table 7.1 Magnitude of Private Resources to Public Schooling in Developing Countries

Country	Measure (year)	Private resources by education level	Sources
Asia			
Cambodia	DPC as % of government educational expenditure (1997)	246% in primary schools	Computed from Bray (1999, pp. 126–127)
China	DPC as % of per-student government budgeted recurrent expenditure (1988)	64% urban primary schools in Shaanxi province 51% in rural primary schools in Shaanxi province 70% in urban primary schools in Guizhou province 49% in rural primary schools in Guizhou province	Computed from Tsang (1994)
	DPC as % of per-student government budgeted recurrent expenditure (1993)	45-70% in rural primary schools in Hebei province	Computed from Tsang (2000)
	Household spending on books and miscellaneous school fees as % of government budgeted recurrent expenditure (1993)	56% in primary schools in Guangdong province	Computed from West (1995)
	DPC as % of recurrent expenditure from budgeted and out-of-budget sources (1996)	68% in Beijing	Computed from Wei and Qiu (2000)
India	DPC as % of public educational expenditure (1979–80)	49% for education system	Computed from Tilak (1985)
	Indirect private cost as % of public educational expenditure (1979-80)	108% for education system	Computed from Tilak (1985)
Indonesia	DPC as % of public educational expenditure (1989)	10% at the primary level	Computed from King (1994)*
Philippines	DPC as % of public educational expenditure (1994)	44% at the primary level, 74% at the secondary level	Computed from Schwartz (1995)*
Myanmar	DPC as % of public educational expenditure (1994)	43% at the primary level	Computed from Evans and Rorris (1994)*
Pakistan	DPC as % of per-student public recurrent expenditure (1979-80)	30% at the primary level	Tsang et al. (1990)
Thailand	DPC as % of per-student recurrent cost (1987)	20% in government primary schools	Computed from Tsang and Taoklam (1992)
	Household contribution as % of per-student recurrent cost (1987)	4% in government primary schools	Computed from Tsang and Taoklam (1992)
	Indirect private cost as % of per-student recurrent cost (1987)	14% in government primary schools	Computed from Tsang and Taoklam (1992)
	Total private cost as % of per-student recurrent cost (1987)	38% in government primary schools	Computed from Tsang and Taoklam (1992)
Vietnam	DPC as % of public educational expenditure (1993)	110% at the primary level, 210% at lower-secondary level, and 260% at upper-secondary level	Computed from World Bank (1995)*
	DPC as % of public educational expenditure (1994)	80% at the primary level, 95% at lower-secondary level, 106% at upper-secondary level	Computed from World Bank (1997)

Table 7.1 (*Continued*)

Country	Measure (year)	Private resources by education level	Sources
Latin America and the Caribbean			
Argentina	DPC as % of total public expenditure by Ministry of Education	4% for education system	Schiefelbein (1986)
Barbados	DPC as % of per-student government expenditure on education (1997)	17% at the primary level, and 19-34% at the secondary level	Tsang et al. (in press)
Brazil	DPC as % of total public expenditure by Ministry of Education	111% for education system	Schiefelbein (1986)
Chile	DPC as % of total public expenditure by Ministry of Education	32% for education system	Schiefelbein (1986)
	DPC as % of government educational expenditure (1996)	62% for Public DAEM primary schools, 79% for Public-Corporation primary schools	Computed from McEwan and Carnoy (2000)
Colombia	DPC as % of total public expenditure by Ministry of Education	51% for education system	Schiefelbein (1986)
	DPC as % of per-student school expenditure (1981) in other public secondary schools	22% in diversified public secondary schools, 32%	Computed from Psacharopoulos (1987)
Guyana	HEE as % of total public educational expenditure (1995)	31% for education system	Computed from Tsang (1997b)
	DPC as % of per-student government recurrent expenditure (1993)	95% at the primary level, and 50% at the secondary level	Tsang (1997b)
Honduras	DPC as % of government educational expenditure (1990)	Between 38% and 77% at the primary level	Computed from McEwan (1999)
Jamaica	HEE as % of total public educational expenditure (1996)	31% for education system	Computed from Tsang et al. (in press)
Trinidad and Tobago	HEE as % of total public educational expenditure (1991)	48% for education system	Computed from Wu (1995)
Venezuela	HEE as % of total public expenditure by Ministry of Education	13% for education system	Schiefelbein (1986)
Africa			
Kenya	DPC as % of per-student government spending (1980)	75% in government secondary schools; 1080% in assisted Harambee secondary schools	Computed from Knight and Sabot (1990, p. 282)
	DPC as % of total cost per student (1981-82)	81% for assisted Harambee secondary schools	Wolff (1985)
East Africa	DPC as % of total cost per student in 9 countries (1981-82)	33% at the secondary level	Wolff (1985)
Tanzania	DPC as % of per-student school expenditure (1981)	12% in government secondary schools	Computed from Psacharopoulos (1987)

*Cited in Bray (1996)

Notes: DPC is the Direct Private Cost. HEE is the Household Educational Expenditure.

DIRECT PRIVATE COSTS OF SCHOOLING

At the primary level, the ratio of total direct private cost to government educational spending ranged between 10 percent in Indonesia to 246 percent in Cambodia; although it was between 30 percent and 80 percent for most countries. At the secondary level, the ratio ranged between 12 percent in Tanzania to over 200 percent in Vietnam in 1993. The ratio averaged about one-third for government schools in Colombia, Barbados, and nine East African countries and about three-quarters in the Philippines and Kenya. For Vietnam, because of an increasing role of government financing, the studies by the World Bank indicate that the magnitude of direct private costs declined substantially between 1993 and 1994. But even in 1994, private spending was still as large as government spending. For the entire education system, the ratio ranged between 4 percent in Argentina to 111 percent in Brazil, with most of the values lying between 30 percent and 50 percent.

In short, direct private costs constitute a significant part of the total funding for public schools in the majority of the developing countries documented in Table 7.1. Table 7.1, however, does not show the magnitude of direct private costs of private schooling. There are reasons to believe that, in many circumstances, the direct private costs of private schooling are much higher than those of public schooling in developing countries. First, tuition is generally the most important source of funding for private schools and can be a relatively large spending item for households.[6] It is a common practice for government primary schools not to charge tuition; and government secondary schools also do not charge tuition in some countries. Second, parents of private schools in some countries have to pay some non-tuition school fees that are not required in government schools. For example, parents may be required to pay a registration or admission fee in order to get their children into a private school; this school fee could be large compared to the tuition fee for an elite private school. Third, public and private schools may serve children from very different socio-economic backgrounds that have a different capacity for spending on education. For example, studies in 10 countries (see Table 7.2) have documented that there are very large differences in private educational spending among households. As expected, such spending is much higher for households with higher income or consumption, and for parents with higher educational attainment, in professional occupations, or from a certain ethnicity. This finding has implications for the relative cost of public and private schools. To the extent that private schools serve proportionately more students from higher socio-economic backgrounds, direct private costs will be relatively higher for private schools.

Table 7.3 compares the direct private costs of public and private schools in six countries for which information is available. While all the studies reported higher direct private cost for private schools, they also showed that there were substantial variations in relative cost across education levels and across countries. Some of these studies pointed out that it was important to distinguish the different types of government schools and private schools within a country for proper comparison.

In Thailand, for example, the total direct private cost of private primary schools averaged 4.7 times that of government primary schools in 1987. In private primary

---

6   However, private schools with heavy government subsidies may not charge tuition (Cuellar, 2001; McEwan and Carnoy, 2000).

Table 7.2 Variations in Household Educational Spending by Family Background in Selected Developing Countries

Country (year)	Measure of Variation	Schooling Level	Sources
Bangladesh (1992)	Ratio of HEE, top-income decile to bottom-income decile	348 (on all levels of education)	Computed from Tsang (1995b)
China	Ratio of per-capita HEE, top-income decile to bottom-income decile (1987)	1.3 in urban areas (on all education levels)	Computed from Tsang (1995b)
	Ratio of per-capita HEE, top-income decile to bottom-income decile (1991)	1.3 in urban areas (on all education levels)	Computed from Tsang (1996)
Guyana (1993)	Ratio of HEE, top consumption quintile to bottom consumption quintile	3.4 (on all education levels)	Tsang (1997b)
	Ratio of HEE, top-spending geographical area to bottom spending geographical area	2.4 (on all educational levels)	Tsang (1997b)
	Ratio of HEE, top-spending ethnic group to bottom spending ethnic group	3.3 (on all educational levels)	Tsang (1997b)
India (1988)	Ratio of HEE per student, top-income group (above 30,000 rupees) to bottom income group (up to 10,000 rupees), in the city of Delhi	2.5 (on all educational levels)	Computed from Kansal (1990)
	Ratio of HEE per student, respondents with college education to respondents with secondary education	1.2 (on all educational levels)	Computed from Kansal (1990)
Indonesia (1992)	Ratio of HEE, top income decile to bottom income decile	6.9 at primary level, 4.1 at lower-secondary level, and 3.8 at upper-secondary level	Computed from Indonesia (1992)*
Jamaica (1995)	Ratio of per-capita HEE, top consumption quintile to bottom consumption quintile	5.6	Tsang et al. (in press)
	Ratio of per-capita HEE, Kingston (Capital) area to rural area	2.2	Tsang et al. (in press)
Mongolia	Ratio of HEE, top-consumption quintile to bottom-consumption quintile (1995)	5.7	Computed from World Bank (1996)*
Pakistan (1980)	Ratio of DPC for boys, top-income quintile to bottom-income quintile	12.0 in urban primary schools, 9.3 in rural primary schools	Computed from Tsang et al. (1990)
	Ratio of DPC for girls, top-income quintile to bottom-income quintile	15.2 in urban primary schools, 9.3 in rural primary schools	Computed from Tsang et al. (1990)
	Ratio of HEE, top-income quintile to bottom-income quintile	16.9 in urban areas (all levels of education), 16.0 in rural areas (all levels of education)	Computed from Tsang et al. (1990)
	Ratio of HEE, fathers with university education to fathers with no schooling	4.2 in urban areas (all levels), 11.2 in rural areas (all levels)	Computed from Tsang et al. (1990)
	Ratio of HEE, fathers who are professionals to fathers who are skilled workers	3.0 in urban areas (all levels), 3.9 in rural areas (all levels)	Computed from Tsang et al. (1990)

Table 7.2 (*Continued*)

Country (year)	Measure of Variation	Schooling Level	Sources
Thailand (1987)	Ratio of DPC, top-10% income group to DPC of bottom-20% income group	2.6 in government primary schools, 7.7 in private primary schools	Computed from Tsang and Kidchanapansich (1992)
	Ratio of DPC, fathers with higher education to fathers with no education	3.4 in government primary schools, 1.1 in private primary schools	Computed from Tsang and Kidchanapansich (1992)
	Ratio of DPC, fathers who were company executives to fathers who worked in agriculture	2.7 in government primary schools, 2.4 in private primary schools	Computed from Tsang and Kidchanapansich (1992)
	Ratio of DPC, fathers who were Christians to fathers who were Muslims	2.3 in government primary schools, 1.3 in private primary schools	Computed from Tsang and Kidchanapansich (1992)
Vietnam (1996)	Ratio of HEE, top-quintile consumption group to bottom-quintile consumption group (1996)	2.6 at primary level, 2.3 at lower-secondary level, and 2.0 at upper-secondary level	World Bank (1997)
	Ratio of HEE, urban to rural (1993)	2.5 at primary level; 2.4 at lower-secondary level; and 1.6 at upper-secondary level	World Bank (1997)
	Ratio of HEE, top-quintile consumption group to bottom-quintile consumption group (1993)	6.1 in government primary schools; 4.9 in government lower-secondary schools; and 3.3 in government upper-secondary schools	World Bank (1995)*
	Ratio of HEE, urban to rural (1993)	3.3 in government primary schools; 2.5 in government lower-secondary schools; and 1.7 in government upper-secondary schools	World Bank (1995)*

*Cited in Bray (1996)

Notes: HEE is the Household Educational Expenditure. DPC is the Direct Private Cost.

schools, households spent a total of 3,262 bahts per student per year, consisting of 1,676 bahts on tuition and 1,586 bahts on non-tuition items. Households of government primary schools spent an average of 695 bahts per student per year, all on non-tuition items, since they paid no tuition fee (Tsang and Kidchanapansich, 1992, Table 9.4.1). The average for government schools masks large differences in non-tuition household educational spending among different types of government schools. Parents spent 601 bahts in ONPEC schools (government schools mostly found in rural areas), 1,227 bahts in Bangkok schools (urban government schools in the national capital), and 1,213 bahts in Municipal schools (urban government schools in other municipal areas). Thus, the *non-tuition spending* of households of private schools, which are mostly located in urban areas, was about 30 percent higher than that of urban government schools. This study indicates that it is important to distinguish between the different types of government schools, especially between rural and urban ones.

Table 7.3 Direct Private Costs of Public and Private Schools, Selected Countries

Country (year)	Level of schooling	Unit cost of public schools (local currency)	Unit cost of private schools (local currency)	Ratio of unit cost (private to public)	Sources
Chile (1996)	Primary	173,575 pesos	336,329 pesos	1.94	Computed from McEwan and Carnoy (2000)
Colombia (1981)	Secondary	4,270 pesos, INEM schools	12,674 pesos	2.97	Pscharopoulos (1987)
	Secondary	5,787 pesos, Other schools	12,674 pesos	2.19	Pscharopoulos (1987)
Indonesia (1992)	Primary	48,388 rupiah	87,070 rupiah	1.80	Indonesia (1992)*
	Junior secondary	138,405 rupiah	168,356 rupiah	1.22	Indonesia (1992)*
	Senior secondary	233,157 rupiah	279,806 rupiah	1.20	Indonesia (1992)*
Philippines (1992-93)	Primary	645	5176	8.02	Borromeo (1995)*
	Secondary	1122	4599	4.10	Borromeo (1995)*
Tanzania (1981)	Secondary	432 sh.	2491 sh.	5.77	Psacharopoulos (1987)
Thailand (1987)	Primary	695 bahts	3,262 bahts	4.69	Tsang and Kidchanapansich (1992)
	Lower-secondary	2,570 bahts	4,710 bahts	1.83	Myers and Chalongphob (1992)*

*Cited in Bray (1996)

In addition to showing higher direct private costs for private schools at the primary level, a study of Chile highlights the importance of examining different types of private schools. In Chile in 1996, direct private costs averaged (weighted by enrollment) 173,575 pesos in primary schools under public administration, and 336,329 pesos in private schools (computed from McEwan and Carnoy, 2000, Tables 2 and 5). However, private schools in Chile can be classified according to whether or not they receive government funding in the form of a voucher. Direct private costs averaged 237,630 pesos in voucher-receiving private schools, and they were of similar magnitude among Catholic-voucher, Protestant-voucher, and non-religious-voucher private schools. Since both government and voucher-receiving private schools do not charge tuition, this study shows that non-tuition direct private cost of voucher-receiving private schools was 37 percent higher than that of government schools. Parents of private schools that receive no government voucher spent an average of 731,125 pesos in the same year, 4.2 times the average for government schools. In Chile, non-voucher private schools serve children from the highest socio-economic backgrounds and tuition is their main source of funding.

Reported household spending on education may underestimate the total direct private cost of private schools. Though discouraged or even prohibited by the government, some private schools in developing countries charge parents a one-time "admission" fee. This non-tuition school fee can be several times the annual tuition fee, especially for private schools with a good reputation (Tsang, in press; Tsang and Kidchanapansich, 1992; World Bank, 1992). This under-the-table transaction is often un-reported by school staff and by parents. Thus it is difficult to document how prevalent this practice is in developing countries. But researchers should be aware of this likely underestimation of the direct private costs of private schools.

Direct private costs are important to consider not only for proper cost accounting purposes, but also because they have strong implications for educational quality and equity (Tsang, 1995a; Tsang et al., in press). In many developing countries, they are the major source of funding for important education inputs such as textbooks and other learning materials. They also could be a heavy economic burden on some households, particularly those from poor and rural backgrounds that could adversely affect school attendance.

Private Contributions to School

Private contributions are often generated from fund-raising activities held by the school. They can come from a wide variety of sources, including parents, individuals, as well as community and religious organizations. The importance of private contributions can vary across countries and across types of schools. Community financing of education has a long tradition in some countries (Bray and Lillis, 1988). In China, for example, *minban* (people-run) schools in rural areas have for decades received community donations, in cash and/or in kind, to support the livelihood of teachers (known as *minban* teachers) and the construction of school buildings. School staff and education officials at various levels are asked to record the amount of donations from various non-government sources (known as "social contributions"). A study by the World Bank (1999) found that social contributions amounted to 13.7 percent of total government spending on education in 1991 and 12.6 percent in 1997 for the country (computed from Table 9.5.3, p. 74). The Harambee schools in Kenya are another example of schools for which community donations, particularly contributed labor and materials in school construction, are important (Bray and Lillis, 1988). In Thailand in 1987, household donations amounted to 4.4 percent of recurrent cost and 3.2 percent of institution cost in government primary schools; the corresponding ratios were 8.9 percent and 5.8 percent in private primary schools (computed from Tsang and Kidchanapansich, 1992).

A common problem in comparing private contributions to public and private schools is the lack of information. School staffs, especially those from private schools, are often reluctant to provide such information for a number of reasons, such as the concern that their school may receive less funding or subsidy from the government, or that they may induce more close scrutiny from regulatory bodies. Operators of for-profit private schools are particularly careful about information on their taxable revenue (from tuition and other school fees, and from private donations) and expenditure. In many developing countries, the government either does not collect or is not effective in enforcing the regulation to collect information on private contributions. Some evidence shows that private contributions can be substantial and can vary significantly among schools in some countries. A study by a World Bank analyst (Wu, 1995) in Trinidad and Tobago found that private contributions could amount to as much as half a million Trinidad and Tobago dollars in 1994 for a "successful" church-run primary school; such an amount was more than half of the average total government spending on an entire government primary school.[7]

---

7 Per-student government spending was 2,444 local dollars in 1994 (Tsang et al., in press). There are about 350 students per primary school.

The underestimation of private contributions is much more likely to be an issue for private schools than government schools, for two reasons. First, government schools are more likely than private schools to be required by the government to report private contributions. Second, the true economic value of private contributions of some private schools is either not reported or underestimated as the next section emphasizes.

INDIRECT PRIVATE COST OF SCHOOLING

In developing countries, children are generally required by law to go to primary school and employers in some of these countries are even forbidden to employ children at such an age. Thus, in most instances, one may assume that indirect private cost of primary schooling is either zero or very negligible. This assumption is untenable at higher levels of schooling, as there are real opportunities for productive activities besides schooling; the economic value of such productive activities varies across settings and households. Indirect private costs for the education sector could be substantial (Tilak, 1985). But even at the primary level, indirect private costs of primary schooling may not be zero or insignificant in some situations. For example, for rural households in poor countries, children are often needed to help with agricultural production, household chores, or the care of younger siblings. For some poor urban households, primary schooling still affects the amount of productive help obtainable from the child.

In a study of primary schools in 1987 in Thailand (Tsang and Kidchanapansich, 1992), opportunity cost was estimated to be the additional number of hours that parents would like their children to help them per day if their children were not in school. A household survey found this to be 1.6 hours per day for ONPEC government schools, 1.3 hours per day for municipal government schools, 0.82 hours per day for Bangkok government schools, and 0.95 hours per day for private schools. In monetary terms, the indirect private cost as a proportion of per-student recurrent cost was estimated to be 14.7 percent for ONPEC government schools, 20.7 percent for municipal government schools, 10.4 percent for Bangkok government schools, and 20.2 percent for private schools.

In most comparative studies of public and private schools, estimates of indirect private cost are not provided because information on such costs is not readily available. School personnel and educational decision-makers are not interested in this cost because it is not associated with usable resources in the operation of schools. The indirect private cost of public and private schools could be different, as parents could come from different socio-economic backgrounds and have different demands for child labor. To the extent that higher-income families have a lower demand for child-labor, schooling represents a smaller sacrifice to them. For example, in Thailand in 1987, indirect private costs of primary education as a proportion of household income amounted to 7.2 percent in government schools and 0.62 percent in private schools, because government schools had students mostly from rural and lower-income households (Tsang and Kidchanapansich, 1992).

Very few comparative studies of public and private schools consider all three categories of private resources. Table 7.4 presents the findings of such a study. It shows the amount and ratio of private resources for sixth-grade students in government and private schools in Thailand in 1987. Private resources per sixth-grade student totaled 3,568 Baht in private schools, 1,291 Baht in ONPEC government schools, 1,700 Baht in Bangkok government schools, and 1,743 Baht in Municipal government schools.

Total private resources for private primary schools were substantially higher than that of the government primary schools. Indirect private cost was not trivial; it constituted 37.5 percent of total private resources for government schools and 12.6 percent private schools in Thailand. The study also found that private resources as a percentage of household income were 14.4 percent for government schools and 4.8 percent for private schools. Thus private resources were a heavier economic burden for government-school households than private-school ones even though private schools received more private resources than government schools. They were also a heavier burden for rural households than urban ones, and for lower-income households than higher-income households.

Table 7.4 Private Resources to Government and Private Primary Schools in Thailand, 1987 (Baht per sixth-grade student per year)

	Government schools				Private schools	Ratio (5)/(4)	Ratio (5)/(3)
	ONPEC schools	Bangkok schools	Municipal schools	All government schools			
	(1)	(2)	(3)	(4)	(5)	(6)	(7)
Direct private cost	600	1234	1195	692	3055	4.4	2.6
Household contribution	155	181	87	153	62	0.41	0.71
Indirect private cost	536	286	461	508	451	0.89	0.98
Total private resource	1291	1700	1743	1353	3568	2.6	2.0

Source: Tsang and Taoklam (1992, Table 9.5)

In summary, private costs of schooling in developing countries: (1) are substantial compared to government education spending for public schools, and particularly for private schools; (2) may exhibit large variations between and within public and private sectors as well as within and across countries; (3) are likely to be underestimated for private schools relative to public schools because of a lack of available information and other factors; (4) are likely to be higher for private schools than public schools because of student backgrounds, school-fee policies, and other factors; (5) are a source of educational inequity for households in different education sectors and from different backgrounds; and (6) are an important financing source for some quality-related education inputs.

COMPARING INSTITUTIONAL COSTS OF PUBLIC AND PRIVATE SCHOOLS

A popular way to compare the costs of public and private schools is based on the per-student institutional expenditures at the school or system level. Institutional expenditures are educational spending data that school personnel, educational policymakers, and educational planners deal with on a regular basis and over which they have some control. Information on institutional costs of government schools is generally available. Average per-student institutional costs can be estimated from information on costs and enrollment.

Table 7.5 compares the average per-student institutional costs of primary and secondary education in five countries for which information is available for both the government and private sectors. Although the ratio of average cost ranges between 0.39 and 1.46, eight out of ten cases in Table 7.5 show that private schools have lower institutional costs than public schools. This finding is consistent with the assertion of private-school advocates who argue that private schools have a stronger incentive to lower costs (as one way of improving cost-effectiveness) and have more autonomy than public schools in decisions regarding spending and the mix of educational inputs (e.g., teachers qualification and teachers salaries). Private schools could be economically more efficient, other things being equal. Section 2, however, emphasizes several caveats to the proper interpretation of the findings in Table 7.5.

First, institutional costs are part of the total cost of schooling. For public schools, they generally do not include direct private costs, private contributions, and indirect private costs.[8] For private schools, they do not include the non-fee direct private costs

Table 7.5 Average Institutional Cost of Public and Private Schools, Selected Countries

Country (year)	Average unit-cost measure	Level of schooling	Average unit cost of public schools (local currency)	Average cost of private schools (local currency)	Ratio of unit cost (private to public)	Sources
Colombia (1981)	Institutional	Secondary	19,314 pesos, INEM schools	12,674 pesos	0.66	Psacharopoulos (1987)
	Institutional	Secondary	18,281 pesos, Other schools	12,674 pesos	0.69	Psacharopoulos (1987)
Dominican Republic (1982–83)	Per-student institutional cost	Secondary	323 RD$	472 RD$, F-type*	1.46	Jimenez et al. (1991)
	Per-student institutional cost	Secondary	323 RD$	209 RD$, O-type*	0.65	Jimenez et al. (1991)
India (1989–90)	Per-student recurrent cost	Secondary schools in urban Uttar Pradesh	2008 rupees	1827 rupees, private-aided	0.91	Kingdon (1996)
	Per-student recurrent cost	Secondary schools in	2008 rupees	999 rupees, private unaided	0.50	Kingdon (1996)
Pakistan (1983–84)	Per-student recurrent cost	Primary	423 rupees	515 rupees	1.22	Jimenez and Tan (1987)
	Per-student institutional cost	Secondary	3539 rupees	2,456 rupees	0.69	Jimenez and Tan (1987)
Thailand (1987)	Per-student institutional cost	Primary	4,795 baht	2,562 baht	0.53	Tsang and Kidchanapansich (1992)
Thailand (1981–82)	Per-student school income	Secondary	4,492 baht	1,762 baht	0.39	Jimenez et al. (1988)

* F-type private schools are high status private schools that are authorized to give examinations; O-type schools cannot give examinations.

---

8 In some countries, government schools charge tuition fees and/or other school fees at the primary and secondary levels. Such fees could be reflected in the estimate of institutional costs if information is available and taken into account in the analysis. The institution costs reported by government schools may already incorporate the private resource from school fees. Information on private contributions is either not reported or unavailable. Thus private contributions are often not taken into account in the estimate of institutional costs.

and indirect private costs; and private contributions may or may not be incorporated. Information on total costs and their funding sources should be examined if one is interested in finding out how many resources are expended in producing a given level of educational output, comparing the cost-effectiveness and relative efficiency of public versus private schools, and understanding the equity implications of resource mobilization for education. The relative cost could change when all resources are accounted for in the production of public and private schooling. For example, in Thailand, the average per-student cost of private primary school amounted to 53 percent of that of the average government primary schools, in terms of institutional cost only; but the relative cost ratio increased to 78 percent when private resources were also included. Thus, without taking account of private resources, the cost of private schooling relative to public schooling will be underestimated and the efficiency of private schooling relative to public schooling will be overestimated. It is not unusual to find that studies that claim a higher relative efficiency for private schools are subject to this problem (Jimenez and Lockheed, 1995).

Second, average unit costs based on an aggregate system often mask large variations among different types of schools in the public and private sector. And such aggregate estimates are not appropriate for cost or cost-effectiveness comparison. Consider again the example on Thailand. Most of the government primary schools are located in rural areas and private schools are primarily located in urban areas; comparing the system of government schools with the system of private schools is essentially comparing rural government schools with urban private schools. A more appropriate comparison is between private schools and government schools in municipal areas.[9] The cost of private schooling relative to government schooling was 93 percent (see Table 7.6), which is very different from the 53 percent figure shown in Table 7.5. In other words, the efficiency of private schools relative to government schools in Thailand was almost cut in half when all the costs were taken into account and when the appropriate comparison of school groups was made. Kingdon's (1996) study of urban schools in Uttar Pradesh, India, demonstrated the large differences in quality and costs between different types of private schools. Private-aided schools are almost twice as expensive as private-unaided schools but are comparable to government schools, in terms of per-student recurrent cost.[10] Large differences in per-student cost were also reported in a recent study of Chile (McEwan and Carnoy, 2000).[11] In 1996, per-student cost was estimated to be 430,000–440,000 pesos for two types of government schools; 456,000–493,000 pesos for religious voucher-receiving schools; 393,000 pesos for non-religious, voucher-receiving schools; and 731,000 pesos for private non-voucher schools (the most elitist schools). Thus, some private schools were more expensive and some were less expensive than government schools. Cost differences between government schools and non-religious, voucher-receiving schools (the largest category among private providers) were not very large. In the Dominican Republic,

---

9 Traditional government and traditional private schools are real policy alternatives in urban Thailand, but not in rural areas. Bangkok schools are a unique category of government schools because of the very high cost of land.

10 Private-aided schools are privately managed schools with government funding while private-unaided schools are privately managed schools without government funding.

11 It does not include private contribution and indirect private cost.

Table 7.6 Average Per-Student Costs of Primary Schools in Thailand, 1987 (baht/student/year)

	Government schools				Private schools	Ratio (5)/(4)	Ratio (5)/(3)
	ONPEC schools	Bangkok schools	Municipal schools	All government schools			
	(1)	(2)	(3)	(4)	(5)	(6)	(7)
Recurrent	3,630	2,778	2,208	3,505	1,663	0.47	0.75
Capital	766	8,228	1,156	1,290	899	0.70	0.78
Institutional	4,396	11,006	3,364	4,795	2,562	0.53	0.76
Private resources	1,291	1,700	1,743	1,353	3,568	2.64	2.04
Total	5,540	12,533	5,028	6,003	4,667	0.78	0.93

Notes: Institutional cost is the sum of recurrent and capital costs. Total cost equals institutional cost plus private resources minus school fees and household contributions to school.

Source: Tsang and Taoklam (1992), cited in Tsang (1995)

high-status private schools were found to be more expensive than government schools while low-status private schools were less expensive, in terms of per-student institutional cost (Jimenez, Lockheed, Luna, and Paqueo, 1991).

Third, a number of measurement errors could potentially affect the accuracy of the estimates of institutional cost, resulting in an underestimation of the institutional costs of private schools. To begin, information on some of the institutional costs of private schools either does not exist or is not accessible; this could lead to an imprecise estimate or underestimate. In addition, donated inputs could be either not reported or under-reported, resulting in a significant underestimation of institutional cost. A good example is religious schools for which contributions by the concerned religious organization can be substantial. Such contributions may include instructional services provided "free" by the clergy or at below-market salaries and the use of "free" facilities owned by the religious organization (Levin, 1987). Thus, the reported institutional expenditure by these private schools will not represent the true institutional cost for operating such schools. Moreover, measurement error could arise when school-income data in a given year are used in place of information on costs (resources utilized in the schooling process).[12] In a given year, school income may not be equal to school expenditure;[13] and school income does not include other school costs (e.g., non-fee direct private costs, donations in kind, indirect private costs). An example of the use of school-income data is a study of the cost-effectiveness of public and private secondary schools in Thailand (Jimenez et al., 1988). The researchers were careful in pointing out in the text of the published study that their use of school-income data obviously produced rough cost estimates. The cost-estimation section of the published study was somewhat equivocal about the relative cost of public and private schools, but the conclusion section was unequivocal in stating that private schools were much less costly than government schools.

---

12 This practice could be due to a lack of information on cost. It also takes time and effort to collect good cost data.

13 A private school may decide to have some savings in order to finance a capital project in the future. Expenditure could be larger than income if the school borrows to erect a school building.

Fourth, Table 7.5 shows relative costs based on average costs at a given scale. Relative unit costs may change if there is a large change in the scale of one or more of the two subsectors. The average cost of a large private sector could be quite different from that of a small private sector. For example, the cost of educating students in the private sector may go up when the sector serves more students with "undesirable" attributes, and when free or low-cost instructional services become more scarce (McEwan and Carnoy, 2000). If one is dealing only with relatively small changes in enrollment, the marginal cost should be estimated. More generally, average costs are affected not only by the scale of operation, but also by input prices, and the technology of educational production. Analytically, the change in average cost with scale involves a movement along a given cost curve, other things being equal. A change in technology of education (or the price of an education input) could shift the cost curve up or down, other things being equal. Relative costs of the two sectors would likely change when there are changes in prices and/or technology. Thus the cost analyst has to make an assessment of the relevance of existing cost estimates.

Fifth, information on costs alone is not enough to determine the relative efficiency of public and private schools. Costs must be related to educational effectiveness. Since the latter part of the 1980s, relatively more empirical studies of the cost-effectiveness of public versus private schools have been undertaken in developing countries. This is certainly an encouraging development in educational research on the subject. Methodologically, these studies can be divided into two groups. The first group, the majority in terms of the number of studies, conducted separate analyses of effectiveness and costs with a subsequent comparison of cost-effectiveness (Jimenez et al., 1988; Jimenez et al., 1991; Jimenez and Lockheed, 1995; Kingdon, 1996; Psacharopoulos, 1987; Winkler and Rounds, 1996). The second group, the minority, consists of studies that assess relative efficiency by estimating a cost function that simultaneously uses information on effectiveness and costs (James, King, and Suryadi, 1996; McEwan and Carnoy, 2000). Some of these studies recognized that public and private schools serve student populations with varying ability and selection bias was taken into account in the statistical estimation of an educational production function,[14] and some of these studies did provide cost estimates for more than one type of private schools and/or public schools.[15] Except for a couple of studies, however, these cost-effectiveness studies did not consider private resources to public schools and non-fee private resources to private schools.[16] Thus, they are subject to potential erroneous estimation of the relative efficiency of private schools. Some of these studies estimated recurrent costs and did not even consider capital costs in the estimation of institutional costs.[17] There is an obvious need to strengthen cost estimation in these cost-effectiveness studies.

---

14 See, for example, Jimenez et. al. (1991) and Kingdon (1996). The Heckman technique was used in the statistical estimation to deal with sample selection bias associated with unobserved variables.

15 See, for example, Jimenez et al. (1991), Kingdon (1996), and McEwan and Carnoy (2000).

16 McEwan and Carnoy (2000) and Psacharopoulos (1987) did consider the direct private costs of public schools. Like other studies, these two studies did not include information on non-fee private resources to public and private schools.

17 See, for example, Jimenez et. al. (1991), Kingdon (1996), and the studies on Colombia, Tanzania, the Philippines, and the Dominican Republic reported in Jimenez and Lockheed (1995).

In summary, comparison of institutional costs of public and private schools (1) could lead to a distorted assessment of relative costs and relative efficiency if not accompanied by estimation of private resources; (2) should recognize the cost implications of institutional diversity and identify appropriate counterpart school groups for analysis; (3) is often plagued by a lack of information on private schools, with a potential bias in underestimating the costs of such schools; (4) should be aware that relative costs could change with scale, input prices, and technology of education; and (5) should be strengthened in cost-effectiveness studies.

IMPLICATIONS FOR EDUCATIONAL POLICYMAKING AND FURTHER RESEARCH

This last section examines the relevance of cost comparisons to educational policymaking. As an illustration, it identifies the cost issues to be addressed in assessing the impact of two related education initiatives that have attracted much attention in many of these countries: increased privatizing of schooling, and achieving quality basic education for all. Informed policymaking regarding these two initiatives often involves a comparative cost analysis.

PRIVATIZATION OF SCHOOLING

Consider first increased privatization of schooling. A useful framework for assessing privatization initiatives is to compare the effects of public and private schooling with respect to objectives of increased efficiency, enhanced equity, expanded choice, and promotion of social cohesion (Levin, 2000). In developing countries, privatization could be promoted to achieve one or more of these objectives. A key argument for proponents is that privatization could lead to more efficient utilization of educational resources (Jimenez and Lockheed, 1995). To assess the validity of this claim, questions should be raised about whether costs are taken into account, whether costs are properly estimated, and whether comparison is made of public and private schools that are genuine policy alternatives. Many of the published studies on cost-effectiveness of public versus private schools have a deficiency in cost estimation that is more likely to lead to an underestimation of the costs of private schools relative to public schools. There is a clear need to strengthen the research on costs in these studies. Some analysts point out that schools may not respond to privatization-induced competition by improving education quality and that privatization could lead to greater inequity in education expenditures and performance for students from different income groups (Parry, 1997; Winkler and Rounds, 1996). More empirical evidence is needed to support the claim that privatization will lead to higher overall quality. It is also necessary to carefully analyze the distribution of education costs (and output) by student backgrounds in order to assess the equity impact of privatization. Moreover, whether children from disadvantaged backgrounds have an opportunity to attend good-quality private schools is a matter of concern. Some observers point out that equity could be enhanced by reducing the cost of private education relative to public education for children from poor backgrounds (e.g., through a government voucher) so that they are not trapped in low-quality public schools; others counter that private schools could attract children from the most-motivated families, leaving public schools with the less "desirable" children (McEwan, 2000).

Increased schooling choices for parents could be a positive effect of privatization as private schools may arise to meet parental tastes not addressed in the public sector. In practice, families with more resources have more choices than families with less resources, in both education sectors.[18] There is potential conflict between choice and equity; and each society has to determine the proper balance between these two objectives. One also has to find out whether private schools (especially those receiving some government subsidy) have admission rules that limit parental choice, such as rules regarding children with special needs and children from less desirable backgrounds. Such rules may be used to lower the education cost of these schools. Finally, privatization could have a negative impact if it leads to increased fragmentation in schooling experiences; and cost could be a factor in socio-economic segregation.[19] There is potential conflict between individual choice and social cohesion in a democratic society (Levin, 1983). In general, increased privatization may or may not have an impact on social cohesion. The role of public policy is important in determining this effect.[20] In fact, some analysts argue that the distinction between the two sectors is not as important as the perceived public good of schools in each sector and the rules governing their operation. Public policies could be designed to make public schools more market-oriented and make private schools serve the public interest (Wolff and de Moura Castro, 2001).

ACHIEVING QUALITY
BASIC EDUCATION FOR ALL

Expanded access, enhanced equity, and increased efficiency are important objectives in developing countries' effort to provide basic education to all (Inter-Agency for Basic Education for All, 1990). The government faces particular challenge in providing quality basic education to marginalized populations;[21] and private schools might be an alternative to public schools in meeting this challenge. Cost analysis is relevant to informing the government's effort to achieve universal basic education. First, proper cost estimation of alternative programs and assessment of financial feasibility are necessary tasks in devising a realistic education plan. Particular attention has to be paid to the costing of programs for marginalized populations, as the unit costs of schooling at given quality for these populations can be quite different from those for non-marginalized groups (Tsang, 1994). Analysis may be undertaken to determine if private schools could be a viable alternative to government schools for

---

18 Resources can be financial and political. Wealthy families can choose to send their children to a high-tuition private school. Families with good connections may be able to place their children in a high-quality public school.

19 Obviously, in many developing countries, cost is already a factor in socio-economic segregation in the public sector. The issue is whether privatization will lead to more fragmentation and segregation.

20 Some countries have strict government regulations for private schooling, for example, with respect to the school curriculum, teacher qualification, and tuition level.

21 They often refer to populations from poor and rural backgrounds, oppressed minority groups, as well as females in some countries.

serving these groups.[22] Past failure in the implementation of basic-education programs in some of these countries has resulted from either incompetent analysis or neglect.

Second, in many developing countries, the government tries to expand access to quality basic education by requiring more cost-sharing by families and by encouraging more private contributions. The expansion of private schooling can be partly explained by the need to address excess demand for schooling because of limited capacity in public schools or low-quality of some public schools (James, 1995). And private schooling could be an effective strategy to induce additional private spending on education.[23] Private contributions to public schools could augment public spending on public schools and could be used to improve quality. To the extent that private resources are relatively more plentiful for schools that serve higher-income families, there is a potential conflict between access and equity. This conflict could be mitigated if increased private financing is combined with a government policy to increase the priority of government spending on poor communities and to strengthen basic-education programs targeted at disadvantaged groups (Verspoor and Tsang, 1993).

Third, proper costing is highly relevant in a society's decision on whether or not to make basic education truly compulsory, for both children and government officials. If basic education is made a legally binding right of all citizens (UNICEF, 1993), the government should be compelled to confront the full cost of the attainment of such a right for all within a certain time frame. If basic education is simply regarded as part of an overall strategy for development with profitable return, the government will be wise to promote the development of basic education but it will not be subject to a legal requirement. The first position is more likely to benefit marginalized population groups and enhance equity. Fourth, information on costs is needed to assess the cost-effectiveness of public and private initiatives for delivering basic education programs. Like the privatization initiative, proper estimation and comparison of costs are essential. But the attention should be focused on the relative efficiency of the two types of schools with respect to marginalized populations.

Given increased attention across countries to accountability and efficiency in resource utilization in education, unmet demand for quality education, parental choice in schooling, as well as substantial inequity in education, proper comparison of the costs of public and private schools should remain a focus of educational-policy analysis. The need for further and better research is obvious. Research on the costs of public versus private schools faces both technical and non-technical barriers in these countries. Technical barriers may include a lack of cost data, a lack of expertise, and a lack of awareness among education decision-makers of the usefulness of cost analysis. Non-technical barriers could be derived from ideological and political considerations. Some decision-makers and analysts may have a pre-conceived view of public

---

22 In some countries, private schools charge high tuition fees and they are found mostly in urban areas (Tsang, in press). In some other countries, however, the government continues to provide funding for schools in rural areas but it allows community organizations to manage the school (Cuellar, 2001). Government policy has a strong influence on the role to be played by private schools.

23 In some countries, the government has invited private bodies to manage schools that are funded by the government (James et al., 1996). The purpose is increased efficiency instead of additional resource mobilization.

versus private schooling. Some may want to keep the discussion of desired educational goals at a rhetorical level and not want to confront the full costs of education programs to achieve these goals. Thus, they are not interested in proper cost estimation and comparison. Cost analysis may even be manipulated to provide supporting evidence for some pre-conceived policy options or to minimize undesirable results. Findings on the relative costs of public versus private schools will likely remain contentious.

REFERENCES

Belfield, C. (2001). *Political preference and the privatization of education: Evidence for UK* (Occasional Paper No. 18). New York: National Center for the Study of Privatization in Education, Teachers College, Columbia University.

Borromeo, R. (1995). *Cost-effectiveness of education in the Philippines: Comparative analysis of public and private school programs.* Manila, Philippines: Fund for Assistance to Private Education.

Bray, M. (1996). *Counting the full cost: Parental and community financing of education in East Asia.* Washington, DC: The World Bank.

Bray, M. (1999). *The private costs of public schooling: Household and community financing of primary education in Cambodia.* UNICEF.

Bray, M. and Lillis, K. (Eds.) (1988). *Community financing of education: Issues and policy implications in less developed countries.* Oxford: Pergamon Press.

Coleman, J., Hoffer, T., and Kilgore, S. (1982). *High school achievement: Public, Catholic, and private schools compared.* New York: Basic Books.

Cuellar, H. M. (2001). *Decentralization and privatization of education in El Salvador: Assessing the experience.* Paper presented at the Comparative and International Education Conference, Washington, DC.

Evans, K., and Rorris, A. (1994). *Cost effectiveness of primary education in Myanmar.* Yangon: UNICEF.

Indonesia, Government of. (1992). *SUSENAS survey.* Jakarta, Indonesia: Author.

Inter-Agency for Basic Education for All. (1990). *Meeting basic human needs: A background report for the World Conference on Basic Education for All.* New York: Inter-Agency Commission, United Nations.

James, E. (1995). Public-private division of responsibility for education. In M. Carnoy (Ed.), *International encyclopedia of economics of education* (2nd ed., pp. 450-455). Pergamon Press.

James, E., King, E., and Suryadi, A. (1996). Finance, management, and costs of public and private schools in Indonesia. *Economics of Education Review, 15*(4), 387-398.

Jimenez, E., and Lockheed, M. (1995). *Public and private secondary education in developing countries: A comparative study.* Washington, DC: World Bank.

Jimenez, E., Lockheed, M., Luna, E., and Paqueo, V. (1991). School effects and costs for private and public schools in the Dominican Republic. *International Journal of Educational Research, 15*(5), 393-410.

Jimenez, E., Lockheed, M., and Wattanawaha, N. (1988). The relative efficiency of public and private schools: The case of Thailand. *The World Bank Economic Review, 2*(2), 139-164.

Jimenez, E., and Tan, J. (1987). Decentralized and private education: The case of Pakistan. *Comparative Education, 23*(2), 173-190.

Kansal, S. (1990). Disparity in income and levels of living among teachers in Delhi. *Economic and Political Weekly, 25,* 2547-2554.

King, E. (1994). *Who pays for education in Indonesia? The role of government and families.* Paper presented for the workshop on New Strategies for Financing Education and Health in Developing Countries, University of Sussex, Institute of Development Studies.

Kingdon, G. (1996). The quality and efficiency of private and public education: A case-study of urban India. *Oxford Bulletin of Economics and Statistics, 58*(1), 57-81.

Knight, J., and Sabot, R. (1990). *Education, productivity, and inequality: The East African natural experiment.* Oxford University Press.

Levin, H. M. (1983). Educational choice and the pains of democracy. In T. James and H. M. Levin (Eds.), *Public dollars for private schools: The case of tuition tax credits* (pp. 17-38). Philadelphia, PA: Temple University Press.

Levin, H. M. (1987). Education as a public and private good. *Journal of Policy Analysis and Management, 6*(4), 628-641.

Levin, H. M. (2000). *A comprehensive framework for evaluating educational vouchers* (Occasional Paper No. 5). New York: National Center for the Study of Privatization in Education, Teachers College, Columbia University.

Levin, H. M., and McEwan, P. J. (2001). *Cost-effectiveness analysis: Methods and applications* (2nd ed.). Thousand Oaks, CA: Sage.

McEwan, P. J. (1999). Private costs and the rate of return to primary education. *Applied Economics Letters, 6,* 759-760.

McEwan, P. J. (2000). The potential impact of large-scale voucher programs. *Review of Educational Research, 70*(2), 103-149.

McEwan, P. J. (2001). *The relative effectiveness of private and public schooling in Argentina and Chile.* Paper presented at the Comparative and International Education Conference, Washington, DC.

McEwan, P. J., and Carnoy, M. (2000). The effectiveness and efficiency of private schools in Chile's voucher system. *Educational Evaluation and Policy Analysis, 22*(3), 213-239.

Myers, C., and Chalongphob, S. (1992). Education and economic development: Issues and options for policy and reform. In *Educational options for the future of Thailand: The 1991 year-end conference.* Bangkok, Thailand: Thailand Development Research Institute.

Parry, T. (1997). Decentralization and privatization: Education policy in Chile. *Journal of Public Policy, 17*(1), 107-133.

Peterson, P., Myers, D., Howell, W., and Mayer, D. (1999). The effects of school choice in New York City. In S. Mayer and P. Peterson (Eds.), *Earning and learning: How schools matter* (pp. 317-339). Washington, DC: Brookings Institution Press and Russell Sage Foundation.

Psacharopoulos, G. (1987). Public versus private schools in developing countries: Evidence from Colombia and Tanzania. *International Journal of Educational Development, 7*(1), 59-67.

Rangazas, P. (1997). Competition and private school vouchers. *Education Economics,* 5(3), 245-263.

Schiefelbein, E. (1986). *Education costs and financing of policies in Latin America: A review of available research.* Washington, DC: World Bank.

Schwartz, A. (1995). *The Philippines: Cost and financing issues in education.* Washington, DC: World Bank.

Tilak, J. (1985). *Analysis of the costs of education in India* (Occasional Paper No. 10). New Delhi, India: National Institute of Educational Planning and Administration.

Tsang, M. (1988). Cost analysis for educational policymaking: A review of cost studies in education in developing countries. *Review of Educational Research, 58*(2), 181-230.

Tsang, M. (1994). Costs of education in China: Issues of resource mobilization, equality, equity, and efficiency. *Education Economics, 2*(3), 287-312.

Tsang, M. (1994). *Cost analysis of educational inclusion of marginalized population.* Paris: IIEP, UNESCO.

Tsang, M. (1995a). Public and private costs of schooling in developing countries. In M. Carnoy (Ed.), *International encyclopedia of economics of education* (pp. 393-398). Pergamon Press.

Tsang, M. (1995b). *Household expenditure on education in Bangladesh and China.* Paper presented at the American Educational Research Association Conference, San Francisco, CA.

Tsang, M. (1996). *Household expenditure on education in China.* Presentation made at the Western Regional Conference of Comparative and International Education Society, Honolulu.

Tsang, M. (1997a). Cost analysis for improved policymaking in education. *Educational Evaluation and Policy Analysis, 19*(4), 18-24.

Tsang, M. (1997b). *The financing of education in Guyana: Issues and strategies* (Economic and Sector Studies Series No. RE3-97-001). Washington, DC: Inter-American Development Bank.

Tsang, M. (2000). The economic burden of compulsory schooling on families in poor areas in China. In M. Tsang, X. Wei, and J. Xiao (Eds.), *Economic analysis of education policy* (pp. 1-20). Beijing, China: Education Science Press.

Tsang, M. (in press). School choice in the People's Republic of China. In D. Plank and G. Sykes (Eds.), *School choice and school reform: The experience of eight countries.* New York: Teachers College Press.

Tsang, M., Fryer, M., and Arevalos, G. (in press). *Education in the Caribbean region: Policy issues and financing strategies.* Washington, DC: Inter-American Development Bank.

Tsang, M., and Kidchanapansich, S. (1992). Private resources and the quality of primary education in Thailand. *International Journal of Educational Research, 17*(2), 179-198.

Tsang, M., and Taoklam, W. (1992). Comparing the costs of public and private primary education in Thailand. *International Journal of Educational Development, 12*(3), 177-190.

Tsang, M., Zaki, M., and Ghafoor, A. (1990). *Household educational expenditures in Pakistan.* East Lansing, MI: College of Education, Michigan State University.

UNICEF. (1993). *Convention on the rights of children.* New York.

Verspoor, A., and Tsang, M. (Eds.). (1993). *Case studies in financing quality basic education.* Washington, DC: Education and Social Policy Department, World Bank.

Wei, X., and Qiu, L. (2000). Household income and rate of economic burden of household educational expenditure in urban China. In M. Tsang, X. Wei, and J. Xiao (Eds.), *Economic analysis of education policy* (pp. 21-39). Beijing, China: Education Science Press.

West, L. (1995). Provision of public services in rural PRC. In C. Wong (Ed.), *Financing local government in the People's Republic of China* (TA 2118-PRC). Manila, Philippines: Asian Development Bank.

Willms, D. (1983). Do private schools produce higher levels of academic achievement? New evidence for the tuition tax credit debate. In T. James, and H. M. Levin (Eds.), *Public dollars for private schools: The case of tuition tax credits.* Philadelphia, PA: Temple University Press.

Winkler, D. R., and Rounds, T. (1996). Municipal and private sector response to decentralization and school choice. *Economics of Education Review, 15*(4), 365-376.

Wolff, L. (1985). *Controlling the costs of education in Eastern Africa: A review of data, issues, and policies* (Staff Working Paper No. 702). Washington, DC: The World Bank.

Wolff, L., and de Moura Castro, C. (2001). *Public or private education for Latin America: That is the (false) question.* Washington, DC: Inter-American Development Bank.

World Bank. (1992). *Nepal: Critical issues in secondary education.* Washington, DC: Author.

World Bank. (1995). *Vietnam: Poverty assessment and strategy.* Washington, DC: East Asia and Pacific Regional Office, World Bank.

World Bank. (1996). *Mongolia: Poverty in a transition economy.* Washington, DC: Author.

World Bank. (1997). *Vietnam: Education financing.* Washington, DC: Author.

World Bank. (1999). *Strategic goals for Chinese education in the 21st century* (Report No. 18969-CHA). Washington, DC: Author.

Wu, K. (1995). *Trinidad and Tobago: Education sector financing study.* Washington, DC: World Bank.

NEW EMPIRICAL EVIDENCE

8

HOW COST-EFFECTIVE ARE LECTURES? A REVIEW OF THE EXPERIMENTAL LITERATURE

Celia Brown and Clive Belfield*

INTRODUCTION

As a method of evaluation, cost-effectiveness analysis is relatively simple in its principles, with a thorough presentation given by Levin and McEwan (2001). However, these simple principles belie the complexity of cost-effectiveness analysis in practice. Perhaps these complexities explain the dearth of proper cost-effectiveness studies, a dearth identified by Levin (2001) and emphasized in Chapters 2, 3, and 4 of this book.[1] Indeed, these contributions offer a comprehensive overview of the extant literature; and—inevitably—they respond with calls for more high-quality research. Although this call is understandable, it is made repeatedly (see Levin, 1988).

But there is an alternative response, the one adopted here. This response is to make use of the extant evidence on effectiveness, augmented with cost estimates. This

* The authors appreciate the comments of Patrick McEwan on earlier drafts on this paper.

1 Rightly, Schiefelbein et al. (1999, p. 53) comment on how "current knowledge about cost-effectiveness in education is extraordinarily inadequate." If possible, this may be an understatement. Cost-effectiveness seems to be willfully overlooked in evaluations: there is no cost-effectiveness analysis of important educational programs such as 'Success for All' (see Slavin, Madden, Dolan, and Wasik, 1996). And much economic analysis is either methodologically problematic (see Barber and Thompson, 1998; Udharvelyi, Colditz, Rai, and Epstein, 1992) or insufficiently lucid (e.g., conflating cost-effectiveness with cost-benefit analysis, as in Van der Drift, 1980). The difficulty of drawing inferences simply from cost analysis is illustrated by a review of the cost-effectiveness analysis of non-completion for further education in the UK: Fielding, Belfield, and Thomas (1998) find that, under further scrutiny, the conclusions from a simple cost analysis undertaken by the Audit Commission and Office for Standards in Education (1993) require substantial modification. In particular, cost analysis that fails to adjust for actual student attendance can give misleading results.

approach is efficient, because the extant research on effectiveness is sizable. (For example, Russell, 1999, reviews over 90 trials on the educational impact of information technology, as against other educational modes.) It also allows for generalizations as to what educational practices are cost-effective. Most importantly, it would allow for a reasonably rapid development of the cost-effectiveness literature. The ideal approach would be for cost analysis to proceed simultaneously with effectiveness analysis and for the former to be incorporated into the research design *ab initio*. But this is clearly not happening at the present time; thus a synthetic approach appears much more appealing, at least to offer approximate answers to pressing resource-use questions.

Specifically, in this paper we undertake a cost-effectiveness review of the lecture mode of (higher) education. We compare this mode with four other modes, measuring their effectiveness by how well each mode imparts information to students, relative to lectures. Lectures are the main mode of instruction in most universities, and therefore a prime candidate for cost-effectiveness analysis. But a literature review establishes—as anticipated—scant economic research on their efficiency (see Bacdayan, 1997; Zietz and Cochran, 1997; on computer-aided instruction, see Lewis, Dalgaard, and Boyer, 1985; Levin, Glass, and Meister, 1987). Confining our analysis to specific experimental research, the cost-effectiveness evidence base is not adequate as it stands: practically no experiments either report or analyze costs. However, it may be possible to assess cost-effectiveness if costs are imputed across the evidence on effectiveness. This is the main aim of our paper, reviewing the evidence to offer an economic evaluation of lectures as a mode of education.

Our cost-effectiveness review is structured as follows. In Section 2, we report our research method for analyzing the evidence on the effectiveness of lectures and for imputing costs. This necessitates a robust method of imputation and the construction of a costing template. In Section 3, we present the results of the review, estimating the relative cost-effectiveness of lectures compared to other modes of instruction. In Section 4, we subject these estimates to a sensitivity analysis as a check for robustness. In Section 5, we discuss the results, with three objectives: (1) to see what stylized facts can be drawn about the cost-effectiveness of lectures; (2) to evaluate the usefulness of such an evidence base for management and organization of provision; and (3) to explore the methodological requirements for cost-effectiveness reviews. Thus, our discussions relate to both points adverted to above: they serve to emphasize— as do the other authors in this volume—the necessity of cost-effectiveness analysis, and they illustrate how effectiveness data can be re-used—practically and efficiently—with imputation about costs.

Research Method for Cost-Effectiveness Analysis

Research Question and Protocol

The question at issue is the relative cost-effectiveness at imparting information of lectures as compared to alternative modes of education. The other four modes are: personalized instruction, discussion modes, independent study, and "other modes." We apply cost-effectiveness analysis to the extant evidence on effectiveness. The research method for this review follows several discrete stages, as set out in the following protocol.

The first stage of our review is to specify the sample selection strategy. The evidence base for answering the research question is taken from Bligh (2000). Bligh selected research which was experimental, in that it compared lecture-based groups to other forms of education, with randomization or purposive allocation of students to each group. Using experimental evidence has two advantages for assessing cost-effectiveness.[2] First, the differences in cost can be isolated to the actual program (rather than to differences in resource investment by students). Second, it makes the cost analysis easier: all that is required are net cost differences between the lecture-based group and the alternative treatment group. Bligh's selection includes 298 papers from published and unpublished evaluations of lectures as a mode of education. The treatment groups can be classified into four modes: (1) personalized systems of instruction, (2) discussion/enquiry modes, (3) independent study, and (4) other modes. We use these modes for comparison against lectures.[3]

The second stage of the review is to evaluate each study, with an explicit statement of the quality and methods of research that merit inclusion in our sample. Bligh's criteria allow use of all the studies that satisfy the initial sample selection strategy, with no compelling grounds for excluding any particular study for its poor quality.

However, for our purposes, it must be possible (a) for the interventions to be grouped and to be comparable under review; (b) for costs imputation to be undertaken; and (c) for effectiveness to be expressed in a standard metric.

On the issue of comparability of interventions and cost-effectiveness meta-analysis, Levin (1988) raises both general and specific concerns. The general concern is that the two approaches—cost-effectiveness analysis and meta-analysis—were developed to address different purposes. Nonetheless, meta-analysis has proved to be highly adaptable for other contexts (e.g., in health research) and for integration with analogous methods of research synthesis (see Cooper and Hedges, 1994). Essentially, meta-analysis requires that the units really are comparable, and this requirement should be assessed pragmatically. The specific concern is that meta-analysis often generalizes from averages (e.g., average effect sizes), and yet these averages do not refer to an actual program that can be costed. In the research review

---

2   Experimental evidence has several methodological advantages in identifying effectiveness. Trials allow for control of variables that may strongly influence educational achievement and attainment, such as family background, peer effects and parental interest (see Altonji and Dunn, 1996; Feinstein and Symons, 1999). For training programs, Bassi (1984) finds non-random selection of participants generates numerous difficulties for estimating effects. It is also possible that the assessment method in a trial will be uniform across the two modes. In actual education systems, there may be some variation in the assessments applied across providers (for a discussion, see Brasington, 1999). Enrollment may also be strategic: some enrollees may have dips in earnings which serve to allocate or direct them into training programs for example (Heckman and Smith, 1999). Therefore, using trials should satisfy Levin's (1988, p. 57) assertion that *"cost-effectiveness analyses should consider the quality and appropriateness of the effectiveness evaluations on which they are based"* (emphasis in the original).

3   More specific details on these modes is available; e.g., if the instruction included demonstrations, individualized instruction, mastery learning or computer-aided instruction. So the modes could be sub-categorized. However, four categories are manageable for analysis and yield reasonable sample sizes. A list of the specific interventions is available from the authors.

conducted here, each individual research study is analyzed. Although our exposition is in terms of four modes of education, the best individual trials are also identified. This approach should then avoid the problems of "fallacious aggregation" across non-comparable studies.

To undertake cost imputation, sufficient information should be available on the resource use for each trial. Preliminary investigation of the education literature indicates that such information is rarely adequate (for education for health professionals, see Brown, Belfield, and Field, 2001). We therefore constructed a simple template against which to estimate the additional costs of the experimental arm. This template, discussed further below, allows imputation of costs that are standardized across each trial.

Regarding effectiveness and the need for standardization, the measures were standardized into a Cohen-effect size of the alternative mode compared to lectures (Cooper and Hedges, 1994). In most cases, these effect sizes also had to be calculated independently by the authors (sometimes based on p values). From the point estimates (and confidence intervals) of the effect size estimates, a simple trichotomy of more, less, or equally effective can also be derived.

The third stage of the review involves the synthesizing of results from the collection of evidence. Two approaches are used. The first approach involves two steps. We identify the cost-effectiveness of lectures as against the other modes of education across four quadrants of a matrix: lectures can either be relatively more or less effective and relatively more or less costly than the alternative mode. Each experiment will therefore fall into one of the four costs-by-effects quadrants. Then, we draw inferences based on the frequencies in each of the four cells via a simple vote count: the numbers in each cell reflect the relative cost-effectiveness of lectures. The second approach is to use the effect sizes and net incremental costs across each trial. This approach allows cost-effectiveness to be estimated numerically and more precisely.

An alternative representation of cost-effectiveness is to map interventions figuratively. The basic ideas are represented in Figure 8.1. There, cost-effective and cost-ineffective quadrants are identified, along with a fitted diagonal line that divides the set of interventions into those where cost-effectiveness is either increasing or decreasing.

Cost Template

We use a template to estimate costs. Necessarily, for an approach which links imputed cost data to existing effectiveness data to be meaningful, the derivation of the cost data must be rigorous. As part of the research protocol, we therefore describe our estimation of costs in detail here.

To impute costs, a template was derived, breaking the cost items into components or ingredients, as per Levin and McEwan (2001).[4] Costs are divided into four ingredients. One cost is the time of provider staff, which includes instructional time, but also time for material preparation, for induction, and for assessment. Two other

---

4   In many cases educational effectiveness researchers use classification systems to explain their interventions which do not have a ready interpretation in terms of resource use (see for example Freudenstein and Howe, 1999; Davis et al., 1999). Findings are therefore not always reported in a way that allows for ready translation into the ingredients approach.

FIGURE 8.1 COST-EFFECTIVENESS PROPORTIONS

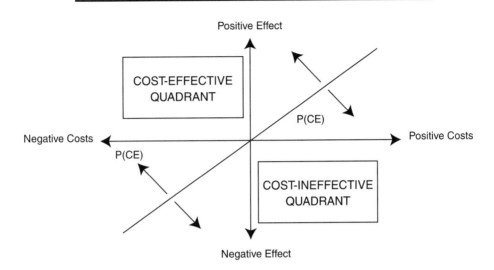

costs are the "software" physical inputs (e.g., learning materials) and the "hardware" physical inputs (e.g., premises and overheads). The final cost ingredient is student effort, to include assembly of learning materials, contribution to the class and outside of class, and psychic engagement in learning. Our approach is to consider an aggregate cost-effectiveness measure, including all costs regardless of who incurred them. Clearly, the cost-effectiveness of particular modes will differ if a provider perspective is adopted: shifting costs from instruction to discussion groups, for example, will lower costs to the provider and raise costs to the student (in terms of preparation and effort in class). This sophistication cannot be incorporated here.

For each intervention, the resources necessary were estimated relative to the lecture mode; this estimate was based on the authors' reading of each study.[5] Across particular ingredients, this change could be positive or negative: moving from lectures to independent study, for example, typically reduces provider staff time but increases student effort. These changes to ingredients are expressed in standard units, and prices are attached to these units. An additional hour of staff time, for example, is priced using the appropriate salary scale. This amount is estimated at $220 per instructional hour (and so reflects the hours of preparation and assessment before and after each instructional hour). For the "software" physical inputs, a figure of $44 per hour was estimated. For the "hardware" physical inputs, an amount of $56 per hour was used. Costs are per participant, measured in year 2000 dollars, and were also adjusted for the duration of each course. For students, a wage and materials cost

---

5 This task is simplified by the close comparability across the modes; many ingredients are the same in either the lecture or the comparison mode. Some resource requirements do differ but many of the trials are specifically set up so that only the mode of instruction is different (e.g., the premises are the same for both modes).

estimate of $12 per hour is used as the opportunity cost.[6] (Rather than deflate the costs to the actual date of each intervention, we assume each intervention was to be implemented at current prices, so as to yield a standard cost metric.)

In general, this imputation method may be sensitive to two factors. One is that the unit changes in resources required are mis-measured; the other is that the prices of the inputs are inaccurate. Typically, the former arises because the studies do not fully describe what materials are used in the intervention; and the latter arises because actual costs were not reported. This sensitivity is addressed in subsequent analysis.

In order to assist the accuracy of imputing costs, a set of stylized facts about the cost function for education programs was applied. Across lectures and the treatment groups, the distribution of provider costs was held to closely approximate that for generic education programs: two-thirds of costs being for teaching staff; one-tenth involving curriculum materials and other forms of support; and the remainder on physical premises, etc. This dis-aggregation is reasonably robust for the standard lecture-based mode (Koshal and Koshal, 1995, 1999a). Generally, treatment modes that increase the amount of human resource are likely to be particularly costly.[7] For the treatment modes, it was conjectured that: (a) personalized systems of instruction require more resources for instruction/staffing and for planning; (b) discussion/ enquiry modes require more study effort than lectures; and (c) independent study requires less instruction and more study by the enrollees.

RESULTS

THE COST-EFFECTIVENESS EVIDENCE BASE

From the papers reported by Bligh (2000), the final sample of sufficient quality is 54 lecture-comparison interventions across 38 papers. The sample of 54 treatment modes breaks down across the four modes as follows: four, personalized system of instruction; 15, other modes; 17, independent study; and 18, discussion modes. The interventions are relatively small-scale: the mean (standard deviation) number of students in the experimental group is 47 (44); and the mean (standard deviation) number of instructional hours per intervention is 13 (10).

Research was rejected from our sample for a number of reasons. For 63 papers, these modes were essentially no different from the lecture mode; e.g., because of a

---

6 Full salary costs per instructional hour are derived from Ragan, Warren, and Bratsberg (1999), with an assumption of 100 instructional hours per year. The "software" and "hardware" costs were estimated as proportions of these salary costs, based on a review of cost function studies (Koshal and Koshal, 1999b). The earnings opportunity costs for students are derived from high-school earnings from the National Longitudinal Survey of Youth reported in Light (1999), with supplemental materials costs added. All figures are transformed into 2000 dollars. All costs are subject to sensitivity analysis, as reported below.

7 Inouye, Miller, and Fletcher (1997) compare the costs of five important U.S. elementaryschool programs to improve reading: the variation in their costs reflects the differing intensity of the programs in terms of resources for instructors. Waterford and DISTAR were relatively intensive in terms of hardware investments; Writing to Read was moderately labor-intensive in its use of para-professionals; and Success for All and Reading Recovery—the high-cost programs—were highly labor intensive.

cross-over design in instruction whereby students received each mode but at different time periods. For 92 papers, the relevant paper could not be traced by the authors (the main reason being that the publication was not in a peer-reviewed journal or was in a discontinued publication). For 89 papers, the relevant paper was unpublished and the only printed evidence was a citation abstract of one paragraph. For 16 papers, either the outcome was not a learning outcome, or there was no actual lecture delivery, or it was not possible to calculate effect size. Of these reasons, the main concern is publication bias against the untraceable (92) or unpublished papers (89). We consider this bias below.

The Effectiveness of Lectures

We begin with an assessment of the relative effectiveness of lectures, across the 298 trials reported by Bligh (2000). Over half of the studies (52 percent) show no significant difference in effectiveness between lectures and the alternative modes; the lecture mode is more effective in over one quarter (27 percent) of the studies, and less effective in one-fifth (21 percent). These 298 trials can be split by mode. Based on 45 trials, lecture delivery appears to be clearly more effective than modes using personalized systems of instruction (as 44 percent of trials show lectures to be more effective). From 109 trials, lecture delivery appears similarly effective to discussion and inquiry modes (19 percent favor the former mode, but 23 percent favor the latter, and 58 percent are inconclusive). Similarly, 40 trials show lectures and independent study appear equivalent in effectiveness (with 25 percent favoring lectures, and 23 percent against). Finally, from 104 trials, lecture delivery appears more effective than "other" modes: 26 percent (19 percent) of trials show lectures to be more (less) effective. This much can be inferred from effectiveness analysis applied at a very broad level of generality (see Bligh, 2000 for a more thorough exposition). However, this discussion of effectiveness is preliminary to a full economic evaluation.

More detailed analysis of effectiveness is reported in Table 8.1. This is based on direct inquiry into each paper, but only using the available sample of interventions. These show the mean effect size across the four modes, and we use a fixed effects weighting to adjust for the quality of each study.[8] Three modes—independent study, personalized systems and discussion modes—are less effective than lectures; only the other mode has a positive effect size. None of these modes appears to be an improvement on lectures, using tests of statistical significance. Pooling the sample, lectures appear to be relatively effective, with a net mean effect size from using an alternative mode at -0.1563. However, measured per instructional hour, the net mean effect size is -0.0002 (i.e., the lecture mode involves more hours of instruction).

Costs of Interventions

Relative incremental costs per participant are reported in Table 8.2. The range of cost differences is -$2308 to +$3366, with a mean (standard deviation) cost difference of $52.38 ($1137.66) across all modes. On average, two of the modes are less costly than lectures—independent study and discussion—and two of the modes are more

---

8 This is based on the variance of the effect size (Shadish and Haddock, 1994).

Table 8.1 Weighted Effect Size Relative to Lectures For Imparting Information

	Weighted Effect Size Relative to Lectures		
	Mean	Standard deviation	N
Treatment mode			
Other modes	0.0970	0.0653	15
Independent study	−0.0379	0.0445	17
Discussion and enquiry modes	−0.0382	0.0504	18
Personalized systems of instruction	−0.8736	0.0658	4
All treatment modes			
Mean effect size	−0.1563	0.0271	54
Effect size per-hour	−0.0002	$3.8*10^{-5}$	54

Table 8.2: Per Participant Incremental Costs Relative to Lecture Provision

	Per participant Incremental Costs Relative to Lecture Provision		
	Mean	Standard deviation	N
Treatment mode			
Other modes	1127.69	1768.36	15
Independent study	−411.57	968.43	17
Discussion and enquiry modes	−387.74	702.06	18
Personalized systems of instruction	2449.51	658.02	4
All treatment modes			
Total	52.38	1137.66	54

costly—personalized systems and other modes (although the last of these has a large standard deviation).

Most interventions involved substituting one input for another, with changes to the input mix rather than investing more resources into a particular mode. Of the 54 interventions, 33 involved changes to the staffing mix of delivery; 38 to the materials; 40 to student effort; and 11 to the physical inputs to education. However, also of importance is the duration of the intervention. Duration has a clear influence on costs: 10 of the interventions were one hour (or less), but 30 of the interventions were the length of a higher-education module/semester.

COST-EFFECTIVENESS OF LECTURES

We now link the effectiveness and cost information together. As a simple exposition, we look at the proportion of interventions in each mode that may either be clearly accepted as cost-effective or clearly rejected as not cost-effective relative to lectures. Modes that are unambiguously cost-effective are ones where the costs are lower, but the point estimate of effectiveness is higher. Modes that are definitely not cost-effective are ones where the costs are higher, but effectiveness is lower.

These categorical statements can be applied to our sample of interventions. Of the 18 discussion mode papers, 5 would be immediately rejected as not cost-effective and 3 would be clearly accepted as cost-effective. Of the 4 personalized system papers, 2 would be rejected and none would be accepted. Of the 17 independent study papers, 4 would be rejected and 6 accepted. Finally, for the 15 other modes, 9 would be rejected and only 2 accepted as more cost-effective.

On this cost-effectiveness vote count, only independent study emerges as more likely to be a cost-effective mode relative to lectures. Discussion modes and the personalized system appear less cost-effective than lectures. Lastly, the other mode appears to be the least cost-effective.

In the aggregate, 37 percent of interventions would be rejected as clearly not cost-effective and only 20 percent are clearly cost-effective. For the remainder—almost half of the interventions—a financing constraint should be applied to justify any extra investment: these interventions are more effective, but also more costly.

A graphical representation of our results is given in Figure 8.2, plotting each intervention against the lecture mode in terms of relative costs and relative effects. One approach to measuring cost-effectiveness is to look at the distribution of interventions in each of the four quadrants. The top left quadrant identifies the most cost-effective modes and the bottom right quadrant the least cost-effective. This method is analogous to our simple tabulation of cost-effectiveness. However, it also indicates modes where there are large gains for only a small increase in costs. Three

FIGURE 8.2 COST-EFFECTIVENESS RELATIVE TO LECTURES BY MODE

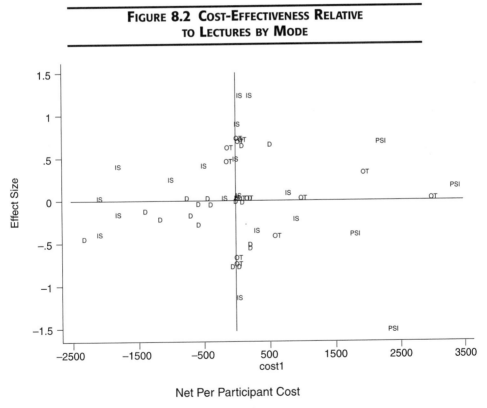

Net Per Participant Cost

NOTES: IS (Independent Study); D (Discussion/enquiry mode); PSI (Personalized System of Instruction); and OT (Other). Costs are in 2000 dollars.

of the independent study interventions, for example, show particularly large effect sizes, for zero or trivial changes to costs. Such interventions are likely to be highly cost-effective.

Overall, Figure 8.2 shows that there does appear to be a cost-effectiveness trade off: where alternative modes to lectures are more effective, they are also more costly. Given that many interventions did not involve substantially greater resource investment, it may in fact be legitimate to use effectiveness analysis—critically, though, this legitimacy must be established (and the variance of costs is high).

A third approach would be to use cost-effectiveness ratios. These ratios must be defined precisely, because the interpretation depends on how the ratio is calculated. One approach is to use an incremental cost-effectiveness ratio, derived as the ratio of per-participant net costs over the effect size. This is the measure used by Gomel et al. (1998). However, this ratio would have to be adjusted to compensate for the fact that both costs and effect sizes can be either negative or positive. Thus, a negative ratio could arise because costs are lower but effect size positive (this would be cost-effective) or because costs are higher and effect size lower (this would be cost-ineffective). Also, because many interventions have zero effect size, this incremental cost-effectiveness ratio is not always determined.

However, cost-effectiveness rankings can be derived from Figure 8.2. Any of the interventions in the top-left quadrant should be implemented over lectures: all cost less than lectures and yet are more effective. None of the interventions in the-bottom-right quadrant should be implemented. For the more cost-effective trials, a cost-effectiveness ratio can be derived as costs over the effect size. This ratio gives a measure of the resource impact from generating a unit effect size.

There are six trials that use independent study modes that are clearly cost-effective. Two of these are more cost-effective because they are lower cost but have an effect size of zero. For the other four studies, the resource savings are $4578, $1784, $1266, and $28. There are two trials that use the other mode, and these generate a resource saving of $262 and $191. For the discussion mode, cost-effectiveness is only generated because the costs are lower, but the effect size is zero. For personalized instruction, there are no clearly cost-effective studies. Thus, three independent study trials generate the best cost-effectiveness ratio scores; and these are followed by two other modes; and then the "remaining" independent study trial.

SENSITIVITY ANALYSIS

VALIDITY CHECKS

The purpose of the review has been to seek general statements about the relative cost-effectiveness of the lecture mode over alternative modes. However, we recognize that a review of this form may be sensitive to the way the data are combined.[9] Our check addresses the internal validity of the evidence base on the cost-effectiveness of

---

9 Another consideration is to restrict the sample to recent interventions. Some of the studies are over 30 years old and may be rejected as being out-of-date for the purposes of cost-effectiveness analysis. One may question whether or not the causal links still obtain—lectures are now much more interactive or visually stimulating than the basic "chalk and talk" mode which prevailed at the time some studies were conducted. Of

lectures: specifically, we have identified potential sources of bias or measurement error from publication and from imputation of resource costs.[10]

PUBLICATION BIAS

One approach to addressing publication bias is to consider the inclusion criteria for analysis. There are three main concerns over the inclusion criteria. First, some of the studies are not available to us and this may generate publication bias. As a simple test, we plot the effect sizes against sample size to identify if they are distributed in a funnel shape (Cooper and Hedges, 1994). This plot in Figure 8.3 is reasonably comforting: the spread of effect sizes (positive and negative) increases as the sample size decreases and there is no obviously missing "chunk" of interventions from the bottom left-hand corner of the plot, as typically occurs with publication bias (Shadish and Haddcock, 1994).

An alternative investigation of publication bias is to compare the effectiveness of our sample with Bligh's population of 398 studies, as described above. Bligh's population shows 27.2 percent of interventions were relatively effective; the respective figure for our sample is 28.7 percent. Plausibly, our sample includes more research where the alternative mode is a statistically significant improvement on lectures. On inspection of all the trials, this over-sampling arises because publication bias favors such results (rather than arising because of a bias in our methods of retrieving and collating the research). However, as our analysis finds that the alternative modes are less cost-effective than lectures, the bias works against our conclusions rather than for them.

Finally, the studies in our sample are on average from research conducted more recently. In part this reflects the improved reporting conventions used in research, so that effect sizes were calculable, and this in turn suggests that fewer of the unavailable studies were likely to meet our quality criteria. (For the obtained sample, 16 of 54 papers were rejected on quality grounds.) As well, older studies are likely to have less external validity, given changes in the culture of education and in the technologies of modes such as independent study. The omission of older research may in fact improve the external validity of our findings.

RE-ESTIMATION OF COSTS AND PRICES

Perhaps the most important sensitivity analysis is to check the accuracy of the costs data, because these are imputed. There are a number of well-documented practical

---

course the other mode may have advanced technologically also: the point here is that the rate of change of technology may not have been stable across the two modes, and it is unlikely that the prices of the inputs for the two activities have remained the same. Critically, the price of a computer-based, distance-learning program relative to the price of an hour of lecturer time has changed substantially since 1980 (Levin et al., 1987).

10 Few other studies have been subject to sensitivity analysis or compared using equivalent methods. This is important, because decisions as to what is cost-effective may differ, depending on the assumptions used to estimate costs. Krueger (2000), for example, finds that the STAR experiment yields a rate of return of 6 percent (and so is applying cost-benefit analysis, not cost-effectiveness analysis); Prais (1996), looking at the same experiment, finds that there are many more cost-effective re-organizations to provision.

FIGURE 8.3 FUNNEL PLOT

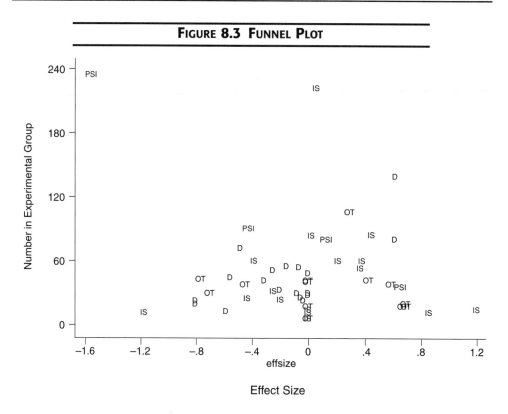

Effect Size

difficulties in estimating costs directly. Breneman (1998, pp. 364–367) describes the difficulties of getting consistent and reliable cost information on U.S. college remediation programs (because of confidentiality by colleges); Harbison and Hanushek (1992) chart similar problems in accessing data in their cost-effectiveness analysis of Brazilian education. These difficulties are compounded when the educational program draws on budgets from multiple sources. These practical difficulties may make cost imputation appear economical and justifiable as a proxy for "real" costs.[11]

The specific check on costs employed here was to apply different prices to each of the inputs. This is equivalent to estimating different unit values. Three alternative vectors for the sets of prices were used, where these were distinguished by their pric-

---

11 Other common problems with costs analysis may be obviated as a result of the general method adopted here. One such problem is effort. Although effort within an educational setting may be estimated based on the duration of the course, less readily measurable is the (unrecorded) effort of students in response to each mode. (In their analysis of the cost-effectiveness of learning in higher education, for example, Zietz and Cochran [1997] assume that the cost of inducing extra effort from the enrollees is zero). A second problem is that, typically, costs within the public sector may not be available, because market prices for the inputs may be unavailable and the depreciation of assets involved in one mode of delivery may differ from that for another. For the method applied here, however, these problems are only significant to the extent that they vary across the groups. Using experimental literature, it may be legitimate to assume these factors are differenced away.

ing of different inputs: vector 2 used high materials costs; vector 3 priced student effort at double the expected wage. Vector 4 was taken from the only paper in the sample to report costs (Harding, Riley, and Bligh, 1981). Each vector was applied to estimate costs, to derive vote-counts of clearly cost-effective and cost-ineffective interventions, and to re-draft Figure 8.2.

The alternative vectors did produce some variation in the costs as represented in Table 8.2. Specifically, vector 4 caused each of the modes to appear more costly than the lecture mode. However, under vectors 2 and 3 the signs of the relative average cost per mode were unchanged from the principal vector. In other words, these two vectors did not change the conclusion about whether a mode cost more than lectures; they only had an effect on how much more it cost. The alternative vectors preserved the ranks of costs: the personalized instruction mode was the most costly, and the discussion mode the least costly. For the last two re-applications, the results are largely unaffected. Re-deriving the vote–counts to identify clearly cost-effective and cost-ineffective interventions made little impact on the results. The only notable effect was that application of vector 4 served to strengthen the argument that the discussion mode was not cost-effective relative to lectures: no interventions in this mode appeared to be definitely cost-effective using this vector. Similarly, re-drafting Figure 8.2 added little explanatory power. (In part this reflects the fact that the quadrants indicate relative cost-effectiveness). Overall, we can be reasonably confident of the findings reported in Tables 8.1 and 8.2 and the above discussion.

USING COST-EFFECTIVENESS ANALYSIS

Our results suggest that, based on the experimental evidence, there is no mode of education that is more clearly cost-effective than lectures for imparting informa-tion. Although some modes appeared to be more effective than lectures, they were in many cases more costly, with a high variance in costs. The personalized instruc-tion mode was both more costly and less effective. For the discussion/inquiry and independent study modes, costs were lower, but so was effectiveness. None of these results suggest that lectures can be replaced so as to achieve more cost-effective pro-vision for imparting information.

In part, these nugatory results are from experiments that are relatively small-scale. The intention is not to entirely change a mode of delivery, but simply to augment a particular mode with either extra lectures or the alternative mode.[12] It is therefore debatable whether such changes to education provision can yield sub-stantive effects. Moreover, even where there are clear indications that one mode is more costly than another, using this evidence-base may not be straightforward. Specifically, whether managers can use the information from such cost-effective-

---

12 In a catalog of 27 interventions to boost science teaching, for example, Anderson (1990) itemizes few that require a substantial increase in resources. From the perspective of the provider, only four out of the 27 interventions cost more than 10 percent of the cost of lengthening the school day by one hour: these involve giving teachers a reduced work-load, lowering the teacher-student ratio, rotating in alternative professionals (from busi-ness) into the classroom, and moving toward a system of full-year institutes.

ness analysis to raise educational achievement within universities will depend on a number of issues.

First, cost-effectiveness results are contingent on the scale of provision. Where study X, for example, refers to an intervention on t students, its relevance to an intervention applied to 2t students is not certain. The importance of scale-contingency becomes particularly clear when cost-effectiveness analysis is applied, because the marginal cost for an enrollee is not typically the same as the average cost. Costs data show that the cost function is typically U-shaped in enrollments (see Koshal and Koshal, 1995). Discussion groups, say, may be more cost-effective with t-x students than lectures, but less cost-effective with t+x students. Given the differences across modes in the proportions of fixed costs (and because modes will differentially impinge on the capacities of education providers, as well as on their capacity utilization), scale effects may be non-trivial.[13] To make general inferences from the evidence base, we need to know how both the effectiveness function and the costs function vary with scale or enrollment levels. As yet, the evidence base on these functions is not available.

Second, there may be costs of transition between one mode and another. Although one mode is more cost-effective, it may not be possible to transfer provision to that mode, because the resale value of the current resource provision is too low. These adjustment costs may be high, particularly for universities where a substantial proportion of education is delivered through lectures. The cost-effectiveness of the alternative mode may be offset by the liquidation costs incurred in disposal of the existing lecture-related physical assets. Consequently, cost savings from re-organization may not be that substantial: providers may be constrained by resource deployment rules. However, Johnes (1997) estimates subject-based re-organization of higher education and finds potentially large-cost reductions.

Third, the most cost-effective mode for imparting information may not be the same as that for, say, generating increases in graduates' earnings or other social outcomes (for a substantial list of the effects of education, see McMahon, 2000; Herrnstein and Murray, 1994). As well, modes may be differentially effective: lectures, say, may be equally effective across all student abilities, whereas discussion groups may favor high-ability students. Thus the results may not be generalized to school pupils or different schooling systems. Plus, effectiveness may be contingent on a portfolio of modes, rather than only one mode (see the estimates of the benefits of mixing vocational and academic courses in Kang and Bishop, 1989; Mane, 1999). Further, to predict the most cost-effective mode of education, it may be necessary to understand the enrollment decisions and time allocation decisions of students (Bacdayan, 1997). More generally, the concept of effectiveness itself may be subject to debate, perhaps to include multiple measures rather than single-point estimates (see Coe and Fitz-Gibbon, 1998; Teddlie and Reynolds, 2000, p. 324).

Fourth, for reviews of cost-effectiveness to be generalizable, the interventions themselves must have construct validity; i.e., it must be possible to specify the

---

13 Also, the rate of research obsolescence reported above appears—to the authors at least—to be non-trivial. Much evaluative research is of limited usefulness beyond the immediate and proximate circumstances in which the research takes place. This raises concerns about the cost-effectiveness of undertaking cost-effectiveness analysis itself, particularly when evaluations must themselves be justified (Datta, 1999).

intervention as a reasonably stable "technology" (Levin, 1988). Unfortunately, some of these alternative modes may not easily conform to a standard. One mode for classification was "other;" this includes interventions as diverse as laboratory-style learning; modeling with role-play; correspondence study; and audio-visual instruction.[14] This criticism of scientism, however, has ramifications for general research methods in the social sciences.

Fifth, there is the issue of choosing a cost-effective re-organization of provision. The evidence here makes clear that some discussion mode interventions were more cost-effective than lectures, and some were less cost-effective. The same applies to the other mode and to independent study. An unambiguous preference for these modes, say, over lectures cannot therefore be derived: cost-effectiveness depends on how a particular mode is implemented. However, in no case was personalized instruction more cost-effective than lectures. For this mode, an unambiguous preference for lectures can be identified.

A final issue arises where the control over the education is split across agencies. A mode that is cost-effective when viewed from the provider perspective may not be so when viewed from the enrollees' perspective. The most obvious example of this occurs with comparisons between lectures and independent study. Promotion of the latter will be lower cost from the perspective of the provider. Relatedly, the agents responding to a cost-effectiveness analysis may not be able to control some of the costs: from the perspective of enrollees, for example, lectures may be free at point-of-attendance where education is subsidized by government.

Notwithstanding these caveats to simple inference from basic cost-effectiveness analysis, our evidence base suggests that any changes to the mode of provision in universities are unlikely to yield substantial gains in learning outcomes.

REFERENCES

Altonji, J. G., and Dunn, T. A. (1996). The effects of family background on the return to education. *Review of Economics and Statistics, 42*, 692–704.

Anderson, R. D. (1990). Policy decisions on improving science education: A cost-effectiveness analysis. *Journal of Research in Science Teaching, 27*, 553–574.

Audit Commission and Office for Standards in Education. (1993). *Unfinished business: Full–time educational courses for 16–19 year olds.* London: HMSO.

Bacdayan, A. W. (1997). A mathematical analysis of the learning production process and a model for determining what matters in education. *Economics of Education Review, 16*, 25–37.

Barber, J. A., and Thompson, S. G. (1998). Analysis and interpretation of cost data in randomized controlled trials: Review of published studies. *British Medical Journal, 317*, 1195-1200.

---

14 An additional consideration is the reporting of information in the investigations under review. Our investigation has highlighted the terse reporting of effectiveness from most interventions and the almost non-existent costs analysis. More generally, many of the papers failed to specify in detail the nature of the intervention, even as this is a critical element of the research.

Bassi, L. (1984). Estimating the effects of training programs, with non-random selection. *Review of Economics and Statistics, 66,* 36–43.

Bligh, D. A. (2000). *What's the use of lectures?* Jossey-Bass.

Brasington, D. M. (1999). Central city school administrative policy: Ssystematically passing undeserving students. *Economics of Education Review, 18,* 201–212.

Breneman, D. W. (1998). Remediation in higher education: Its extent and cost. In D. Ravitch (Ed.), *Brookings Papers on Education Policy.* Washington, DC: Brookings Institution.

Brown, C.A., Belfield, C.R., and Field, S. (2001). A review of the cost-effectiveness of continuing professional development for the health professions. *British Medical Journal.*

Coe, R., and Fitz-Gibbon, C. T. (1998). School effectiveness research: Criticisms and recommendations. *Oxford Review of Education, 24,* 421–438.

Cooper, H., and Hedges, L. V. (Eds.). (1994). *Handbook of research synthesis.* Russell Sage: New York.

Datta, L.-E. (1999). Seriously seeking fairness: Strategies for crafting non-partisan evaluations in a partisan world. *American Journal of Evaluation, 21,* 1–14.

Davis, D. A., Thomson O'Brien, M. A., Freemantle, N., Wolf, F. M., Mazmanian, P., and Taylor-Vaisey, A. (1999). Do conferences, rounds and other traditional continuing education activities change physician behaviour or health care outcomes? *Journal of the American Medical Association, 282,* 867–874.

Feinstein, L., and Symons, R. (1999). Attainment in secondary schools. *Oxford Economic Papers, 51,* 300–321.

Fielding, A., Belfield, C. R., and Thomas, H. R. (1998). The consequences of drop-outs on the cost-effectiveness of 16–19 colleges. *Oxford Review of Education, 24,* 487–511.

Freudenstein, U., and Howe, A. (1999). Recommendations for future studies: A systematic review of educational interventions in primary care settings. *British Journal of General Practice, 49,* 995–1001.

Gomel, M. K., Wutzke, S. E., Hardcastle, D. M., Lapsley, H., and Reznik, R. B. (1998). Cost-effectiveness of strategies to market and train primary health care physicians in brief intervention techniques for hazardous alcohol use. *Social Science Medicine, 47,* 203–211.

Harbison, R. W., and Hanushek, E. A. (1992). *Educational performance of the poor: Lessons from northeast Brazil.* New York: Oxford University Press.

Harding, C. M., Riley, I. S., and Bligh, D. A. (1981). A comparison of two teaching methods in mathematical statistics. *Studies in Higher Education, 6,* 139–146.

Heckman, J. J., and Smith, J. A. (1999). The pre-programme earnings dip and the determinants of participation in a social programme: Implications for simple programme evaluation strategies. *Economic Journal, 109,* 313–348.

Herrnstein, R. J., and Murray, C. (1994). *The bell curve: Intelligence and class structure in American life.* New York: Free Press.

Inouye, D. K., Miller, H. L., and Fletcher, J. D. (1997). The evaluation of system cost and replicability. *International Journal of Educational Research, 27,* 137–152.

Johnes, G. (1997). Costs and industrial structure in British higher education. *Economic Journal, 107,* 727–737.

Kang, S., and Bishop, J. H. (1989). Vocational and academic education in high school: Complements or substitutes? *Economics of Education Review, 8,* 133–148.

Koshal, R. K.. and Koshal, M. (1995). Quality and economies of scale in higher education. *Applied Economics, 27, 773–778.*

Koshal, R. K., and Koshal, M. (1999a). Demand and supply of educational service: A case of liberal arts colleges. *Education Economics, 7,* 121–130.

Koshal, R. K., and Koshal, M. (1999b). Economies of scale and scope in higher education: A case of comprehensive universities. *Economics of Education Review, 18,* 269–277.

Krueger, A B. (2000). *Economic considerations and class size* (Princeton University Working Paper).

Levin, H. M. (1988). Cost-effectiveness and educational policy. *Educational Evaluation and Policy Analysis, 10,* 51–70.

Levin, H. M. (2001). Waiting for Godot: Cost-effectiveness analysis in education. In R. J. Light (Ed.), *New Directions for Evaluation, 90.* Jossey-Bass.

Levin, H. M., Glass, G. V., and Meister, G. R. (1987). Cost-effectiveness of computer-assisted-instruction. *Evaluation Review, 11,* 50–72.

Levin, H. M., and McEwan, P. J. (2001). *Cost-effectiveness analysis: Methods and applications* (2nd ed.). Thousand Oaks, CA: Sage.

Lewis, D. R., Dalgaard, B. R., and Boyer, C. M. (1985). Cost-effectiveness of computer-aided economics instruction. *American Economic Review, 75,* 91–96.

Light, A. (1999). High school employment, high school curriculum and post-school wages. *Economics of Education Review, 18,* 291–309.

Mane, F. (1999). Trends in the payoff to academic and occupation-specific skills: The short and medium run returns to academic and vocational high school courses for non-college-bound students. *Economics of Education Review, 18,* 417–438.

McMahon, W. W. (2000). *Education and development: Measuring the social benefits.* Oxford: Oxford University Press.

Prais, S. J. (1996). Class-size and learning: The Tennessee experiment—what follows? *Oxford Review of Education, 22,* 399–414.

Ragan, J. F., Warren, J. T., and Bratsberg, B. (1999). How similar are pay structures in similar departments of economics. *Economics of Education Review, 18,* 347–360.

Russell, T. L. (1999). *The no significant difference phenomenon.* North Carolina State University.

Schiefelbein, E., Wolff, L., and Schiefelbein, P. (1999). Cost-effectiveness of primary education policies in Latin America: A survey of expert opinion. *UNESCO Bulletin, 49,* 53–76.

Shadish, W. R., and Haddock, C. K. (1994). Combining estimates of effect size. In H. Cooper and L. V. Hedges (Eds.), *Handbook of research synthesis.* New York: Russell Sage.

Slavin, R. E., Madden, N.A., Dolan, L. J., and Wasik, B.A. (1996). *Every child, every school.* Corwin Press.

Teddlie, C., and Reynolds, D. (2000). *The international handbook on school effectiveness research.* London: Falmer.

Udharvelyi, I. S., Colditz, G. A., Rai, A. M., and Epstein, A. M. (1992). Cost-effectiveness and cost-benefit in the medical literature: Are the methods being used correctly? *Annals of Internal Medicine, 116,* 238–244.

Van der Drift, K. D. J. M. (1980). Cost-effectiveness of audiovisual media in higher education. *Instructional Science, 9,* 355–364.

Zietz, J., and Cochran, H. H. (1997). Containing cost without sacrificing achievement: Some evidence from college-level economics classes. *Journal of Education Finance, 23,* 177–192.

9

A BENEFIT-COST ANALYSIS OF THE ABECEDARIAN EARLY CHILDHOOD INTERVENTION

Leonard N. Masse and W. Steven Barnett

INTRODUCTION

A commonly proposed approach to improving the educational success of children in poverty is the provision of compensatory education programs. Compensatory programs, most notably Head Start, typically begin at age three or four and operate on a school calendar. Such programs seem able to boost cognitive scores and school success, though some evidence suggests that at least some of the effects fade out as children proceed in school (Barnett, 1998). A less common approach is the provision of full-day, year-round child care and preschool services starting soon after birth. These programs can be considered more preventative in the sense that services begin before any marked educational deficit can occur.

The Carolina Abecedarian Study is an experiment in the provision of intensive preschool services to children in low-income families from infancy to five years of age. The program began in 1972, and research on program effects found that experimental group children experienced durable gains in IQ, and achievement in mathematics and reading (Campbell and Ramey, 1995). Comparison of the findings for the Abecedarian preschool project to other interventions suggests that effects may be more persistent if a program is preventative, intensive, and starts very early in life (Ramey and Ramey, 1998).

The increment to academic achievement and cognitive development experienced by the Abecedarian children has been fairly well documented. A question that remains, however, is whether or not expenditures on programs based on the Abecedarian preschool model represent sound social investments. Simply put, are the benefits worth the costs when viewed in the light of the many alternative uses of scarce public and private funds? This paper presents the preliminary findings of a benefit-cost analysis of the Abecedarian preschool program. The primary data sources are follow-up surveys and official school records through age 21.

METHODS

SUBJECTS

The program followed an experimental design and originally involved 112 children, mostly of African-American descent, who were born between 1972 and 1977 and whose family situations were believed to put the children at risk of retarded intellectual and social development. A "High-Risk Index" was used to determine risk for retarded cognitive development. The index was constructed based on factors such as household income, parental education, school histories of family members, welfare payments, parental intelligence, and parental occupations (Ramey and Campbell, 1984). Selected background characteristics at program entry were: maternal education of approximately 10 years, maternal IQ of 85, 25 percent of households with both parents, and 55 percent of households on Aid to Families with Dependent Children (Ramey and Campbell, 1984; Campbell, Helms, Sparling, and Ramey, 1998). Between 6 and 12 weeks of age children were randomly assigned to either a preschool program or a control group. By 1978, 104 participants remained in the study and the follow-up at age 21 involved all 104 of these participants.

TREATMENT

The preschool program was center-based with teacher/child ratios that ranged from 1:3 for infants/toddlers to 1:6 for older children. The center was operated from 7:30 a.m. to 5:30 p.m., five days per week, and fifty weeks out of the year, with free transportation available. The curriculum is called "Partners in Learning" and is discussed in Ramey and Ramey (1998). The curriculum emphasized language development, but addressed the needs of children in all developmental domains. Children at the center also received medical and nutritional services. In order to avoid the confounding effects of these factors on intellectual development, the same medical and nutritional services were provided to the children in the preschool control group.

OUTCOME MEASURES

The educational results of the program are summarized in Table 9.1. Early assessments indicated substantial gains in intellectual development. Children in the preschool group consistently outscored children in the control group on standard measures of intelligence (Ramey and Campbell, 1984). At age 8 participants were assessed and it was found that children in the preschool group had IQ scores that were significantly higher than the scores of the control group. Further, at 8 years of age children who had received the preschool intervention also scored significantly higher on a set of achievement tests in mathematics and reading (Campbell and Ramey, 1995).

An additional assessment was conducted at age 12 and the results were similar to those discussed above, indicating durable gains in intelligence and achievement (Campbell and Ramey, 1994). An assessment at age 15 indicated that the effect on IQ tended to "fade" but that the effects on reading and mathematics scores remained positive and significant (Campbell and Ramey, 1995). The most recent assessment at age 21 indicated similar effects with respect to measures of intelligence and achievement. Importantly, the age-21 data demonstrated that the experimental group children were much more likely to have attended a four-year college than the control-group

Table 9.1 Preschool Program Effects Related to Economic Benefits.

	Program Group		No-Program Group	
	Measure	*N*	*Measure*	*N*
Education effects (children)				
IQ (Stanford Binet), age 3*	101	50	84	48
IQ (McCarthey GCI), age 4.5*	101	49	91	46
IQ (WISC-R), age 15	95	48	90	44
Reading achievement (WJ), age 15*	94	48	88	44
Math achievement (WJ), age 15*	93	48	82	44
Ever retained in grade by age 15*	31%	48	55%	44
Special services by grade 9*	25%	48	48%	44
High School graduation by age 19	67%	54	51%	51
Ever enrolled in a 4-yr college by age 21*	36%	53	13%	51
Employment effects at participant's age of 54 months (teenage parents)				
Teenage mothers and post-secondary training	46%	13	13%	15
Teenage mothers and self-supporting	70%	13	58%	15
Teenage mothers and additional births	23%	13	40%	13

Notes: * differences are significant at the 0.05 level of confidence. WISC-R is the abbreviation for the Wechsler Intelligence Scale for Children Revised (Wechsler, 1974). WJ is the abbreviation for the Woodcock-Johnson Psycho-Educational Battery, Part 2: Tests of Academic Achievement (Woodcock and Johnson, 1977). McCarthy GCI is abbreviation for the McCarthy General Cognitive Index. Data on education effects are from Campbell and Ramey (1995), Ramey and Campbell (1984), Clarke and Campbell (1998), and Campbell et al. (2001). Data on employment effects for teenage mothers are from Campbell et al. (1986). A mother was considered to be self-supporting if welfare funds were not used except in the cases where the mother was a student and had made 4 years of educational progress in the 4.5 years since the birth of her child.

children (P=36 percent, C=13 percent, p=0.01).[1] In general, the results from all the assessments supported the claim that the preschool intervention was effective in improving measures of intelligence and achievement over the long-term.

Comparisons of the two groups revealed benefits of the program beyond those discussed above. Campbell and Ramey (1995) reported that preschool participants experienced lower levels of grade retention and placements in special education classes. Clearly, these cost-savings to school districts and families represent real economic benefits of the Abecedarian program. Following the example set by the Perry Preschool Program, researchers examined the relationship between program participation and the incidence of youth crime to an average age of 21 and found no statistically significant differences between the groups (Clarke and Campbell, 1998). The differences in the nature of community life experienced by the Perry families and the Abecedarian families could account for the differing results. Although further examination of the relationship between preschool participation and crime is possible, it does not appear likely that crime reduction and cost-savings to victims will represent significant benefits in the Abecedarian case.

Researchers also investigated the impact of preschool availability on the lives of the subsample of teenage mothers (under 18 years of age) who participated in the study (Campbell, Breitmayer, and Ramey, 1986). When children were approximately 54 months of age, it was found that teenage mothers of preschool children were more

---

1   All tests of significance are two-tailed.

likely to have graduated high school, to have received post-secondary training, to be self-supporting, and less likely to have borne subsequent children. It was also reported that mothers with children in the preschool group were generally more likely to be employed and to obtain jobs with a classification of "skilled or semi-skilled" (Ramey et al., 1983). To the extent that additional training, job experience, and education was realized in increased earnings and/or decreased future reliance on social assistance, the above effects on mothers represent a direct and quantifiable benefit of the program.

Economic Measures and Analysis

This study presents a benefit-cost analysis of the Carolina Abecedarian Preschool Program. As informed by economic theory, our perspective is that education is both a consumption good that confers immediate benefits and an investment good that confers personal and social benefits well into the future (Becker, 1964; Haveman and Wolfe, 1984). Benefit-cost analysis involves estimating the monetary values of streams of cost and benefits in order to measure the program's net value as a social investment.

The benefit-cost analysis of the Abecedarian Project will follow the standard procedures set forth by Thompson (1980) and Levin and McEwan (2001), and followed by Barnett in the analysis of the Perry Preschool Program (Barnett, 1996). The two core parts of a benefit-cost analysis are a detailed estimation of program costs and the identification and estimation of program benefits or effects. In this case, records provided by the program sponsor (the Frank Porter Graham Child Development Center, hereafter FPG) are the primary data sources used for estimation of program costs and effects.

In this preliminary benefit-cost analysis, program costs are estimated for three different resource "settings" in which the program might be offered. Program benefits are generated for four categories for which it was possible to obtain monetary estimates: 1) earnings and fringe benefits of participants, 2) earnings and fringe benefits of future generations, 3) maternal employment and earnings, 3) elementary- and secondary-education cost-savings, and 4) improved health. Estimates of the program's effect on adult education and welfare use are not available at this time. However, in both cases the relative magnitude of the effects is quite small. The effects of the program on crime and delinquency appear to be negligible given earlier research in this area (Clarke and Campbell, 1998).

As the analysis involves streams of cost and benefits over time, estimated benefits and costs are converted into constant dollars (deflated) and discounted to the present using appropriate rates of discount. The rate of discount reflects the opportunity cost of public resources. A range of discount rates from 0 to 7 percent is employed in this analysis. The analysis estimates the present value of benefits minus costs for each alternative rate of discount. Additionally, estimates of the internal rate of return, the rate at which the project benefits are equal to its costs, can be generated.

Results

Table 9.2 presents estimates of the present value of program costs and benefits at various rates of discount. Some of the benefits and costs accrue to the program participants and some to the general public. The distribution of benefits and costs are important to the political viability of an instrument of public policy. It might be relatively easy to show that an intervention provided at little cost to disadvantaged

Table 9.2 Present Value of Per Child Benefits and Costs of the Abecedarian Early Intervention (1999 Dollars)

	Discount Rate		
	3%	5%	7%
Program cost FPG setting[a]	33,486	32,305	31,205
Program cost PS setting[b]	39,137	37,747	36,453
Program benefits			
Participant earnings	46,740	21,454	10,462
Earnings of future generations	6,400	2,269	534
Maternal earnings: ages 32-41[c]	22,215	16,592	12,497
Maternal earnings: ages 42-60[d]	27,758	15,942	9,348
Subtotal	49,973	32,534	21,845
K-12 education	6,963	5,731	4,757
Smoking/health	12,452	2,918	706
Total benefits	122,528	64,906	38,304
Net Present Value: FPG setting	89,042	32,601	7,099
Net Present Value: PS setting	83,391	27,159	1,851

a. Program cost is for the Frank Porter Graham Child Development Center.

b. Program cost is for replication in a public school setting.

c. Maternal earnings through age 41 are estimated using actual data on maternal earnings at ages 32, 35, and 41.

d. Maternal earnings from age 42 to age 60 are extrapolated based on estimates through age 41 and assumes no increase in program effects.

groups provides returns in excess of the cost to that group. However, since public funds are required to provide the program, it is important to examine whether society generally realizes returns in excess of whatever funds and resources are dedicated to the program. In the final benefit-cost analysis, therefore, effects will be allocated to the economic actors (participants and taxpayers) to which they accrue and net present values calculated for each.

PROGRAM COST

Resources employed for a representative sample of program years were identified by FPG. The resources, or program ingredients, were broadly classified according to function (Levin and McEwan, 2001). Categories included labor resources (paid staff and volunteer workers), and non-labor resources (equipment, supplies, facilities, etc.). The cost of reproducing the Abecedarian program according to its resource requirements is clearly relevant for policy purposes. Resources are therefore valued at the prices typically paid by two institutions that might provide such programs on a large scale: public schools and child-care centers. This is in addition to estimating cost based on the actual prices paid by FPG during the program's operation.

TOTAL COSTS

Table 9.3 presents the yearly costs of providing the Abecedarian treatment by program year in the three different cost settings. Average enrollment in the nursery was about 12 infants and the staff/child ratio was 1:3. Average age at entry was 4.4 months. In program years 2 and 3 the average unit of instruction/care was 7 children for both age groups and the staff/child ratio was 1:3.5. In program years 4 and

Table 9.3 Estimated Yearly Costs of the Abecedarian Program in Three Different Settings (Undiscounted 1999 Dollars)

	Abecedarian FPG	Public School	Child-Care
Year 1	10,083	10,934	6,393
Year 2	15,147	16,613	9,514
Year 3	15,147	16,613	9,514
Year 4	11,196	12,302	7,594
Year 5	11,196	12,302	7,594
Totals	62,769	68,764	40,609

5 the average unit of instruction/care was 12 children for both age groups and the staff/child ratio was 1:6.

The undiscounted total resource costs for the FPG and public-school settings are clearly greater than the costs for the child-care setting. A few comments are in order. First, it is not surprising that the cost of executing the program in the FPG and public school settings are similar. FPG paid workers what they considered to be competitive public-school salaries. The difference in the two estimates is due, in part, to the lower cost of living and level of salaries in North Carolina relative to the national average. Second, the relatively low cost of executing the program in a child-care setting is presented mostly as a benchmark. It is unlikely that the input quality necessary to execute a high-quality program could be maintained at the prices and wages paid in this setting. The extent to which cost savings, represented by a movement along the resource continuum from the public preschool setting to the child-care setting, can be discovered while preserving benefits is important even if the program is found to lead to substantial net benefits in the highest cost setting. Although movement away from a successful setting involves risk of lost benefits, this would have to weighed against the probable cost-savings. A full treatment of this issue is beyond the scope of the current work and is suggestive of an area for future research.

COST OF CARE: CONTROL CHILDREN

The cost of the program, properly considered, is the additional cost of the Abecedarian treatment over the cost of child-care arrangements experienced by the control group. Both sets of experiences involve a stream of costs and a stream of benefits. The measurement of benefits is necessarily marginal (i.e., the difference between groups consists of benefits beyond the benefits received by the control group) and the appropriate comparison is with the marginal cost of the Abecedarian treatment.

Data on the child-care experiences of the control children are somewhat limited. Data were collected on the use of center-based, child-care by age. The percentage rates of participation are 18, 29, 67, 78 and 73 for the first five years of life. Compared to national and regional data, these rates seem high, especially for years 3 to 5. Possibly, families that volunteered for the study were exceptionally predisposed to use center based care. There is indication, however, that the community in which the experiment took place was one that was unusually supportive of the care and education of young children (Burchinal, Lee, and Ramey, 1989). To the extent that higher-quality, center-based care was available to the control group, this analysis may underestimate net marginal benefits if the Abecedarian program were provided nationally.

Meaningful cost estimates for the child-care received by the control children require estimates of participation rates and hours of care by type of care. Since the analysis seeks to inform current public policy, the estimation procedure considers the nature of care as it currently exists. Using data from the National Household Education Survey of 1995, estimates of the number of hours a child was in center-based care, relative care, and non-relative care for each of the five program years or age groups are obtained. One of the advantages of using the NHES data is that it permits the estimation of the use of relative and non-relative care arrangements for the control group children. These data are not available from FPG but are clearly important to the calculations of the cost of care for non-treatment children.

The cost estimate for the care of the control children is based on the actual participation rates of the control-group children in center-based child care. In addition, the NHES data is used to obtain estimates of participation rates and hours of care in non-center-based care arrangements. The weekly cost of care for each program year is calculated by multiplying the average number of hours of care by a weighted average (based on participation rates) of the cost of care. Yearly costs are generated for the non-parental care arrangements of the control group children. These estimates are used to calculate the marginal cost of the program.

PARENTAL CARE

The benefit-cost analysis seeks to weigh the marginal benefits that accrue due to program participation against the marginal costs that are incurred. The marginal cost of the program is the difference between the cost of the intervention and the cost of the care experienced by the control-group children. The program provided an average of 40 hours of care per week. The control-group children also experienced care for the same 40 hours but a portion of the care was parental. Since it is the difference in the quality and composition of the care during these 40 hours that leads to program benefits, then it is consistent to obtain a cost for the full 40 hours of care experienced by the control-group children. In order to accomplish this it is necessary to obtain estimates for the parental component of care and to combine these with the estimates for non-parental care.

In order to estimate the cost of parental care a price needs to be assigned to an hour of parental-provided care. Information is available on the prices paid to individuals for the care of young children. The prices of non-relative and relative care are estimated at $2.12 and $1.34, respectively (Hofferth, Brayfield, Deich, and Holcomb, 1991). The price of relative care may be conservatively low, and not reflect market prices, for a number of reasons. Individuals may provide care at a subsidized rate for children of relatives either because of reciprocity agreements between family members (exchange of services) or merely due to a sense of family responsibility. A relative may also receive a lower-than-market wage to reflect the fact that he/she may receive a benefit from participating in the care of a child to which there is some attachment. For these reasons, an hour of parental provided care is valued at the price for non-relative care.

MARGINAL COSTS

The cost of care for the control-group children is subtracted from the cost of care for the program group-children to estimate a yearly net cost for the program at each age or program year. The average marginal yearly costs for the program are $7086

Table 9.4 Present Value of Marginal Costs of the Abecedarian Program in Three Cost Settings (1999 Dollars)

Discount Rate	Abecedarian FPG	Public School	Child-Care
0%	35,430	41,425	13,270
3%	33,486	39,137	12,521
5%	32,305	37,747	12,066
7%	31,205	36,453	11,642
10%	29,691	34,673	11,058

at FPG, $8385 in a public preschool setting and $2654 in a child-care setting. Table 9.4 presents the present value of the marginal costs under various rates of discount. As detailed above, the cost of implementing the Abecedarian program in a public preschool is far more expensive than implementation in a child care setting. Both options are presented as suitable endpoints for the analysis. Benefit-cost analysis is an important component of a full program evaluation but it cannot provide answers to all relevant policy questions. Measures that are cost-saving and quality-preserving are clearly relevant as policymakers consider movement away from the public preschool model and to the child-care model. The benefit-cost analysis, at the minimum, should provide information on the magnitude of the required movement.

COMPARATIVE COSTS

The average annual total cost of the Abecedarian Program is approximately $13,000 (1999 dollars). By comparison, the annual amounts for Head Start and the Perry Preschool Program are approximately $6500 and $8600, respectively (Barnett 1996; USDHHS, 2000). The Abecedarian treatment is clearly more intensive than the other two and this is reflected in its higher costs. This analysis is partially aimed at determining whether or not the higher costs of the Abecedarian Program are associated with sufficient benefits to justify the intervention on purely economic grounds.

At the federal level, the United States spends approximately 12 billion dollars (1999 dollars) on the early care and education of young children (CEER, 1999). State governments spend an additional 5 billion dollars and direct expenditures by families (not accounting for parental-provided care) exceed 20 billion dollars (Barnett and Masse, 2000). What would be the effect on funding levels of providing the Abecedarian program to all poor children? How much additional funds would have to be allocated by government to early care and education?

According to Hofferth, Shauman, Henke, and West (1998), there are approximately 4.1 million children in each age cohort from birth to age 4. Assuming that 25% of these children are poor, then the target population for the Abecedarian program totals 5.125 million children. The total annual cost of providing the Abecedarian program to poor children in the United States is therefore approximately 67 billion dollars. This is 3–4 times the level of current federal and state expenditures for early-childhood education and about twice the level of total current expenditures (including federal, state and household expenditures).

The costs of the program may seem prohibitively high for replication on a large scale. Governments and policymakers may experience "sticker shock" at first but must bear in mind that costs alone offer little guidance. The costs of a program must be compared against the benefits that the program generates. Benefit-cost ratios that are greater than one for acceptable rates of discount indicate that a program is worthy of consideration regardless of the absolute level of program costs.

PARTICIPANT EARNINGS

Earnings are forecasted on the basis of educational attainment based on the standard method first presented in Miller and Hornseth (1967). Using cross-sectional data from the Bureau of the Census, earnings estimates are obtained by age, race, and gender for various categories of educational attainment (United States Bureau of the Census, 1998). Each category corresponds to an estimated stream of lifetime income. An individual's estimated lifetime income depends on educational attainment at age 21 and the probability of higher-educational attainment later in life.

FPG provided data on the educational levels of the Abecedarian control- and program-group participants at age 21. The schooling levels of the participant fell into eight categories (less than 9 years, 9 to 11 years, GED enrollee, GED graduate, high-school graduate with no college credits, some college but no degree, enrolled in an AA program, and enrolled in a BA program). In order to estimate future earnings it was assumed that educational status at age 21 did not necessarily represent an individual's final educational status. It was therefore necessary to calculate the expected value of an individual's future stream of income. In order to accomplish this, it was necessary to assign probabilities to each level of future educational attainment (nine census categories) for each level of current educational status (eight study categories). The conditional probabilities were based on the results of United States Department of Education longitudinal studies that follow the educational advances of specific age cohorts (Adelman, 1999; Boesal, Alsalam, and Smith, 1998; McCormick et al., 1999) and cross-sectional data on high-school dropout and graduation rates (USDOE, 1998). For each level of current education, the expected value of future income is the sum of the products of the probability of obtaining each level of higher education and the present value of the income stream associated with each educational level.

The procedure for estimating lifetime earnings therefore involved several steps. First, earnings for ages 22–65 were estimated using cross-sectional data for the nine levels of future educational attainment. Second, these earnings were multiplied by the probability that a participant would survive to each age. Survival rates were estimated from data from the National Center for Health Statistics (1998). Discounted lifetime earnings were then calculated for each level of future educational attainment. The estimated probabilities for future educational attainment were then employed to calculate the expected value of discounted lifetime earnings given the level of educational attainment at age 21.

The simple use of cross-sectional data assumes that there is no productivity-induced growth in real income over the lifetimes of participants. Government data show that the output per-hour of all persons employed grew at an average annual rate of 2.3 percent over the period from 1948–1997. More recently, the average annual rate in gross domestic product per-worker-hour was 1.2 percent over the period from 1979–1990 and was 1.3 percent over the period from 1990–1997 (Bureau of Labor Statistics, 2000). In this analysis, therefore, earnings are adjusted assuming a 1.0 percent growth in real income.

Table 9.5 Estimated Program Effects on Participant Compensation after Age 21, Earnings of Future Generations, and Schooling Costs (1999 Dollars)

Discount Rate	Compensation	Future Generations	Schooling
0%	170,608	54,295	9,486
3%	46,740	6,400	6,963
5%	21,454	2,269	5,731
7%	10,462	534	4,757

The estimates for the program effects on lifetime compensation beyond age 21 are presented in Table 9.5. Compensation includes base salary and fringe and employer-provided benefits that are valued at 20 percent of base salary. In this preliminary benefit-cost analysis results are not presented by gender. It is noted however that gender differences in program effects on academic achievement and attainment seem to have translated into effects with respect to earnings. The mechanism through which female participants are more likely than male participants to realize a marginal effect on higher-educational attainment and earnings is an area of research that warrants further attention.

The program effect on lifetime compensation beyond age 21 is approximately $47,000 at a discount rate of 3 percent. Overall, lifetime compensation beyond age 21 is somewhat conservatively estimated. The use of cross-sectional data assumes that age-earnings profiles are relatively stable over time. In particular, it assumes that the labor-force participation rates of men and women that gave rise to the current cross-sectional earnings data will prevail over the working lives of our sample. However, the labor-force participation rates of women have shown a significant upward trend over the past 50 years for women of all ages (Fullerton, 1999). Using 1998 cross-sectional data, the labor-force participation rates for women aged 35–44 is estimated at 77 percent. However, Fullerton (1999) estimates that in 2015 this rate will have increased to 82 percent. For women aged 45–54, the 1998 and 2025 estimates are 76 percent and 82 percent, respectively. Similarly, Fullerton's estimate of 59 percent for the LFP in 2025 of women aged 55–64 can be used as an estimate for the LFP of Abecedarian women when they reach this age interval (approximately 2035). The estimate employed for this age-group using cross-sectional data is 51 percent.

In 1998, 2015, 2025, and 2035, the Abecedarian participants (were) will be approximately 23, 40, 50 and 60 years of age. The use of 1998 cross-sectional data, therefore, seems to underestimate the labor-force participation of program participants by approximately 5 percent to 6 percent at ages 40 and 50 and 8 percent at age 60. Therefore, projecting female earnings based on cross-sectional data is conservative and leads to estimates that are below the actual earnings that will be realized by program participants.

EARNINGS OF FUTURE GENERATIONS

In this section, the magnitude of benefits that accrue to the descendants of the Abecedarian participants is explored. There are a number of clear mechanisms through which benefits from the preschool program may be transmitted across generations. In theory, most benefits that accrue to program participants are sources of benefits for the children of participants. These include effects on academic achievement, educational attainment, earnings, criminal behavior, welfare use, educational cost-savings, job-satisfaction and status, self-esteem, pro-social behavior, household management, fertility and birth weight. As is the case with the effects for the program participants, some of these effects are difficult to monetize and will remain unmeasured. The overall ratio of program benefits to costs is conservatively estimated for this reason.

There is a significant amount of evidence that supports the positive relationship between parental education and income and the educational attainment and income of children (Birdsall and Cochrane, 1982; Wolfe and Behrman, 1985; Singh, 1992; Glewwe and Jacoby, 1994; Leigh, 1998). Measures of household income and family background are standard variables used in estimating wage and earnings functions (Cohn and Geske, 1990). Using cross-sectional data, Peters (1992) presents the conditional probabilities of a child's income attainment given the income attainment of the father or male head-of-household. In general, the probability that a child's income attainment is greater than or equal to that of the parent is greater than 0.50. Peters (1992) also estimates an earnings function and finds that the elasticity of child-income with respect to the income of the father is approximately 0.26. Estimates from other studies range from 0.07 to 0.44 (Atkinson, 1981; Behrman and Taubman, 1985; Solon, 1992).

In order to estimate the program's effect on the earnings of future generations, elasticities presented in Altonji and Dunn (1990) are employed. Using data from the National Longitudinal Surveys of Labor Market Experience, Altonji and Dunn derive estimates of the elasticity of child income with respect to the income of parent. In particular, they find that the elasticity of the income of a son (daughter) with respect to the income of the father is equal to 0.210 (0.335). The elasticity of the income of a son (daughter) with respect to the income of the mother is equal to 0.148 (0.348).

In order to use these elasticities to estimate the earnings of future generations, it is first assumed that they can be applied to undiscounted lifetime earnings. It is also assumed that the program effect on generation one (G1) parental income can be considered an increment to income relative to the base-level achieved by the control group. Using the program effects by gender, the percentage change in G1 income associated with each effect is calculated. Employing the elasticities given above, the corresponding change in generation-two income (G2) associated with the calculated change in parental income is calculated. Once the program effect in G2 income is calculated, the process can be repeated and effects calculated for future generations in an iterative manner. For the purpose of this analysis, estimates for the combined program effects on generations two through four are provided.

In Table 9.5 the discounted values for combined incomes of future generations are presented. It is assumed, conservatively, that each participant (parent) has one child at age 25 and that the children will have earned income from age 22 to age 65. The overall effects are the weighted average of the individual effects for males and females. We can see from Table 9.5 that the program effects on the earnings of future generations are not economically insignificant. At an interest rate of 3 percent, these effects equal $6400 per participant, an amount equal to approximately 12 percent of the per-child cost.

ELEMENTARY AND SECONDARY EDUCATION

The effects of the program on the elementary- and secondary-education costs of participants were estimated. School histories were constructed for 99 of the study participants based on data that was originally gathered from official school-record data by FPG. For each participant, a school placement was assigned to every year that a child was in school. The major distinction was between special education placements and regular educational placements, with the former being more resource intensive and, hence, more costly.

Costs were mapped onto the schooling histories in the following manner. A school year that involved at least one special education category was assigned the yearly estimate for special education. All other school years were assigned the cost estimate for regular education. The estimates for the costs of regular education and special education are adjusted from data presented in Parrish, O'Reilly, Duenas, and Wolman (1997), which are based on data from the national cost study conducted by Moore, Strange, Schwartz, and Braddock (1988). According to Parish and colleagues, the average annual real rate of growth in per-pupil special education costs over the period from 1968 to 1986 was 4.1 percent. The corresponding rate for regular education was 2.1 percent (Parrish et al., 1997). Assuming that education costs grew at these rates over the period from 1986 to 1999, revised national estimates for the costs of regular education and special education are $7405 and $17125, respectively, in 1999 dollars.

In Table 9.5 the program effects on educational costs are presented. At a discount rate of 3 percent the cost reduction was equal to $6963, an amount equal to approximately 20 percent of program cost in the FPG setting. It was expected, however, that the savings from reduced rates of grade retention and special education would be somewhat larger. Campbell and Ramey (1995) reported that the rates of placement in special education by the end of grade 9 were 25 percent and 48 percent for the program group and control group, respectively (n=92). These rates represent the percentage of children that had ever received special education services by the end of grade 9. The current reexamination of the schooling data results in comparable estimates of 31 percent and 49 percent for the program and control groups (n=99, p=0.0672). The difference between the two estimates is likely due to the change in the sample size over the years as more complete schooling data became available.

In addition to the above measure, the percentage of total school years in special education was calculated for the program and control groups. The program effect using this measure was not nearly as pronounced. The estimates for the program and control groups were found to be 12 percent and 18 percent, respectively (p=0.0082). Since years in special education are more directly related to cost than the former measure, the expected program effect is somewhat reduced.

SMOKING AND HEALTH

Data collected by FPG indicate that there are differences in the rates of smoking between the program- and control-group children, although the rates seem high relative to national average data. However, any program or policy that can reduce smoking rates has the clear potential to generate significant economic benefits. The benefits include, but are not limited to, improvements in health and longevity, and reductions in the cost of health care.

National data indicate that there are a number of strong associations between smoking and certain demographic characteristics (USDHHS, 1997). First, individuals with less than a high-school degree currently smoke at a rate of 47 percent, which is nearly four times the rate of 12 percent for college graduates. Second, smoking is negatively associated with the level of income. At household income levels that are less than 150 percent of the poverty level, the rate of adult smoking is 38 percent. At household income levels that are 300 percent of the poverty level, the corresponding rate is 25 percent. The national data also suggest that individuals that live in households that do not include both biological parents are more likely to be smoking as adults. It can be argued that these data indicate that situations that involve certain forms of stress raise the possibility that an individual will smoke, in part, as a reaction to his/her situation in life (USDHHS, 1998). In this view, policies aimed at reducing stress from these sources for any reason should consider as a benefit the possible effect of the policy or program on the rate of smoking for the target group.

Data on smoking by participants come from a 1993 youth risk behavior survey conducted by FPG. The rates of smoking for the control-group and program-group were estimated at 55 percent and 39 percent, respectively (p=0.106). The results are clearly suggestive, if not strictly significant from a statistical point of view. In order to estimate the economic value of the program's effect on the rate of smoking, it is necessary to translate these rates into monetary returns. For the purposes of this analysis, the effects on morbidity (illness) prior to death are ignored and the focus is only on the value of differences in expected mortality between the two groups. Ignoring the effect of smoking on illness prior to death simplifies the estimation procedure at the cost of underestimating potential benefits by potentially significant amounts. However, the effect on mortality may still contribute significantly to program benefits and this suggests a future area for research. In any case, data on smoking behavior should be collected in follow-ups of early intervention programs.

Cutler and associates use national data to estimate the life expectancy of individuals who either are or had been regular smokers by age 20 (Cutler et al., 2000). Being a non-smoker at age 20 increases longevity by approximately 6.5 years. In order to value these additional years of life, an economic estimate of the value of an additional year of life is needed. It is assumed that additional years gained occur after the average age for life expectancy by gender. The value of a life (L) is associated with the years from 70–76 for male non-smokers and for the years 77–82 for female non-smokers. The estimates for L are then discounted to program entry and the discounted values are multiplied by the average difference in smoking rates between the two groups in order to obtain estimates of program effects.

In order to execute the above simple procedure the non-simple task of attaching a value (L) to a year of life is necessary. There is a vast literature in the area of health economics that corresponds to the economic value of an increase in mortality and/or a decrease in morbidity (Adams and Young, 1999; Manning et al., 1989; Miller, Calhoun, and Arthur 1990; Moore and Viscusi, 1988; Oster, Colditz, and Kelly, 1984; Tolley, Kenkel, and Fabien, 1994). For example, values are associated with decreases in government expenditures on Medicaid, an individual's willingness to pay for reductions in health risks, income loss due to premature death, and property loss or damage due to fire. Following the example of Cutler et al. (2000) and Gruber and Zinman (2000), in their respective works for the National Bureau of Economic Research, the range for the value of a year of life that emerges from this literature is between $100,000 and $200,000 (1999 dollars).

Table 9.6 presents the estimates for the program effects on smoking and the economic value of increased longevity. Similarly, the discounted values of increased longevity between males and females were not significantly different and, therefore, average values were used to calculate program effects. It is clear from Table 9.6 that

Table 9.6 Program Effects on the Value of Life due to Decreased Rates of Smoking and Increased Longevity (1999 Dollars)

Value of life	Discount Rate	Program Effect
$100,000	0%	78,000
	3%	8,301
	5%	1,945
	7%	471
	10%	60
$150,000	0%	117,000
	3%	12,452
	5%	2,918
	7%	706
	10%	90
$200,000	0%	156,000
	3%	16,602
	5%	3,890
	7%	942
	10%	119

the benefits from a reduction in the rate of smoking are not insignificant. At a discount rate of 3 percent, the estimates of program effects range from approximately $8000 to $17,000, with an average estimate of $12,450 dollars. It is also clear from the estimates that the assumption that benefits accrue in the last years of life results in a large reduction in benefits at higher rates of discount. Although not explicitly measured here, there are benefits from reductions in the consumption of cigarettes that occur in the present. General health is improved and individuals can lead more active and productive lives. There is also arguably a benefit in the reduction of the number of individuals captive to a physical addiction that exceeds whatever benefits individuals may experience due to the act of smoking. However, even ignoring these benefits and the substantial benefits from reduction in the pain and suffering associated with illness, program effects on the rate of smoking result in benefits that are equal to approximately 30 percent of the marginal cost of the Abecedarian program in a public school setting.

In some sense the effect on smoking is an unexpected result. The program had its main goal of improving the cognitive ability of young children and increasing the probability of school and workplace success later in life. However, a relative increase in cognitive ability, coupled with significant differences in achievement and school-related experiences, can arguably result in the program-group children making relatively more productive choices about personal health. The general nature of this finding may be limited by the fact that the smoking rates were much higher for the Abecedarian participants relative to the national population. Measured benefits for a different population of children will likely be less than those presented here. However, given the great concern over youth smoking, and the strong relationship between youth and adult smoking, the results here are particularly encouraging.

MATERNAL PRODUCTIVITY AND EARNINGS

The provision of five years of full-time child-care decreases the opportunity cost to mothers of the choice to pursue employment, training, education, and other productivity-enhancing activities. According to Ramey and colleagues (2000), the mothers of the Abecedarian program-group children experienced gains in employment and

Table 9.7 Program Effects Due to Increased Maternal Earnings (1999 Dollars)

Value of life	Discount Rate	Program Effect
Ages 32-41	0%	35,000
	3%	22,215
	5%	16,592
	7%	12,497
Ages 42-60	0%	66,500
	3%	27,758
	5%	15,942
	7%	9,348
Total	0%	101,500
	3%	49,973
	5%	32,534
	7%	21,845

earnings relative to the mothers of the control-group children. Self-reported income data were available on maternal earnings at participant ages of 12, 15, and 21. Corresponding maternal ages were approximately 32, 35 and 41. Based on these data, a yearly program effect of $3500 per child is estimated.

Table 9.7 presents the program effect on maternal earnings for various rates of discount. The program effects through age 41 are estimated based on the actual earnings of mothers from ages 32 to 41. The program effects from ages 42 to 60 are extrapolations based on the effects through age 41 and assume, conservatively, that there is no increase in the earnings differential between the two groups. Due to a lack of earlier data on maternal earnings, the estimates are also conservative in that they assume that the earnings differential does not occur until maternal age 32. Despite these assumptions, the program effect on maternal earnings is quite substantial and is approximately equal to the per child cost of the intervention in the FPG setting at a discount rate of 5 percent.

This preliminary analysis indicates that an important benefit of the program is the effect of fully subsidized preschool on the labor-market success of mothers. This issue, by itself, is important to the child-care debate because program effects on the household go beyond those that involve the children receiving care. Maternal employment is clearly related to labor-market experience, training, and earnings, all of which promote self-sufficiency and an improved quality-of-life for all members of the household. Society benefits as well from improvements in the productive capacity of female workers and from a decrease in the need for social assistance. Although there is a large supply of research on the effect of child-care on maternal employment, there is little experimental evidence and econometric studies have produced mixed results (Kimmell, 1998). The results of this analysis with respect to maternal employment, therefore, are encouraging and warrant further attention.

DISCUSSION

The last two lines of Table 9.2 present the net present values of benefits and costs at three different rates of discount for program replication in the FPG and public-school settings. In both cases the net present value is greater than zero for discount rates up to 7 percent. The same is clearly true for replication in the lower-cost, child-care setting. If we include all measured benefits, then the internal rate of return for the Abecedarian intervention appears to be slightly greater than 7 percent. The positive results are not highly sensitive to the presence or exclusion of any one benefit. Excluding maternal earnings from ages 42–60 yields an internal rate of return of between 5 percent and 7 percent in the FPG and the public school resource settings. Excluding forecasted participant earnings and the earnings of future generations also results in an internal rate of return between 5 percent and 7 percent. Excluding the estimates for smoking and health still results in an internal rate of return greater than 7 percent. If we confine attention to the benefits that accrue mainly to the children (participant earnings and smoking/health), then the rate of return to the program is between 3 percent and 5 percent. Overall, the rate of return to the Abecedarian project is no less than 3 percent and is likely higher than 7 percent.

The Abecedarian program results in healthy returns for the investment of public resources targeted at a disadvantaged group. This occurs even when viewed in the light of significant unmeasured benefits from improved education, such as the personal consumption value of learning and educational experiences, increases in civic and pro-social behavior, increases in the overall quality-of-life, and improvements in personal decision-making and household management (Haveman and Wolfe, 1984). In addition, Donohue (1999) argues that lower rates of discount or estimated internal rates of return may actually be appropriate if government programs help future generations avoid some irreversible damage. Market rates of return, and hence market rates of discount, may not lead to appropriate decisions if markets alone cannot bring about the desired program effects. If the goal is to increase the income and prospects of a disadvantaged group, and there exists no other clear mechanism for doing so, it may make sense to apply a lower rate of discount to projects that accomplish this goal. An alternative is to recognize that a dollar of program benefit to a target group has more value than a dollar of program cost to others. Favoring the disadvantaged group may help improve distributional equity at the expense of efficiency in resource allocation. In this case, the effects of program participation on the educational attainment, productivity, and earnings of at-risk children result in an improvement in overall social equity. Change in equity remains, therefore, a potentially large unmeasured benefit of the Abecedarian program.

It is unlikely that the results of the Abecedarian program can be replicated perfectly in all settings and for all populations. The benefits that accrued to the participants were due to the marginal differences in the quality of the care received by the program-group children and the quality of the care received by the control-group children in the first five years of life. In the cases where the care currently being received is of a higher quality, then the marginal effects will not be as great. However, if attention is limited to the 25 percent of our nation's children that are estimated to be living in poverty, then the results of the study are more directly applicable.

Replication in other settings will also affect the magnitude of specific benefits. It is possible that the effects on the smoking behavior of participants may not be as great outside of North Carolina and the southern region of the United States. However, this is a relatively minor measured benefit. More importantly, it is also very possible that the effects of the intervention on criminal behavior may be more pronounced in higher-crime areas. We would, therefore, not be surprised if the Abecedarian intervention resulted in greater program effects and returns than estimated above if replicated on a large scale for at-risk children in areas where the quality of care currently being received was relatively low.

The issue of the *optimal* form and intensity of a preschool program cannot be settled with the encouraging results of the Abecedarian project. How many years of full-time quality preschool and child-care are needed to produce the results outlined above? As a matter of research, more information is needed on the long-term results of programs that vary the amount and form of care before this issue can be settled. As a matter of principle, all children should receive quality care in the first five years of life. A concern for the lives of the children considered to be most "at-risk" can, by itself, direct public resources to an intervention that will provide quality experiences to children and, over the long run, result in benefits that exceed costs.

REFERENCES

Adams, K. E., and Young, T. L. (1999). Costs of smoking: A focus on maternal, childhood, and other short-run costs. *Medical Care Research and Review, 56*(1), 3–29.

Adelman, C. (1999). *Answers in the tool box: Academic intensity, attendance patterns, and Bachelor's degree attainment.* Washington, DC: U.S. Department of Education, Office of Educational Research and Improvement.

Altonji, J. G., and Dunn, T. A. (1990). *Family background and labor market outcomes* (Final Report to the United States Department of Labor). Washington, DC: Bureau of Labor Statistics.

Atkinson, A. B. (1981). On intergenerational income mobility in Britain. *Journal of Post-Keynesian Economics, 3,* 194–217.

Barnett, W. S., and Masse, L. (2000). Funding issues for early care and education in the United States. In *USA background report for the OECD thematic review.* Washington, DC: Office of Educational Research and Improvement.

Barnett, W. S. (1996). *Lives in the balance: Age-27 benefit-cost analysis of the High/Scope Perry Preschool Program* (Monographs of the High/Scope Educational Research Foundation, Number 11). Ypsilanti, MI: High/Scope Press.

Barnett, W. S. (1998). Long-term cognitive and academic effects of early childhood education on children in poverty. *Preventive Medicine, 27,* 204–207.

Becker, G. S. (1964). *Human capital.* New York: Columbia University Press.

Behrman, J., and Taubman, P. (1985). Intergenerational earnings mobility in the United States: Some estimates and a test of Becker's intergenerational endowments model. *Review of Economics and Statistics, 67,* 144–151.

Birdsall, N., and Cochrane, S. H. (1982). Education and parental decision-making: A two-generation approach. In L. Anderson and D. M. Windham (Eds.), *Education and development.* Lexington, Massachusetts: DC Heath.

Boesal, D., Alsalam, N., and Smith, T. M. (1998). *Educational and labor market performance of GED recipients.* Washington, DC: U.S. Department of Education, Office of Educational Research and Improvement.

Burchinal, M. R., Lee, M. W., and Ramey, C. T. (1989). Type of daycare and preschool cognitive performance of disadvantaged children. *Child Development, 60,* 128–137.

Bureau of Labor Statistics. (2000). *Multifactor productivity trends, 1997.* Available: http://www.bls.gov/news.release/prod3.-nws.htm.

Campbell, F. A., Breitmayer, B., and Ramey, C. T. (1986). Disadvantaged single teenage mothers and their children: Consequences of free educational day care. *Family Relations, 35,* 63–68.

Campbell, F. A., Helms, R., Sparling, J. J., and Ramey, C. T. (1998). Early childhood programs and success in school. In W. S. Barnett and S. S. Boocock (Eds.), *Early care and education for children in poverty*. New York: State University of New York Press.

Campbell, F. A., and Ramey, C. T. (1994). Effects of early intervention on intellectual and academic achievement: A follow-up study of children from low-income families. *Child Development, 65*(2), 684–689.

Campbell, F. A., and Ramey, C. T. (1995). Cognitive and school outcomes for high-risk African American students at middle adolescence: Positive effects of early intervention. *American Education Research Journal, 32*(4), 743–772.

Campbell, F. A., Ramey, C. T., Pungello, E., Sparling, J., and Miller-Johnson, S. (2001). Early childhood education: Young adult outcomes from the Abecedarian Project. *Applied Developmental Science.*

Center for Early Education at Rutgers (CEER). (1999). *Federal expenditures on early care and education* (CEER Fact Sheet No. 1). New Brunswick, NJ: CEER.

Clarke, S. H., and Campbell, F. A. (1998). Can intervention early prevent crime later? The Abecedarian Project compared with other programs. *Early Childhood Research Quarterly, 13*(2), 319–343.

Cohn, E., and Geske, T. G. (1990). *The economics of education*. New York: Pergamon Press.

Cutler, D. M., Gruber, J., Hartman, R. S., Landrum, M. B., Newhouse, J. P., and Rosenthal, M. B. (2000). *The economic impacts of the tobacco settlement* (Working Paper 7760). Cambridge, MA: National Bureau of Economic Research.

Donohue, J. J. (1999). Why we should discount the views of those who discount discounting. *Yale Law Journal, 108*, 1901–1910.

Fullerton, H. N. (1999, December). Labor force participation: 75 years of change, 1950–1998 and 1998–2025. *Monthly Labor Review.*

Glewwe, P., and Jacoby, H. (1994). Student achievement and schooling choice in low income countries: Evidence from Ghana. *Journal of Human Resources, 23*(3), 843–864.

Gruber, J., and Zinman, J. (2000). *Youth smoking in the U.S.: Evidence and implications* (Working Paper 7780). Cambridge, MA: National Bureau of Economic Research.

Haveman, R., and Wolfe, B. (1984). Schooling and economic well-being: The role of nonmarket effects. *Journal of Human Resources, 19*(3), 377–407.

Hofferth, S., Shauman, K. A., Henke, R. R., and West, J. (1998). *Characteristics of children's early care and education programs: Data from the 1995 National Household Survey*. Washington, DC: National Center for Education Statistics, U.S. Department of Education.

Hofferth, S., Brayfield, A., Deich, S., and Holcomb, P. (1991). *National Child Care Survey, 1990*. Washington, DC: Urban Institute Press.

Kimmel, J. (1998). Child care costs as a barrier to employment for single and married mothers. *Review of Economics and Statistics, 80*(2), 287–299.

Leigh, J. P. (1998). Parents' schooling and the correlation between education and frailty. *Economics of Education Review, 17*(3), 249–358.

Levin, H. M., and McEwan, P. J. (2001). *Cost-effectiveness analysis: Methods and applications* (2nd ed.). Thousand Oaks, CA: Sage.

McCormick, A. C., Nunez, A., Shah, V., Choy, S., and Knepper, P. R. (1999). *Life after college: A descriptive summary of 1992–93 Bachelor's degree recipients in 1997.* U.S. Department of Education, Office of Educational Research and Improvement.

Manning, W. G., Keeler, E. B., Newhouse, J. P., Sloss, E. M., and Wasserman, J. (1989). The taxes of sin: Do smokers and drinkers pay their way? *Journal of the American Medical Association, 261,* 1604–1609.

Miller, H. P., and Hornseth, R. A. (1967). *Present value of estimated lifetime earnings* (Technical Paper Number 16). Washington, DC: U.S. Department of Commerce, Bureau of the Census.

Miller, T. R., Calhoun, C., and Arthur, W. B. (1990). *Utility-adjusted impairment years: A low-cost approach to morbidity valuation.* Washington, DC: Federal Highway Adminstration.

Moore, M. T., Strange, E. W., Schwartz, M., and Braddock, M. (1988). *Patterns in special education service delivery and cost.* Washington, DC: Decision Resources Corporation.

Moore, M. J., and Viscusi, W. K. (1988). The quantity-adjusted value of life. *Economic Inquiry, 26,* 369–388.

National Center for Health Statistics. (1998). United States abridged life tables, 1996. *National Vital Statistics Reports, 47*(13).

Oster, G., Colditz, G. A., and Kelly, N. L. (1984). *The economic costs of smoking and benefits of quitting.* Lexington, MA: DC Heath and Company.

Parrish, T. B., O'Reilly, F., Duenas, I. E., and Wolman, J. M. (1997). *State special education finance systems, 1994–1995.* Palo Alto, CA: Center for Special Education Finance, American Institutes for Research.

Peters, H. E. (1992). Patterns of intergenerational mobility in income and earnings. *Review of Economics and Statistics, 74,* 456–466.

Ramey, C. T., and Campbell, F. A. (1984). Preventive education for high risk children: Cognitive consequences of the Carolina Abecedarian Project. *American Journal of Mental Deficiency, 88*(5), 515–523.

Ramey, C. T., et al. (1983). Group day care and socially disadvantaged families: Effects on the child and the family. *Advances in Early Education and Day Care, 3,* 69–106.

Ramey, C. T., et al. (2000). Persistent effects of early intervention on high-risk children and their mothers. *Applied Developmental Science.*

Ramey, C. T., and Ramey, S. L. (1998). Prevention of intellectual disabilities: Early interventions to improve cognitive development. *Preventive Medicine, 27,* 224–232.

Singh, R. (1992). Underinvestment, low economic returns to education, and the schooling of rural children: Some evidence from Brazil. *Economic Development and Cultural Change, 40*(3), 645–664.

Solon, G. (1992). Intergenerational income mobility in the United States. *American Economic Review, 82,* 393–407.

Thompson, M. S. (1980). *Benefit-cost analysis for program evaluation.* Beverly Hills, CA: Sage Publications.

Tolley, G., Kenkel, D., and Fabian, R. (1994). *Valuing health for policy: An economic approach.* Chicago: University of Chicago Press.

United States Bureau of the Census. (1998). *Money income in the United States: 1997* (Current Population Reports, Series P60–200). Washington, DC: Government Printing Office.

United States Department of Education (USDOE). (1998). *Dropout rates in the United States, 1996* (Report 98–250). Washington, DC: National Center for Education Statistics.

United States Department of Health and Human Services (USDHHS). (1997). *Fertility, family planning, and women's health: New data from the 1995 National Survey of Family Growth* (Series Report 23). Atlanta, GA: U.S. Department of Health and Human Services, Centers for Disease Control and Prevention.

United States Department of Health and Human Services (USDHHS). (1998). *Tobacco use among U.S. racial/ethnic groups—African Americans, American Indians and Alaska Natives, Asian Americans and Pacific Islanders and Hispanics: A report of the Surgeon General.* Atlanta, GA: U.S. Department of Health and Human Services, Centers for Disease Control and Prevention.

United States Department of Health and Human Services (USDHHS). (2000). *Head Start fact sheet, 2000.* Washington, DC: Administration for Children and Families, Head Start Bureau.

Wechsler, D. (1974). *Wechsler intelligence scale for children—Revised.* New York: The Psychological Corporation.

Wolfe, B. L., and Behrman, J. R. (1985). Who is schooled in developed countries? The roles of income, parental schooling, sex, residence, and family size. *Economics of Education Review, 3*(3), 231–245.

Woodcock, R. W., and Johnson, M. B. (1977). *Woodcock-Johnson Psycho-Educational Battery.* Hingham, MA: Teaching Resources Corporation.

10

IDENTIFYING OPTIMAL CLASS SIZES AND TEACHER SALARIES

*Doug Harris**

INTRODUCTION

The purpose of cost-effectiveness analysis is to help policymakers improve decisions about the use of school resources, in order to obtain the most from every dollar that is spent. While this type of analysis is rare in education, it is quite common in economics. Unfortunately, economics is not always very useful for making real decisions in practice. At the introductory level, it provides principles that are just slightly better than common sense. At the graduate level, economics turns that common sense into complicated sets of equations with relatively precise solutions and specific policy recommendations. However, since few understand these approaches, they simply collect dust, providing little value for policymakers.

Cost-effectiveness analysis (CEA) is a useful means of simplifying the complex models of economics. But does this simplicity come at the expense of providing appropriate policy advice? Under what circumstances is cost-effectiveness sufficient or even better than more sophisticated economic analyses? This chapter addresses these questions by applying cost-effectiveness and a more complex approach—called "optimization"—to the analysis of the class size debate. Specifically, class size reduction policies are compared with those of raising teacher salaries. These two policy reforms are key parts of a much larger debate on education reform. While it is clear that class size reductions have benefits, it is also evident that they have enormous costs. Should class sizes be reduced? Should these resources instead be used to raise salaries? This chapter attempts to answer these questions using two types of analysis. One key conclusion is that the answers may differ depending on the type of analysis used.

Section 2 provides some conceptual background on cost-effectiveness and other approaches that are standard in the economics profession. Section 3 reviews trends

---

* The author wishes to thank Dale Ballou, Clive Belfield, Gerhard Glomm, Hank Levin, Patrick McEwan, David Plank, Jeff Wooldridge, and participants in the Michigan State University Labor Economics Seminar for valuable comments on this paper. Financial support was provided by the U.S. Department of Education's North Central Regional Education Laboratory.

and evidence related to class size and teacher-salary policies. Section 4 discusses the specific considerations necessary to identify appropriate policies for class size and teacher salaries. The results are reviewed and discussed in section 5 (although many of the technical details are confined to the Appendix).

CONCEPTUAL FRAMEWORKS FROM ECONOMICS

The purpose of economics is to study the allocation of scarce resources. A fundamental principle of the field is that the "optimal allocation" occurs where the marginal benefit equals marginal cost. In other words, each resource should be increased until the additional benefit provided by the next unit is less than the additional costs required to obtain that unit.

An important characteristic of marginal benefits is that they generally decrease as inputs increase. For instance, hiring one more teacher in a school will probably improve student outcomes. That teacher would presumably be assigned to the school's most pressing needs. Hiring a second teacher would also provide benefits, but these would be smaller because the first teacher would already have addressed the most pressing needs.

The marginal cost of a resource is often just the market price, at least from the perspective of individual schools and districts, which are too small to influence overall market conditions. If markets are competitive, then the price is constant (i.e., a school can hire as many teachers as it wants at the market wage). Markets are often uncompetitive, but the previous assumptions provide a useful starting point.

These characteristics of marginal costs and marginal benefit are quite helpful for making decisions about school inputs. Specifically, they guarantee that there is some point at which marginal benefits equal marginal costs, as shown in Figure 10.1. It provides an example of the above economic reasoning using an important education resource: the number of teachers hired. The graph indicates that the optimal number of teachers is T^*, where marginal benefits equal marginal costs. Hiring fewer teachers (T_1) would mean that the marginal benefit of hiring an additional teacher would be greater than the marginal cost, so hiring more teachers would be desirable. Shifting the number to T_2 would mean that the additional cost of the last teacher hired is greater than the additional benefits, so the school should cut back on teachers and free up resources for other inputs, such as curriculum, professional development, or teacher salaries.

Figure 10.1 paints a fairly simple picture. Not surprisingly, this type of analysis involves many complicating factors. Most importantly, there is almost always a long list of resources to be chosen. Combined with the fact that school budgets are fixed, this means that the simple rule is no longer valid. It would be quite a coincidence for the rule to hold for every input, while simultaneously using all available resources. To account for this, economic theory suggests that decision-makers should choose inputs so that the ratio of marginal benefits to marginal costs is the same for all inputs. To take a simple case, suppose that the marginal cost is $1 dollar for each input. In this case, we should choose inputs so that the benefit we receive from the last unit of input is also equal for all of them. If the marginal benefit were higher for one resource, then we would buy more of that one and less of others. Because marginal benefits are declining, this process would eventually equalize all of the ratios (see equation [4] in the Appendix). This approach, based on marginal benefits and costs, is referred to as the "optimization approach."

FIGURE 10.1 MARGINAL BENEFITS
AND MARGINAL COSTS

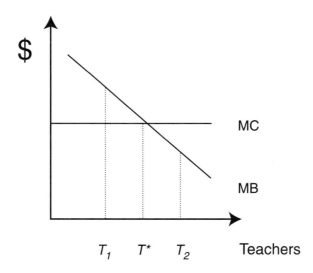

One key challenge in using this approach is that all benefits and costs must be *translated into dollar values.* This is intuitive for costs—schools have budgets and pay for resources with money. Translating benefits into dollars is much more complicated, but necessary to avoid an "apples-and-oranges" comparison with costs. Therefore, the increased sophistication and precision of the optimization approach is offset by the challenge of measuring benefits.

Cost-effectiveness analysis (CEA) and cost-benefit analysis (CBA) attempt to simplify the optimization approach. CEA is also more flexible. It does require that costs are measured in monetary terms, but it does not require this for benefits. Instead, outcomes are measured in whatever units seem appropriate (e.g., test scores and dropout rates). The effects of reform on these outcomes are then compared, along with their costs. This allows researchers and policymakers to consider a wider range of education outcomes that are not easily monetized.

On the other hand, CEA requires that the goals be arbitrarily set. Ideally, we would want test scores to be as high as possible; who is to say that scores should go up by 10 percentiles? Why not 5 or 15? The reason, of course, is that resources are limited and doing one thing will come at the expense of other goals. The optimization analysis attempts to take these other goals into account, maximizing the overall well being of students and society.

Cost-benefit analysis (CBA) is a third approach to policy analysis. This method is most similar to the optimization approach, in that, benefits need to be converted into dollar values. The key difference is that CBA focuses on *total* benefits and costs instead of *marginal* benefits and costs. First, a specific policy is considered (e.g., lowering class sizes from 22 to 15). If the total benefits of the policy are found to exceed the total costs, then the policy should be adopted. This may sound like a small difference compared with the optimization approach, but, as section 4 indicates, the results can vary substantially.

One disadvantage of CBA is that it often does not work well when the main policy variable can take on many values. For instance, many different class sizes are possible. Considering only one strategy, such as a reduction from 22 to 15 students per class, is likely to produce misleading results. Even if the benefits exceed the costs, it is likely that the optimal class size is something other than 15.

A second weakness of cost-benefit analysis, at least in its actual applications, is that it usually focuses on only one resource. It is possible, even likely, that many policies could yield positive net benefits. Since policymakers are almost always considering multiple options, focusing on just one is unlikely to provide useful policy guidance. Section 3 below discusses a specific CBA of class size reductions.[1]

The theme of the above discussion is that different approaches are appropriate under different circumstances. Cost-effectiveness analysis is best used when policy outcomes are difficult to translate into dollar values. The optimization approach should be used when benefits can be "dollarized" and policy variables can take on many values. Finally, CBA is appropriate when benefits can be dollarized and policy options are few and discrete. Using any one of them under other circumstances is likely to produce misleading or even incorrect policy recommendations.

BACKGROUND ON CLASS SIZES AND TEACHER QUALITY

Before applying the above techniques to the analysis of class size and teacher-salary policies, recent trends and research on these policies are considered. Table 10.1 below indicates that the pupil-teacher ratio declined from 25.8 to 16.2 between 1960 and 1999, which corresponds to a 61 percent increase in the number of teachers hired (assuming a constant student population). Real teacher salaries appear to have increased by 46 percent over the same time period.

There are several reasons to believe that the increases in teacher salaries displayed in Table 10.1 are exaggerated. Baumol (1967) shows that service industries, such as education, experience low-productivity-growth compared with industries requiring large capital investments. The implication is that the high-productivity-growth indus-

Table 10.1 Public School Resources in the U.S., 1960–1999 (1999 dollars)

Year	Pupil-Teacher Ratio	Teacher Salaries
1960	25.8	$27,972
1970	22.3	$37,574
1980	18.7	$33,848
1990	17.2	$40,647
1999	16.2	$40,582

Source: National Center for Education Statistics (2001)

---

1 For more detail on the technique of CBA, see, for example, Layard and Glaister (1994) and Mishan (1988).

tries will be willing to pay workers higher wages, requiring low-productivity-growth industries to match these increases, or otherwise lose their workers to other higher-paying jobs. This effect is compounded in education by the fact that schools have traditionally relied heavily on females whose opportunities have grown considerably in recent decades. The net effect is that the Consumer Price Index is likely to under-estimate inflation in education, and thus overestimate growth in salaries. Rothstein (1997) confirms this view. Also, Lakdawalla (2001) finds that teacher salaries have declined by as much as 30 percent in the last half-century relative to professions requiring similar qualifications.

It is clear that the changes in spending indicated above do not accurately reflect the changes in real instructional resources available to schools. While it is clear that *teacher quantity* has increased, it is likely that *teacher quality* has declined. Theory and evidence supporting this argument are presented later.

There is little, if any, research available that would justify this policy of increasing teacher quantity, while decreasing teacher quality. Some papers have focused on the costs of these individual policies. Many others have focused on the separate benefits of class size reduction and higher teacher salaries. However, real economic analysis requires considering all of these factors simultaneously, balancing of the costs and benefits of multiple programs.

THE ECONOMICS OF CLASS SIZE AND TEACHER SALARIES

Section 2 provides a general framework for analysis, while section 3 provides background on class size and teacher-salary policies. This section attempts to link the two, presenting several considerations that are important in applying the economic frameworks to these policy areas.

It is useful to think of class size and teacher salary as mechanisms for affecting the quantity and quality of teachers, respectively. Other mechanisms also exist, but these two comprise a substantial share of school resources and are frequent subjects of debate. The quality-quantity framework is also useful because it highlights the interrelationships between the two policies. First, smaller classes affect teacher quality, as well as quantity. If schools hire the best teachers first, then the additional teachers hired to reduce class size will necessarily be of decreasing quality.[2] In this sense, class size reduction is equivalent to lowering the standard for teachers. Quality standards prohibit applicants from teaching if they do not meet minimum criteria. Lowering the standard or reducing class size would, therefore, allow lower quality teachers into the classroom.

A second relationship is that the cost of increasing quantity increases with the level of quality. For instance, if policymakers decided to raise average salaries to raise quality, then hiring more teachers to reduce class size would also be more expensive. Each additional teacher hired would require greater budgetary resources. Studying the two policies together allows these relationships to be directly incorporated in the economic model.

---

2 Ballou and Podgursky (1992, 1994) and Ballou (1996) argue that schools do not select the best teachers. If they were correct, then the potential gain in teacher quality from teacher standards would be lessened. However, the gain would not be eliminated unless teachers were chosen completely at random.

The quality-quantity framework does raise important measurement issues. Measuring teacher quantity is fairly easy, but how can we measure teacher quality? Many studies have provided evidence about various teacher characteristics that are associated with high student performance. One that shows up consistently is teacher test scores, such as college entrance exams and certification tests. Many researchers have found that these scores are significantly related to teacher classroom performance. Whether this is because these teachers are "smarter" or because test scores are correlated with some unobserved individual factor does not really matter here. What does matter here is that teacher test scores provide an accurate signal of teacher performance.

One implication of the above discussion is that lowering class size may have both a positive and a negative effect. The positive effect is that students receive more personal attention and are subject to fewer distractions from other students. For instance, in the 1980's, Tennessee conducted an experiment that included random assignment of 12,000 students to small and large classes for grades kindergarten through three. The average large class had approximately 22 students and the average small class had 15 students. The findings were generally positive, especially for disadvantaged students (Finn and Achilles, 1999; Krueger, 2000; Nye, Hedges, and Konstantopolous, 1999; also see Chapter 6). Similar results were found in a quasi-experimental evaluation of the Wisconsin SAGE program (Molnar et al., 1999).

In 1996, the State of California implemented a large-scale class size reduction, costing nearly $1 billion per year. Stecher and Bohrnstedt (2000) find that this program resulted in a decline in average teacher qualifications and that the "decline in teacher qualifications was greatest in schools serving students most in need" (p. 1). These findings—consistent with the previous discussion—highlight the potential harm that class size reduction can have on teacher quality. Moreover, the results suggest that these unintended effects fall disproportionately on disadvantaged students.

The evidence above helps to define a general economic model for the present analysis. The model will require four basic categories of information in order to assess the optimal allocation of resources: (1) the effect that changes in class size and teacher salary have on teacher quantity and quality; (2) the effect of teacher quantity and quality on students' academic achievement; (3) the effect of students' academic achievement on students' future wages; and (4) other important parameters that could alter the results, especially the discount rate and productivity growth rate. The productivity growth rate is important because any given level of human capital will produce increasing levels of output in the workplace, providing additional monetary benefits.[3]

Information regarding these categories is taken from non-experimental education production functions. Regarding category (1), the relationship between class size and teacher quantity is straightforward—the number of teachers required to reduce class size by a certain amount can be calculated using simple arithmetic. The effects of class size and teacher salary on quality are more complicated. Manksi (1987) finds that a one-percent increase in the number of teachers leads to a three-tenths standard deviation decrease in teacher SAT scores. This estimate is used to estimate the

---

3 This last category is not discussed here in detail, although the chosen range of values is listed in Table 10.6 in the Appendix.

negative effect of class size reduction on teacher quality. Manski also finds that a one-percent increase in salaries would increase average teacher SAT scores by 0.0098 standard deviations. Figlio (1997) finds a similar value. This means that a full unit, or one standard deviation increase, would require a 100 percent increase in average salaries or double the current average salary of $40,582.

Evidence on the relationship between teacher quality and student achievement, category (2), comes from Strauss and Sawyer (1986) who find that a one standard deviation in teacher-test scores leads to a 0.5–0.8 standard deviation gain in student test scores. The effect of teacher quantity on student achievement comes from the Tennessee STAR class size reduction discussed earlier.

Economic theory suggests that schooling should increase the productivity of each worker by raising their "human capital," thus leading to increased wages. A large number of studies have attempted to estimate this relationship, providing evidence on category (3). O'Neill (1990) finds that a one standard deviation increase in scores on the military AFQT tests were associated with a 7 percent increase in wages for whites and a 10.6 percent increase in wages for blacks. Blau and Kahn (2001) find that a one standard deviation leads to a 7.6–16.4 percent increase in wages for men and a 3.3–16.7 increase for women. Bishop (1989) shows that test-score measurement error is likely to attenuate the test score effect on wages. After making corrections for this problem, and after including years of schooling and other control variables, he finds that a one standard deviation increase in test scores yields a 19 percent increase in future wages. Krueger (2000) discusses several other studies on this subject, yielding similar results. The base values and ranges for these and other parameters are described in the Appendix. More detailed discussion is provided in Harris (2001).

RESULTS

COST-EFFECTIVENESS ANALYSIS

The results in Table 10.2 are based on the equation (3) in the Appendix, which is simply a mathematical formalization of CEA. Similar results could just as easily be calculated from the literature review in the previous section and information about the costs of class size and teacher salaries.

The second row of the last column indicates that average teacher salaries in 1999 were $40,582. The number below it ($41,090) means that average salary must be increased $508 to increase student test scores by 0.01 standard deviations. As a simple way to see where the estimate comes from, recall Manski's (1987) finding that a 1

Table 10.2 Input Levels and Costs for Test Score Gains

	Test Score Gain	Class Size	Teacher Salaries
1999 input levels	—	16.2	$40,582
Required input level	0.01σ	15.0	$41,090
	0.05σ	10.7	$43,490
	0.10σ	7.0	$47,370
Additional	0.01σ	$210	$31
expenditures per	0.05σ	$1,287	$163
pupil	0.10σ	$3,251	$402

percent increase in teacher salaries leads to a 0.0098 standard deviation increase in student test scores. One percent of $40,582 is $406. (The difference between this value and the $508 in the table is due to the non-linear functional form assumed in the formal model. See the Appendix.) The raise of $508 amounts to $31 per-pupil.

Accomplishing the same 0.01 standard deviation gain in test scores by lowering class sizes appears to cost more—$210 per-pupil. The Tennessee STAR study found that a class size reduction of approximately seven students increases test scores by 0.10 standard deviations. This reduction amounts to a 47 percent increase in the number of teachers. A 0.01 standard deviation increase would only require one-tenth the additional teachers, or a 4.7 percent increase in the number of teachers. At the base values for class size and teacher salary, instructional spending per-pupil is $2,500. Thus, a rough estimate of the required expenditure per-pupil is 4.7 percent of $2,500, or $120 per-pupil. (Again, this differs somewhat from the $210 figure in the table.)

OPTIMIZATION ANALYSIS

How do these results compare with the more sophisticated optimization analysis? Before answering that question, it is important to return again to the differences between these two types of analysis. It was stated earlier that the main difference lies in the requirement of translating benefits into dollar values. Here, student test scores are translated into dollar values through the anticipated effect of these scores on student's future wages. This amounts to multiplying the benefits of class size and teacher salaries by a single number. Since the approach to estimating costs are the same in each case, the general conclusion of the two analyses must be the same in this particular case; that is, the optimization approach will also suggest that relatively more resources should be allocated to teacher salaries. This conclusion is confirmed by the results in Table 10.3, which are based on the optimization problem (1) and objective function (11) in the Appendix.

Each parameter in the model has a range of possible values, which are displayed in Table 10.6 in the Appendix. Nearly every possible combination of parameter values was used. The "minimum" value in Table 10.3 is the lowest value obtained from this process of sensitivity analysis. The "maximum" is the largest value. This represents the reasonable range of optimal values. Most of the variation is due to different assumptions about the discount rate and the rate of productivity growth.

The class size column indicates that average class sizes should be somewhere between 8.4 and 39.5. The actual 1999 value of 22.2 is within this range. However, teacher salaries are not within the optimum range: they should be raised from $40,582 to at least $56,500 per teacher. As suggested earlier, this provides stronger evidence for raising salaries compared with reducing class sizes.

Does the similarity in results between Tables 10.2 and 10.3 suggest that the results of CEA and the optimization approach will always be the same? The answer is cer-

Table 10.3 Comparing Optimal Input Levels with 1999 Levels

Restrictions	Input	
	Class Size	Teacher Salary
1999 input levels	16.2	$40,582
Min	8.4	$56,500
Max	39.5	$151,700

tainly "no." The similarity in this case is due to two strong assumptions: (a) that the effects of schooling on human capital are determined by their effects on test scores; and (b) that there are no other benefits produced by either input, other than human capital. Relaxing either assumption could produce very different results in the optimization approach. With regard to the second assumption, there is considerable evidence that education affects crime, participation in community affairs, and other outcomes that also have value (e.g., Haveman and Wolfe, 1984, 1994; Levin, 1989). Harris (2001) provides estimates of how large these other benefits would have to be to justify the current level of inputs.

So far, it seems apparent that reducing class sizes is neither cost-effective nor optimal. This conclusion is further reinforced by the fact that the benefits attributed to class size reduction do not include the negative effect of class size reduction on teacher quality. If the negative effects were included, then the benefits of class size reduction would look smaller and this policy would compare even less well with policies aimed at addressing teacher quality. Thus, the earlier results give class size reduction the benefit of the doubt, but it is still not sufficient to justify the policy. (See Table 10.5 in the Appendix for specific estimates of the positive and negative effects.)

These conclusions seem to contradict the results from Krueger (2000) who found that class size reductions pass the cost-benefit test, conducting a secondary analysis of the Tennessee STAR experiment. Strictly speaking, Krueger is correct in his interpretation of his results. However, he only considered one possible policy—class size reduction—and chose not to consider other possibilities, such as teacher-salary increases. He also assumes that there is no negative effect of class size reduction, an assumption also made in this chapter.

In addition, Krueger's approach highlights the weakness of CBA when the policy variable can take on many values. Even if he had considered other reforms, and even if there was agreement on the actual costs and benefits of class size, the optimal class size calculated based on marginal costs and benefits would be larger than those found using Krueger's CBA. A wide range of policy changes can pass a cost-benefit analysis. The advantage of the optimization approach is that the policy advice is much more precise and does not depend on the often arbitrary decision about which specific policy change should be considered.

CONCLUSION

The results here suggest that policymakers have gone too far in reducing class sizes, even at lower grade levels. This conclusion lies in stark contrast to the prevailing policy wisdom that is devoid of cost analysis or consideration of alternative resource uses. The policy discussion also ignores the negative effect that reducing class size has on teacher quality. While more research is certainly necessary, the results here suggest that serious consideration should be given to alternative policy reforms.

It is likely that raising teacher salaries is one of the most expensive ways to raise teacher quality. Other options include professional development and improved working conditions. The fact that teacher salaries still seem to be more cost-effective than hiring more teachers further reinforces the above conclusions. In other words, perhaps the most expensive approach to raising teacher quality is still more cost-effective than reducing class size.

The results here also provide useful evidence for researchers whose responsibility it is to carefully consider the different methods. The results here are quite similar for both the cost-effectiveness and optimization approaches. However, cost-benefit analysis yields a very different conclusion—in fact, the opposite conclusion. Such differences would not be surprising if different estimates were made regarding benefits or costs in general. In this case, the difference in results is due to two aspects of methodology: the number of options considered and the focus on total benefits and costs instead of marginal benefits and costs.

In referring to the oft-repeated calls for education reform, Hanushek states, "it is startling how little any of the reports, or the reform movement itself, draw upon economic principles in formulating new plans" (1996, p. 29). One apparent reason for this is that economic *principles* alone provide little value for policymakers. What is needed is economic *evidence* that includes the costs and benefits of specific policy options. The purpose of economic analysis, and this chapter, is to do just that—provide evidence that helps policymakers improve education decisions.

REFERENCES

Ballou, D., and Podgursky, M. (1992). Buying quality: Will higher pay improve the teaching workforce? Unpublished manuscript, University of Massachusetts at Amherst.

Ballou, D., and Podgursky, M. (1994). Recruiting smarter teachers. *Journal of Human Resources, 30*(2), 326–338.

Ballou, D. (1996). Do public schools hire the best applicants? *Quarterly Journal of Economics, 111*(1), 97–133.

Baumol, W. J. (1967). Macroeconomics of unbalanced growth: The anatomy of urban crisis. *American Economic Review, 57*(3), 415–26.

Bishop, J. (1989). Is the test score decline responsible for the productivity growth decline? *American Economic Review, 79*(1), 178–197.

Blau, F., and Kahn, L. (2000) Do cognitive test scores explain higher U.S. wage inequality? Unpublished manuscript.

Figlio, D. (1997). Teacher Salaries and teacher quality. *Economics Letters, 55,* 267–271.

Finn, J., and Achilles, C. (1999). Tennessee's class size study: Findings, implications, and misconceptions. *Educational Evaluation and Policy Analysis,* 21(2), 97–110.

Hanushek, E. (1996). Outcomes, cost, and incentives in schools. In E. Hanushek and D. Jorgenson (Eds.), *Improving America's schools : The role of incentives.* Washington, DC: National Academy Press.

Harris, D. (2000). Different methods, different results: New approaches to meta-analysis with applications to education production functions. Unpublished manuscript, Michigan State University.

Harris, D. (2001). *Optimal school and teacher inputs.* Unpublished manuscript.

Haveman, R. H., and Wolfe, B. L. (1984). Schooling and economic well-being: The role of non-market effects. *The Journal of Human Resources,* 14(3), 377–407.

Haveman, R., and Wolfe, B. (1994). *Succeeding generations: On the effects of investments in children.* New York: Russell Sage Foundation.

Krueger, A. (2000). *Understanding the magnitude and effect of class size on student achievement* (Working Paper #121). Washington, DC: Economic Policy Institute.

Lakdawalla, D. (2001). *The declining quality of teachers* (Working Paper No. 8263). Cambridge, MA: National Bureau of Economic Research.

Layard, R., and Glaister, S. (1994). *Cost benefit analysis.* New York: Cambridge University Press.

Levin, H. (1989). Economics of investment in educationally disadvantaged students. *American Economic Review*, 79(2), 52–56.

Manski, C. F. (1987). Academic ability, earnings, and the decision to become a teacher: Evidence from the National Longitudinal Study of the High School Class of 1972. In D. A. Wise (Ed.), *Public sector payrolls.* Chicago: University of Chicago Press.

Mishan, E. J. (1988). *Cost-benefit analysis: An informal introduction* (4th ed.). Cambridge, MA Unwin Hyman Ltd.

Mishel, L., Bernstein, J., and Schmitt, J. (2001). *The state of working America.* Washington, DC: Economic Policy Institute.

Molnar, A., Smith, P., Zahorik, J., Palmer, A., Halbach, A., and Ehrle, K. (1999). Evaluating the SAGE program: A pilot program in targeted pupil-teacher reduction in Wisconsin. *Educational Evaluation and Policy Analysis*, 21(2), 165–177.

National Center for Education Statistics. (2001). *Digest of Education Statistics, 2000* (NCES–2001–034). Washington, DC: Author.

Nye, B., Hedges, L., and Konstantopoulos, S. (1999). The long-term effects of small classes: A five-year follow-up of the Tennessee class size experiment. *Educational Evaluation and Policy Analysis*, 21(2), 127–142.

O'Neill, J. (1990). The role of human capital in earnings differences between back and white men. *Journal of Economic Perspectives*, 4(4), 25–45.

Rothstein, R. (1997). *Where's the money going? Changes in the level and composition of education spending, 1991–1996.* Washington, DC: Economic Policy Institute.

Stecher, B., and Bohrnstedt, G. (Eds.). (2000). *Class size reduction in California: The 1998–99 evaluation findings.* Sacramento: California Department of Education.

Strauss, R. P. and Sawyer, E. A. (1986). Some new evidence on teacher and student competencies. *Economics of Education Review*, 5(1), 41–48.

APPENDIX

This appendix provides details on the equations referred to in the main text (for further discussion, see Harris, 2001). The government's objective in this model is to maximize the present discounted value of economic output net of education costs. Specifically, the government chooses school inputs s to solve

$$\max_{s} \sum_{t=0}^{\infty} (1 - \delta)^t \, (y_t - c)) \tag{1}$$

$$s.t. \quad \begin{aligned} y_t &= y(\rho, h(s, \varphi, \gamma)) \\ c &= c(s, p) \end{aligned}$$

where economic output y_t is a function of productivity growth ρ, and human capital $h(\cdot)$. (Note that ρ refers to technological gains as opposed to increases in human capital.) Human capital, in turn, is a function of school inputs and a vector of education production function parameters φ and γ. Only permanent policies are considered; therefore, output varies over time only because of productivity growth. The economic cost of education c is a function of the same education inputs, as well as input shadow prices p. Output and costs are discounted by δ.

Equation (1) assumes that the level and allocation of resources are determined simultaneously. In reality, this is a two-step process whereby policymakers and voters set resource levels; then, schools and school districts determine the allocation of these resources among inputs. As a result, it is worth considering a different version of (1) in which schools face a resource constraint. The problem schools now face is

$$\max_{s} \sum_{t=0}^{\infty} (1 - \delta)^t \, y_t \tag{2}$$

$$s.t. \quad \begin{aligned} y_t &= y(\rho, h(s, \varphi, \eta)) \\ \bar{c} &= c(s, p) \end{aligned}$$

where $\bar{c}$ is the fixed level of education resources (costs). No results are reported in the text using this model because the basic conclusion does not change very much: schools appear to be devoting too many resources to teacher quantity regardless of the specific resource constraints faced by high- and low-spending schools.

Finally, the government may set a desired level of academic achievement $\bar{a}$ and then solve for the optimal allocation of resources, yielding the problem

$$\min_{s} \sum_{t=0}^{\infty} (1 - \delta)^t \, c \tag{3}$$

$$s.t. \quad \begin{aligned} \bar{a} &= a(s, \eta)) \\ c &= c(s, p) \end{aligned}$$

This is simply a more formal means of describing cost-effectiveness analysis. The practical differences between this approach and less formal methods are not great, as shown in the text. The solutions to problems (1) and (2), labeled s^*, satisfy the following:

$$\frac{MB_{s_1^*}}{MC_{s_1^*}} = \cdots = \frac{MB_{s_2^*}}{MC_{s_2^*}} \tag{4}$$

where MBs_i is the marginal benefit of input s_i and MCs_i is the marginal cost of input s_i.

Academic achievement appears is one signal of human capital. Thus, human capital is modeled as

$$h = a^\gamma \tag{5}$$

where $0 < \gamma < 1$. Evidence presented below suggests that achievement comprises only a small portion of human capital.

Achievement is assumed to be determined by the Cobb-Douglas function

$$a = s_1{}^{\varphi_1} s_2{}^{\varphi_2} \tag{6}$$

where $0 < \varphi_i < 1$. This implies decreasing returns to scale in all inputs.

Substituting (6) into (5) yields

$$h = (s_1{}^{\varphi_1} s_2{}^{\varphi_2})^\gamma \tag{7}$$

This discussion in the text suggests that teacher quality Q can be modeled as a function of the quantity of teachers T and teacher salaries $Tsal$, such that

$$Q = T^{\eta_1} Tsal^{\eta_2} \tag{8}$$

where $-1 < \eta_1 < 0$, and $0 < \eta_2 < 1$. This specification is consistent with those commonly used in the education production function literature.

Substituting T for s_1 and Q for s_2 in (7), and inserting (8), yields a reduced form human capital function of

$$h = (T^{\varphi_1 + \varphi_2 \eta_1} Tsal^{\varphi_2 \eta_2})^\gamma \tag{9}$$

where $\varphi_2 \eta_2$ is hypothesized to be positive; i.e., teacher salaries lead to increased teacher quality and additional student human capital. The term $\varphi_1 + \varphi_2 \eta_1$ may be positive or negative, since its two parts are hypothesized to be of different signs. The first term refers to the potentially beneficial effect of class size reduction. The second refers to the potentially negative impact on teacher quality.

The specification of (9) does not allow for a unique solution to the optimization problems (1) and (2). It is displayed here anyway because it highlights the interrelationships between quality and quantity; it is also similar to the assumptions made in the education production function literature.

The human capital function used in this paper to calculate the results is

$$h = \lambda_T \ln T + \lambda_Q \ln Q \tag{10}$$

where λ_T and λ_Q are parameters relating each input to student human capital. This form of the function allows for a unique solution using the objective function

$$(y_t - c) = (1 + \rho)^t (\lambda_T \ln T + \lambda_Q \ln Q) - (p_T T + p_Q QT) \tag{11}$$

Empirical estimates of the parameters in (11) are summarized in Table 10.4 and 10.5 (see Harris, 2001 for a detailed discussion). The former table lists the range of values for each individual parameter, citing the papers from which they were obtained. The individual parameters are then multiplied together and displayed in Table 10.5. These yield the reduced-form parameters in equation (9). These values are then transformed from the elasticity form to a linear-log form, consistent with the specification of (10). The transformation was done using the means of T and Q displayed in Table 10.1. The transformed values can be found in the right-hand column of Table 10.5.

Several other parameters used in this model are summarized in Table 10.6. To obtain the base value for teacher quality it is necessary to calibrate the cost function in (11) based on current values for T and total instruction spending, which are computed from the previous tables. The cost of raising teacher quality by one standard deviation, p_Q, is estimated to be \$67,000 using the results from Manski (1987). The value for p_T is set to \$30,000 per-teacher, but does not affect the results. Any change in p_T simply alters the base value for the base value for Q, having little impact on the results. The base value for Q is difficult to interpret because its main purpose is to serve as a base from which marginal changes can be made.

Table 10.4 Parameters in the Human Capital Function (Elasticity Form)

Parameter	Independent variable: Dependent variable	Structural Estimates			Studies
		Min	Base	Max	
η_1	$T{:}Q$	−4.500	−3.000	−1.500	Manksi (1987)
η_2	$Tsal{:}Q$	+0.220	+0.600	+0.980	Figlio (1997), Manksi (1987)
φ_1	$T{:}a$	+0.060	+0.120	+0.180	Krueger (2000)
φ_2	$Q{:}a$	+0.100	+0.200	+0.300	Strauss and Sawyer (1996), Harris (2000)
γ	$a{:}h$	+0.050	+0.080	+0.190	Krueger (2000) and others

Table 10.5 Human Capital Parameters for Various Functional Forms

Parameter	Independent variable: Dependent variable	Elasticity (from Table 10.4)			Linear-Log Base*
		Min	Base	Max	
$\varphi_2\eta_1$	$T{:}a$	−1.350	−0.600	−0.450	n.a.
$\varphi_1+\varphi_2\eta_1$	$T{:}a$	−1.290	−0.480	−0.270	n.a.
$\varphi_2\eta_2$	$Tsal{:}a$	+0.022	+0.120	+0.294	n.a.
$\gamma\varphi_2\eta_2$	$Tsal{:}h$	+0.001	+0.010	+0.056	n.a.
$\gamma\varphi_1$	$T{:}h$	+0.003	+0.010	+0.034	+4.4 (λ_T)
$\gamma\varphi_2\eta_1$	$T{:}h$	−0.257	−0.048	−0.023	n.a.
$\gamma\varphi_1+\gamma\varphi_2\eta_1$	$T{:}h$	−0.245	−0.038	−0.051	n.a.
$\gamma\varphi_2$	$Q{:}h$	+0.005	+0.016	+0.057	+7.0 (λ_Q)

*These adjustments are based on annual wages, including benefits, in 1999 of \$43,700 (Mishel, Bernstein, and Schmitt, 2001).

Table 10.6 Other Parameters

Parameter	Values		
	Min.	Base #1	Max
δ	0.03	0.04	0.05
ρ	n.a.	0.01	0.02
α	n.a.	0.73	n.a.
p_Q	n.a.	$67,000	n.a.
p_T	n.a.	$30,000	n.a.
Q *(calib.)*	n.a.	0.156	n.a.

INDEX

A

Abecedarian early childhood program, 10, 15, 157–173
  benefit-cost methodology for, 158–160
  earnings of future generations, 166–167
  elementary and secondary education costs, 167–168
  maternal productivity and earnings, 170–171
  participant earnings, 165–166
  program cost, 161–165
  smoking and health of students, 168–170
Accelerated Schools Project (Levin), 71, 75n., 77, 81–82, 84, 85, 88–89, 91
accountability, cost analysis and, 21–22, 34
Achilles, C., 98–99, 101n., 182
Adams, K. E., 169
Adelman, C., 165
Adler, M., 71
Algina, J., 83n.
Alsalam, N., 165
alternative financing, cost analysis and, 33, 34
alternatives, in cost-effectiveness analysis, 8, 38, 41, 45
Altonji, J. G., 141n., 167
American Educational Research Association, 22–23, 61
American Institutes of Research, 85
America's Choice, 77, 78, 80, 81, 85, 85n., 86
Anderson, R. D., 151n.
Angrist, J. D., 9
Archibald, S., 91
Arevalos, G., 116n., 118, 120, 123, 123n.
Argentina, 118, 119
Arnolda, G., 2n., 25, 34, 46

Arthur, W. B., 169
assessment, cost analysis and, 33, 34
Atkinson, A. B., 167
at-risk students
  in Abecedarian early childhood program, 158
  critical role of targeting and, 98–101, 106–108
  migrant children, 62
  Title I funds and, 65, 91–92
Audit Commission and Office for Standards in Education, 139n.
Austin (Texas) Independent School District (AISD), 61–62, 63

B

Bacdayan, A. W., 140, 152
Ballou, D., 181n.
Bangladesh, 120
Barbados, 118, 119
Barber, J. A., 139n.
Barnett, W. S., 10, 13, 15, 23, 38–39, 42n., 44, 55, 64, 89, 91, 157–176, 160, 164
Bartell, E., 48
basic education for all, 131–133
Bassi, L., 141n.
Baumol, W. J., 180
Becker, G. S., 160
Begg, C. B., 79
Behrman, J. R., 167
Belfield, C. R., 14–15, 111, 139n., 139–156, 142
Bell, S. H., 9
Berends, M., 77, 79n., 80, 86
Berliner, D. C., 21n.